Reporting the Troubles

Journalists tell their
stories of the
Northern Ireland conflict

Compiled by DERIC HENDERSON and IVAN LITTLE

·THE·
BLACK
·STAFF·
PRESS

In respectful memory of the men, women and children
who died during the Troubles.

For my son Deric. This book was his idea. (DH)

For Victor Gordon, my friend and mentor from the
Portadown Times, who sadly died before he could contribute
to this book. (IL)

First published in 2018 by Blackstaff Press
an imprint of Colourpoint Creative Ltd
Colourpoint House
Jubilee Business Park
21 Jubilee Road
Newtownards BT23 4YH

Reprinted with corrections, October 2018

Printed and bound by CPI Group UK Ltd, Croydon CR0 4YY

A CIP catalogue for this book is available from the British Library

ISBN 978-1-78073-179-7

www.blackstaffpress.com

Contents

Foreword

Senator George J. Mitchell

Twenty years ago the government of the United Kingdom, the government of Ireland, and eight Northern Ireland political parties declared their support for the Agreement that has become known as the Good Friday Agreement, or the Belfast Agreement. Much has been said and written about the long and difficult road that led to the Agreement. Many have deservedly received credit for their roles.

The prime ministers – Tony Blair and Bertie Ahern – and their predecessors laid the foundation for the negotiations and then brought those negotiations to a successful conclusion. Both governments were ably represented by a talented and dedicated corps of civil servants whose work has not been adequately recognised.

The real heroes of the Agreement were the people of Northern Ireland and their political leaders. The people supported the effort to achieve agreement, and afterward they voted overwhelmingly to ratify it. Their political leaders, in dangerous and difficult circumstances, after lifetimes devoted to conflict, summoned extraordinary courage and vision and reached agreement, often at great risk to themselves, their families, their political careers.

But little has been said or written about a small group of courageous men and women who made an enormous contribution to the effort. In this book *Reporting the Troubles*, Deric Henderson and Ivan Little – both experienced Northern Ireland journalists – fill that void. They have compiled the recollections by journalists of events and encounters that made a lasting impression on them. The resulting book will make a lasting impression on readers. It contains accounts of death and life, of loss and survival, of heroism and cowardice, all of which in the aggregate convey the swirl of emotions experienced by those who lived through the Troubles.

Over a span of five years I chaired three separate but related discussions in what came to be known as the Northern Ireland peace process, and I later served for ten years as the chancellor of Queen's University, Belfast. I have seen Northern Ireland at its worst and at its best. Although I am an American and proud of it, a large part of my heart and my emotions will forever be with the people of Northern Ireland. This moving book helps me, and will help any reader, to better understand what happened.

Thomas Jefferson wrote, 'The basis of our government being the opinion of the people, the very first object should be to keep that right; and were it left to me to decide whether we should have a government without newspapers, or newspapers without a government, I should not hesitate a moment to prefer the latter.'

In the turbulent and difficult times in which we live, many disagree. But the journalists in this book provide support for Jefferson's view, to the benefit of all who care about Northern Ireland and history.

Introduction
Deric Henderson and Ivan Little

The start of the Troubles half a century ago caught journalists by surprise. None of us had foreseen that the batoning of marchers by the Royal Ulster Constabulary at a civil rights rally in Derry in October 1968 would light the fuse that set off an explosion of violence that would rage for decades, with over 3,700 deaths.

Exact figures for the toll of the terrorist campaign are impossible to come by but it's estimated that more than 47,500 people were injured and that there were at least 37,000 shootings and over 16,000 bombings.

This was a world before the instant global dissemination of news on social media, and it was almost impossible for the mainstream media to keep abreast of the bedlam in Belfast in particular. In newspaper offices like the *Belfast Telegraph*'s, shortwave radios were pressed into service as news-gathering tools, constantly tuned to broadcasts from the police. The crackling messages from officers on the streets to their bases recorded the non-stop onslaught of terrorist attacks in the city. Along with thousands of ordinary citizens, journalists took it in turns to eavesdrop on the exchanges.

In 1973, freshly arrived from provincial weeklies, we were among the *Belfast Telegraph* reporters who monitored the police channels. We didn't know it at the time, but our professional lives would be dominated by the Troubles for the next forty years. In our old newsroom, for years on end, the morning ritual was the same. Senior reporter John Conway – who went on to become a high-powered BBC news executive in London – turned the dozens of incident reports he received from the RUC press office into an article for the paper called 'the overnight'. Along with our colleagues, we were then sent out to chase the follow-ups on the worst of the attacks. Newspapers and broadcasting organisations from around the UK paid retainers to *Telegraph* staffers for a heads-up on what had happened during the night and what was in the diary for the day ahead.

Sometimes the sheer volume of the terrorist killings was overwhelming. One Monday, a story about ten murders over the weekend was relegated to the inside pages by new attacks that day. In-depth coverage of every incident was out of the question. One day's murders would routinely be overtaken by the next day's atrocities.

It was non-stop, so it was hardly surprising that journalists found solace in bars like the Old Vic, the upstairs lounge bar of Frank McGlade's pub, virtually next door to the *Telegraph*. The Europa Hotel in the centre of the city was another watering hole for English and international journalists who flew in to Belfast to report on the ever-intensifying violence. The Battle of the Bogside, the deployment of the British Army, internment, the no-go areas, Bloody Sunday and Bloody Friday all thrust Northern Ireland on to the world stage of news like never before.

As well as the unprecedented violence, journalists also had to contend with intimidation and bullying, which were rife, not only from the men of violence but also from the men supposedly trying to stop it – the police, the army and the shadowy intelligence operatives. Lies were the stock-in-trade on all sides in the propaganda battle. For journalists, finding the middle ground of the truth was the challenge.

Successive governments tried to constrain broadcasters, particularly BBC journalists, claiming there should be no such thing as impartiality between lawful and unlawful men when it came to media coverage. Even the judiciary put the pressure on. The former Lord Chief Justice Sir Robert Lowry criticised the Corporation over interviewing Sinn Féin politicians and said that he 'felt the BBC would have given Satan and Jesus Christ equal time'.

A number of documentaries were the subject of battles royal between Downing Street and the BBC, and in 1988 Prime Minister Margaret Thatcher went one step further by introducing a blanket broadcasting ban on interviews with political allies of loyalist and republican terror groups. But the media outwitted the Iron Lady by dubbing actors' voices over the words spoken by the likes of Gerry Adams and Martin McGuinness.

In the background too, the RUC persistently tried to identify journalists' sources within the paramilitary organisations.

Reporters who'd built up a large number of terrorist contacts often became reluctant conduits for the killers' claims of responsibility for their brutal attacks. Ivan Little was once threatened with death by the very man who phoned him with UDA and UFF statements. The caller said he and another named *Telegraph* journalist would be killed if the paper didn't change what he claimed was its pro-republican editorial policy. Little was told that he and his colleague had been targeted because their bylines were on the front page; the caller bizarrely assured them there was 'nothing personal' in the threat. Around the same time an English journalist based in a Belfast newsroom was spirited away from the city after republicans claimed he was a British spy using his job to gain intelligence about them.

In the years to come it was loyalists who were to shoot journalists. The

UVF came within inches of killing Jim Campbell of the *Sunday News* at his home, and the LVF later murdered Martin O'Hagan of the *Sunday World*, who, like Campbell, was attacked because he courageously exposed the truth about the terrorists.

Throughout the Troubles, hundreds of young reporters were sent to Northern Ireland from Britain (and further afield) to hone their skills in what was undoubtedly one of the best journalistic training grounds in the world. All the brightest young reporters from Fleet Street, the BBC and ITN came over. In time, ITN opened its own bureau in Belfast, with reporters and camera crews based in Northern Ireland full-time. Until then ITN had relied on UTV staffers to double-job and report for them, only sending in their own teams to cover the major atrocities.

However the establishment of the Belfast office didn't go down well with everyone at ITN because many journalists and camera crews volunteered for stints in Belfast as much for the social life as for the professional challenges. In the old days, the expenses ITN and national newspapers were prepared to pay employees were exceptionally generous – because of the dangers few bosses queried the bills in front of them. A number of journalists even acquired rudimentary printing kits to produce DIY receipts. Gerry Fitt famously told the story of how he once discovered that his name had appeared as a dinner guest for five different English reporters on the same evening. The influx of British journalists into Northern Ireland soon became a two-way street. The experience garnered in the Troubles by fledgling Ulster-born reporters equipped them with skills unmatched by most of their British-based contemporaries, and so it was no surprise that many of them joined national broadcasters and newspapers.

When the slow march to peace began in the '90s, the 'old boys and girls' were the obvious reporters to be sent back to Northern Ireland by their bosses. But covering the twists and turns along the road to the Good Friday Agreement in the wake of the republican and loyalist ceasefires in 1994 took patience and stamina. In the run-up to Good Friday 1998, dozens of journalists from across the world were camped out around Castle Buildings at Stormont as the negotiations involving local politicians and British and Irish premiers Tony Blair and Bertie Ahern dragged on. And on. And on. Journalists, including Deric Henderson, gathered for a team photograph outside Castle Buildings with Senator George Mitchell, the NI Secretary Mo

Mowlam and Irish Foreign Minister David Andrews. This was the deadline, no matter the outcome of the talks – but there was a feeling history was about to be made.

Sure enough, late that afternoon, BBC political correspondent Stephen Grimason was the first journalist to break the news that there had been a meeting of minds between all the parties, except Ian Paisley's Democratic Unionists, who were left out in the cold. Weeks later a referendum showed a majority of voters were backing the power-sharing deal.

After all the years of grief and heartache, of distress and anguish, there was joy and elation when the guns fell silent and when the Good Friday Agreement was ratified. Both of us had worked through the worst of the Troubles and we'd watched as the place was torn apart. This was our home, our people, our families and loved ones. For us, the Troubles were up close and personal.

The idea for this book had been in our minds for some time – when we realised that the fiftieth anniversary of the outbreak of the Troubles was on the horizon, the time seemed right. Over the years, we'd worked with some brilliant print and broadcast journalists from Belfast, Dublin and London – we knew that for all of them their time in Northern Ireland reporting on the Troubles had been hugely significant. For many of them it had been a formative experience; often the events they covered never left them. Martin Cowley, who was at the civil rights march in Duke Street in Derry on 5 October 1968, the day that marked the start of the Troubles, was the first journalist we approached. He accepted straight away – and that enthusiasm and commitment to being involved was the response of almost everyone we contacted.

Over sixty journalists agreed to write about a defining event or person from their experience of reporting the Troubles. They all wanted to contribute and reflect on their memories of stories they had covered and people they had met during some extremely difficult, tense and harrowing years. One or two politely refused, preferring to keep their thoughts to themselves. We're friends with them all, and had space permitted, there could easily have been double the number.

All of the contributors were free to decide what subject to focus on. We didn't get caught up in trying to make the book comprehensive – that's the job of the historian. However, the contributions from these journalists span the three decades of the Troubles – a series of deeply personal and engaged accounts of some of the key moments and personalities that defined and shaped the conflict. More than that, they are a testimony to the huge responsibility the journalists felt, to their commitment to putting things on the record, and to remembering. To adapt a phrase from John Mullin's contribution, this book is 'an epitaph, of sorts'.

US Senator George J. Mitchell, the Northern Ireland Secretary of State Mo Mowlam, Irish Foreign Minister David Andrews and General John de Chastelain, chairman of the Independent International Commission on Decommissioning, with journalists outside Castle Buildings, Belfast, on the day of the signing of the Good Friday Agreement, 10 April 1998.

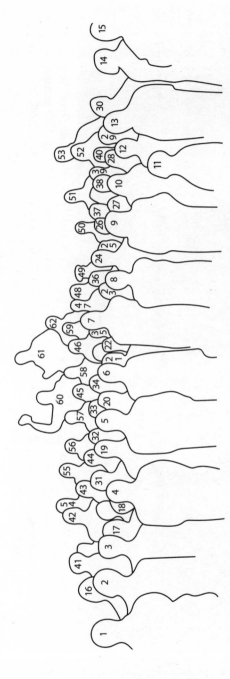

1 Mark McCauley, BBC
2 Daniel Mulhall, Irish government
3 Tim Franks, BBC
4 Denis Murray, BBC
5 John de Chastelain, Independent
   International Commission on
   Decommissioning
6 US Senator George J. Mitchell
7 David Andrews, Irish government
8 Liz O'Donnell, Irish government
9 Mo Mowlam, Northern Ireland
   Secretary of State
10 Letitia Fitzpatrick, UTV
11 John Coghlan, RTÉ
12 Martina Purdy, BBC
13 Eamonn Mallie, Downtown Radio
14 Billy Graham, Irish News
15 Johnny Saunderson, APTV

16 Colin Ross, Northern
   Ireland Office
17 John Devine, Irish Independent
18 Sharon Hall
19 Mark Simpson, BBC
20 Deric Henderson, Press Association
21 Deaglán de Bréadún, Irish Times
22 Ivan Heslip, UTV
23 Alan Lewis, Photopress
24 Harri Holkeri, Independent
   International Commission on
   Decommissioning
25 John Irvine, ITN
26 Hervé Amoric, AFP
27 Karen Patterson, Downtown Radio
28 Melissa Kite, Press Association
29 Dominic Cunningham, Irish
   Independent

30 Paul Connolly, Belfast Telegraph
31 Trevor Yates, ITN
32 Michael Fisher, RTÉ
33 Michael O'Kane, RTÉ
34 Ken Reid, UTV
35 Ian Courtney, OUTV
36 Mark Davey, ITN
37 Ian Graham, Press Association
38 Brendan Wright, RTÉ
39 Jane Dodge, BBC
40 Stephen Grimason, BBC
41 Des O'Flynn, RTÉ
42 Timlin Ó Cearnaigh,
   Raidió na Gaeltachta
43 Hugh Russell, Irish News
44 Eamon McKenna, RTÉ
45 Damian Gaffney, Sky TV
46 Martin McCullough, Press Association

47 Gary Honeyford, Sky TV
48 Anne Cadwallader
49 Martin Cowley, Reuters
50 David Blevins, Sky TV
51 Toby Harnden, Daily Telegraph
52 Jane McSorley, BBC
53 Mark Devenport, BBC
54 Chris Beck, TG4
55 Paddy McEntee, RTÉ
56 Justin Kernaghan, Photopress
57 Gerry O'Brien, RTÉ
58 Jim Donnelly, APTV
59 William Cherry, Pacemaker
60 Paul McErlane, photographer
61 Crispin Rodwell, photographer
62 Brian Little, photographer

© Trevor McBride

A searing image from a tumultuous day when baton-wielding police broke up a civil rights protest in Derry. Scores of demonstrators were injured, among them student Andy Hinds, eighteen (above).

Duke Street, Derry, 5 October 1968
Martin Cowley

Derry was sunny. A fine afternoon for an autumn walk. No need for a heavy coat. I wore a light-grey three-piece suit. But tension pervaded Duke Street. Everyone knew it wouldn't be a stroll.

The Northern Ireland Civil Rights Association (NICRA) planned to march from Duke Street across Craigavon Bridge to the city despite a ban by Home Affairs Minister William Craig.

A crowd of about four hundred moved off in uneven ranks, ignoring a megaphoned police warning. At the rear, RUC officers watched from a hilly street. Word spread that police were also blocking the road some three hundred yards in front.

By dusk, Derry was in ferment and Northern Ireland was changed forever.

The spark was an onslaught by baton-wielding RUC officers that left scores of civil rights demonstrators injured. The police violence was shocking but the north of Ireland had seen street violence before and it had hardly raised an eyebrow elsewhere. 5 October 1968 was different.

During almost fifty years of one-party unionist rule the region was a cold house for the nationalist minority. Central government in London turned a blind eye, choosing not to interfere in how unionists handled the region's internal affairs.

What set Duke Street apart was that this time the whole spectacle was caught 'on tape', up close and very personal in daylight, and screened worldwide. Press photographers captured vivid images and reporters provided graphic accounts. In particular, film shot by RTÉ cameraman Gay O'Brien with sound recordist Eamon Hayes established 5 October as a transformative and historic episode.

Prime Minister Harold Wilson invited Stormont Premier Terence O'Neill to Downing Street and on 22 November O'Neill announced measures effectively setting in train many of the reforms NICRA had sought.

The Duke Street gathering included veteran politicians, NICRA leaders, Derry socialists and housing activists, trade unionists, left-wing republicans, nationalists, labour supporters, liberals, jobless workers, small business owners, teachers, teenage school students and many others. University students

1

arriving late from Belfast with hastily scrawled placards added a frisson of edginess and noise.

Of the many photographs that emerged, one showing a demonstrator, Andy Hinds, surrounded by RUC officers with batons drawn, is an enduring and defining symbol of that epochal day. The image was captured by newspaper photographer Trevor McBride. Hinds, an eighteen-year-old student, is doubled over and clinging to a lamp post and in the firm grip of two officers. One of them, his face contorted in a grimace, towers over the melee with his baton raised aloft.

Westminster MP Gerry Fitt was among many whose injuries needed X-raying. The Nationalist Party leader Eddie McAteer MP was struck with a baton.

O'Brien and Hayes got into the thick of the action, capturing the clamour and frenzy: police rushing to hold marchers back; a few protestors scrambling through; shouting and placard waving; tense eye-to-eye confrontations at the police line; pushing and shoving; the batoning free-for-all.

The standout clip is of a demonstrator, Pat Douglas, facing the police phalanx and pleading, 'Gentlemen, please, for God's sake –' before he suddenly roars in anguished pain and crumples to the ground, jabbed below the belt by an unseen baton.

The camera rolls on, recording deliberate slashing blows and capricious swipes at anyone within reach.

It follows a young man, groggy from baton blows, careering into the road where he is felled by lashes to the head from a police commander's ceremonial blackthorn stick. The youth wears a light-grey three-piece suit.

Under the heading 'Victims of Police Batoning Tell Their Stories', the *Derry Journal* reported: 'Among those treated at Altnagelvin Hospital for injuries sustained in the Duke St scenes was a member of the "Journal" reporting staff, 18-years-old Martin Cowley.'

The article gave my account of being caught between two converging groups of police, batoned and hearing the man with the blackthorn say to other officers, 'That's the boy,' before he lashed out.

When I joined the *Journal* as a trainee reporter in February 1968, I was well up to speed with the prevailing political winds. The first time I heard 'We Shall Overcome' sung in Derry was at an election rally in 1966. It was a time when a string of decisions from Belfast, including the siting of a new university in Coleraine rather than Derry – which also angered liberal unionists – was seen as designed to stymie the city's growth.

The city was a textbook case of the sectarian discrimination that operated under a unionism determined to keep opposition at bay and see off any real or perceived threat to its power and position within the United Kingdom.

Derry was overwhelmingly nationalist but gerrymandering, voting restrictions, extra votes for business owners and control of council housing allocation ensured power was held by the leaders of the minority unionist community.

In the spring of 1968 a small band of campaigners staged protests to highlight the plight of young families in dire housing conditions. I knew most of the activists and had reported on a couple of the protests. Later, some in the group were instrumental in getting NICRA to choose Derry as the march venue.

I wasn't assigned to cover the 5 October demonstration. That was a job for the *Journal*'s senior reporters. But I wasn't going to miss it either.

At Duke Street I was in a quandary. I knew I wanted to walk with the protestors on the road but, being a reporter, albeit officially off duty, professional conflict kicked in. As the march started I distinctly remember opting to remain on the footpath, walking the two hundred or so paces in parallel to within a few yards of the police line, and standing among spillover demonstrators as speakers addressed an impromptu meeting. Thus – and having neither shouted nor shoved, chanted nor cheered – I have always thought of myself as having been a supportive spectator not an active participant. Recently though, I got a fresh and forthright perspective. I read for the first time in fifty years a carbon copy of a statement I had typed a few weeks after 5 October. Unknown to me, the five faded pages of cheap newsroom copy paper, held by a rusted clip, had lain in a drawer in my late mother's home.

I had written, 'On the 5th October I went to Duke Street and took part in the Civil Rights march. As a supporter of the Civil Rights campaign and a citizen of Derry I was exercising my right to free lawful assembly and my right to march where I pleased. As a reporter, although I had not been officially assigned to cover it, I took notes, both mental and written, before and during the march.'

From that, it is clear to me that, rather than going to a different vantage point to observe the demonstration, my decision to walk along the pavement, within arm's reach of it, was my way of taking part.

It was the only means by which I could satisfy my determination to show solidarity while maintaining some notion of journalistic detachment and a reporter's curiosity to see how things would turn out. I wrote the statement in response to an appeal for witness accounts and for long afterwards avoided reliving the memory of my experience. I rarely talked about it in detail and twenty years passed before I wrote a newspaper article about it.

Another forgotten or mentally buried aspect emerged from the statement.

I was surprised to read that when I caught the eye of the officer with the blackthorn I thought he would come to my rescue.

'I remember feeling a bit relieved. I thought he would know me. He turned to me and I was waiting for him to give some sign of recognition but he didn't … I shouted "Press" and then started to run.'

I had seen him in court often and a couple of months earlier had sat across the table from him at a press conference in his office. Why he lunged at me in Duke Street shouting something like, 'That's him, that's the boy, I want him,' I'll never know.

Maybe he didn't like reporters mixing politics and protest.

Maybe he just didn't like the suit.

Martin Cowley is a former London editor of the *Irish Times* and Reuters Ireland correspondent.

How an ex-B Special owes his life to a lady on the Falls Road

Ray Managh

A nightmare encounter on the Falls – when gunmen, suspected of being Shankill Road members of the B Specials, opened fire on a group that had earlier taken part in a street riot – marked my most terrifying experience throughout years of reporting the Troubles.

The attack, in which through sheer luck no one died, was to be the last straw for the British government's tolerance of an official armed militia, some members of which had been suspected of backing loyalists in violent attacks on Roman Catholic areas. A year later the force was history.

Compared with other bloody nights of rioting, things had been relatively quiet on the Falls Road – some petrol bombing and missile throwing, but nothing as serious as I was used to reporting for the Belfast *News Letter*, when I covered the nightly street battles from Divis Flats to the Springfield Road, Ballymurphy and New Barnsley.

It was probably due to the reasonably inconsequential nature of the street protests that I found myself behind the lines that night on my hunt for a better story, mixing with those who had earlier been spearheading the rioting. Reporting always from behind the lines of the security forces lacked adventure. Abandoning that safety barrier was to risk life and limb, as I was to find out.

Large groups of people inevitably gathered at street corners to discuss the success or otherwise of the latest attack by or against the security forces. I was in the middle of such a group when the B Specials opened fire on us.

As shots rang out and bullets ricocheted off the brick walls above our heads, one of the group suddenly put a rifle to his shoulder and returned fire in the direction of the corner on the Shankill side of the Falls from where the attack had been launched.

A gun battle broke out between the shooters and the lone gunman who, in the darkness, had surreptitiously crept into our group with a concealed gun. No one had noticed him join us and, when the shooting broke out from our midst, we quickly decided to leave him to it, dashing for cover down a side street to escape what was now a hail of bullets pinging off walls.

Panic had struck and as we rushed almost blindly down the ill-lit street a door opened and a voice shouted, 'In here. In here.' I followed the pack into the hallway and what appeared to be the safety of someone's home. Seconds after the door closed behind me I realised I should have kept running.

If I had escaped from the proverbial frying pan I quickly realised I faced a potential roasting. I was ushered into a front room packed with men and women, most of whom would have been in the middle of earlier rioting and all of whom wanted to know the reason for the gunfire. I was in an IRA safe house.

I could hear comments like 'the black bastards' above the din and the babble of conversation as news of the attack was outlined and exaggerated. A second room in the house was also packed with anti-loyalists, anti-Protestants and most particularly anti-B Specials. The terror of discovery now engulfed me.

Never had I experienced fear like it before, nor have I felt such terror since, despite the closest of encounters with serious danger in reporting the Troubles.

I knew of photographer colleagues who had been apprehended at street disturbances, blindfolded and taken for questioning by the IRA before eventually being released, thankfully unharmed.

It was a little middle-aged woman in an apron, obviously the lady of the house, who turned out to be my saviour and liberator from what I saw as a doomed situation. As she approached through the crowd I could see over her head that a group was making tea and distributing it with biscuits from a kitchen at the back of the hallway.

I was still trying to recover my breath when she said, 'What's wrong with you?' To this day I don't know what she had seen in my face that caused her to see that I was in a predicament.

'I'm in desperate trouble,' I blurted out. 'I have a wife and child over in East Belfast and I've only just heard that shooting has broken out there too. I need to get to them.' There was desperation in my voice; sheer terror more honestly, but it worked.

Yes, I did have a wife and a child on the east side of Belfast but as far as I knew they were perfectly safe. She quickly called a man from one of the rooms. 'This young man has a wife and child in East Belfast ... take him out of here and get him on his way,' she said.

He did what he was told, checking the street before allowing me to step outside, then loping ahead of me from street corner to street corner whistling signals, dramatically if perhaps unnecessarily. Shortly afterwards he pointed towards the city centre and said, 'Good luck.'

In a phone box at Belfast City Hall I dropped in a few coins and breathlessly outlined my experiences to my night editor Dan Kinney. Like all good journalists the news was all that mattered to him at that moment. 'I'll transfer you to copy. Give us the story, Ray,' he said.

I never did find out who that woman was or whether she somehow suspected I shouldn't be there. While I still see her as my deliverer from potential disaster there was no way I could have told her I would champion her anonymously on the front page of my newspaper next morning for 'saving my life'.

I still believe, had I stayed in that house or even have been caught sneaking off in the middle of a gun battle, that I would have been sussed out as a journalist; perhaps blamed for spying on an enclave of republicans, if not members of the IRA.

It was also a night when men would have willingly pulled the throat out of a member of the hated B Specials who had launched what they saw as yet another deadly attack on their community.

I often contemplate my fate had the people in that house found out I was a not-long-retired member of Brackey Platoon of the Ulster Special Constabulary* in East Tyrone – an ex-member of the hated B Specials. That I had also been a past secretary of Brackey Loyal Orange Lodge No. 165 would have been trivial in comparison.

That woman may never have known she was the hero of a front page report outlining how I owed my life to her and the young man who led me to safety. But I doubt if the Paisley-supporting Belfast *News Letter* of that era was part of the morning reading over breakfast in the heart of the Falls.

Ray Managh is a freelance high court reporter in Dublin. He previously worked for the *News Letter*, *Tyrone Constitution*, *Belfast Telegraph*, BBC and *Irish Independent*.

---

* The Ulster Special Constabulary, of which I am proud to have been a member, recruited from November 1920; its last patrols were carried out on 31 March 1970. Past membership never coloured my journalistic reporting throughout all of the Troubles, but the force became the victim of what has been described as a vicious and mendacious IRA-led propaganda campaign, widely believed in Great Britain and ably assisted by the thuggery of a handful of its members – dressed in civilian clothes – against civil rights marchers.

That I might have fallen to one of their bullets in the shameful and potentially murderous gun attack on the Falls Road that night is an irony that has stayed with me.

It was my journalistic colleague, former *Irish Press* editor and author Tim Pat Coogan, who has chronicled the history of the IRA, who paid the Ulster Special Constabulary its greatest compliment when he said, 'The B Specials were the rock on which any mass movement by the IRA in the North has inevitably foundered.'

Their knowledge of the areas in which they worked, lived and operated, and the daily movements of the people in and out of those areas were the bane of IRA activity throughout Northern Ireland. The IRA set out to force them out of existence and succeeded.

The night Paisley said I worked for the Papist Broadcasting Corporation
Martin Bell

I first set foot in Northern Ireland in November 1968 to report a court case following the civil rights demonstrations in Londonderry/Derry. I learned soon enough about the importance of place names and other badges of identity.

I was working for BBC TV news in London and hardly a cub reporter. I had already reported from war zones in Vietnam, Nigeria and the Middle East, and been tear gassed twice in civil commotions in Paris and Chicago.

But nothing had prepared me for Northern Ireland. It was special and close to home and verging on a sort of civil war. Two of the fiercest gun battles I have ever witnessed were in Belfast – on the Shankill Road between loyalist paramilitaries and the 3rd Light Infantry in October 1969, and in Lenadoon Avenue at the breakdown of the IRA ceasefire in July 1972.

The closeness to home meant that the people we were reporting on cared passionately about what we showed and what we said – every frame and every word of it. The BBC's early evening news in those days was just before six. The streets turned quieter at that time, as the main players – rioters, demonstrators or just plain spectators – went indoors to watch our version of the day's events. Then they would return to the streets and tell us in the plainest language what they thought of it. *Tell the truth* was their universal instruction to all of us.

A citizen of Belfast wrote to the BBC complaining that an explosion in her street had not been shown on television. She wondered, had the national broadcaster grown so unfeeling? Or was it a part of a sinister conspiracy to suppress the truth?

It was always the BBC that drew the incoming fire. Our rivals at ITN could run similar reports with nothing like the same degree of intimidation.

The metropolitan reporters like myself became uncomfortably well known. A group of loyalists in Dungannon sent me a message that they intended to send me home in a coffin. A lady in mid-riot on the Newtownards Road set upon me with her umbrella, complaining that we were filming something that was not happening. I attended a civil rights meeting at Limavady Town Hall, and had to escape through a lavatory window and hoof it across the fields.

And the Reverend Ian Paisley – whom I suppose I helped to make famous – waged a continuous campaign against us. I remember a prayer meeting in

Armagh, attended by two thousand of his supporters. 'There is one man here,' he said at the top of his voice, 'who is no friend of the Protestant and loyalist people. That man is Martin Bell of the PBC, the Papist Broadcasting Corporation.' He urged his people not to harm a hair of my head. Then he turned and pointed slowly, 'He's standing over there in the sheepskin coat!' So they roughed me up a bit. Then he said, 'Brethren, let us now bow our heads and pray for deliverance from all our foes.'

Thank goodness there were no rolling news channels in those days. Imagine what the rioters could have done with it, adding a burning satellite truck to the barricades of trucks and buses.

Censorship? Of course there was censorship, although I denied it at the time. In August 1969 I was completing a report about Catholics being burned out of their homes off the Falls Road. I sensed a presence in the edit room behind me. It was that of Waldo Maguire, the BBC's controller in Northern Ireland, who was worried about the after-effects of the coverage. 'You can't call them Catholics,' he said. 'They will have to be *refugees*.'

'Look Waldo,' I said, 'there is a woman wheeling her belongings in a pram with a crucifix on top of it: she's not a Protestant, is she?'

But still I had the time of my life. I patrolled the streets constantly. I fact-checked compulsively. I made friendships that last to this day. I have nothing but the fondest memories of my five years, on and off, in this remarkable corner of the island of Ireland.

The hotels were special too. In Londonderry we stayed in the Melville, where my cameraman one morning asked for egg and bacon without the bacon. 'Bacon is compulsory, sir!' said the waiter.

The Grand Central in Belfast was a hotel before it became a barracks. My cameraman, who had a taste for Irish whiskey, turned his room into a bar and hung a sign there: 'Emergency Powers'.

Best of all was the Europa, one of the great press hotels of the world. On one of the many occasions when it was blown up, the water supply failed. The manager, Harper Brown, gave us a half-bottle of champagne each to brush our teeth with. The bar was renamed in his honour.

Over those years I must have stood time and again on just about every street corner in Belfast. But then they changed the street corners.

Martin Bell was a foreign affairs correspondent for the BBC. He later became an independent MP.

The 'honey-trap' killings of three Scottish soldiers
Martin Lindsay

It was a normal Wednesday night in McGlade's bar, a favourite Belfast city centre watering hole for journalists. Most of the hacks enjoying a pint that night had filed their copy or their broadcast pieces and were winding down, with, perhaps, one ear trained on the streets, where IRA bombs and gunfire had become common background noise in 1971.

Earlier that afternoon, three young Scottish soldiers filed out of Girdwood military barracks. Dressed in civvies, they were heading into Belfast for a few pints – they too were winding down from the pressures and perils of patrolling streets where terrorism was rife.

1st Battalion Royal Highland Fusiliers Dougald McCaughey, 23, John McCaig, 17, and his brother Joseph, 18, had six hours to let their hair down before heading back to Girdwood – and the daily grind of foot patrols, vehicle checkpoints and guard duty.

As they strolled along the Antrim Road, the privates – along with three other Fusiliers – planned to visit city centre bars, and perhaps get to know the locals. By early evening, they had done just that and were also invited to a house party – but that was one gathering they would never attend.

Back at McGlade's and an hour or so before 10 p.m. closing, some journalists began leaving the bar – and their hurried departures were the first signs that something had happened. I had just finished my drink, when I got a phone call about an 'incident' in North Belfast.

When I reached the scene at White Brae, Ligoniel, the journalists from McGlade's were huddled in the darkness. A lone policeman stood nearby, blocking our way to the scene of whatever had happened there.

I strolled over to speak to him but he was he was carrying out his orders to the letter and wasn't prepared to talk to the press – including me. So I gave up asking about the 'incident' and, instead, began a general conversation about the Troubles.

After about twenty minutes and for no apparent reason, the policeman stopped me in mid-sentence and gripped my arm. 'I can tell you what happened, but you mustn't tell your colleagues. Do you agree?'

I nodded. Then he whispered these chilling words, 'There are three dead Scottish soldiers, lying in a ditch. Shot. Young fellows. In civvy clothes.' He added that they were identified as soldiers by military markings on their socks.

The following morning, the *Belfast Telegraph* and the other papers and broadcasting outlets moved into top gear to find out how the first multiple murders of the Troubles had been carried out and by whom.

Only three soldiers had been killed, in separate incidents, before those horrific murders in March 1971, and those soldiers had been on duty. Now three young Scottish Fusiliers, unarmed and off-duty, had been butchered – after enjoying a few pints in downtown Belfast.

Journalists swooped on city centre pubs trying to establish where the soldiers had been drinking and, more importantly, with whom. The search soon narrowed to Mooney's and Kelly's Cellars, and the murders were dubbed the 'honey-trap killings' when it emerged that women *might* have lured them to their deaths.

Detectives, using witness statements and interviews with fellow Fusiliers, gradually built up a picture of what had happened. After reaching the city centre, McCaughey went into the main GPO, in Royal Avenue, to withdraw money from his savings account. The McCaig brothers went with him. The three other Fusiliers embarked on a shopping trip for cigarettes, stationery and magazines for their mates back at the barracks.

The first pint stop for the McCaigs and Dougald McCaughey was the Abercorn bar in central Belfast. An off-duty paratrooper told detectives he saw them around 2.30, drinking with two men with southern Irish accents. He also saw two young women, who he described as 'pick-ups', sitting nearby.

When the Fusiliers left the Abercorn to walk to nearby Mooney's bar, witnesses claimed they were now accompanied by five men. It was while in Mooney's that someone – probably one of their new-found 'friends' – suggested going to Kelly's Cellars.

Eyewitnesses claimed that at 6.30 p.m. five men entered the bar, including the Fusiliers. This was the last time anyone saw the soldiers alive – except for the Provos, who lured them from that pub, with the promise of a house party and girls to round off the day.

Ironically, when they left Kelly's and got into a waiting car (possibly a grey Austin Cambridge), Girdwood officers posted them as being absent without leave. The Fusiliers from whom they had become separated earlier had already returned to barracks by taxi.

The Fusiliers had now only a matter of minutes to live. The car snaked its way through the back streets of the city centre, probably heading to Ligoniel via the Crumlin Road.

At White Brae, investigators believe the Fusiliers got out to relieve themselves by the roadside, and as they did so, their Provisional IRA killers struck – shooting them in the back of the head with a .38 revolver and a 9mm semi-automatic pistol. When the bodies were found they were lying on top of each other; one intact and two broken beer glasses were nearby.

Locals heard shots around 7.25 p.m. and shortly afterwards three children were returning from searching for a donkey when one of them, Brenda Keilty, made the gruesome discovery. A passing motorist went to a nearby pub and raised the alarm. Other witnesses spoke of seeing an Austin Cambridge and a red Mini leaving the scene. The Mini's occupants appeared to be covered by a white sheet.

The next day, tens of thousands took to the streets of Northern Ireland, laying scores of floral tributes and demanding tougher security and an unrelenting hunt for the killers. Among them were thousands of shipyard and aircraft workers.

The army responded by raising the minimum age of soldiers serving in Northern Ireland to eighteen. Former Irish Guards officer and Stormont Premier James Chichester-Clark demanded extra troops and, when Downing Street didn't give him what he wanted, he resigned. Brian Faulkner became the new prime minister.

Despite investigations by the RUC and Metropolitan police, no one has been charged with the murders, but the campaigning Fusiliers' families know of three suspects, still living in the Irish Republic. Two of them were the actual gunmen.

One of the men spotted drinking with the Fusiliers that day bore a striking resemblance to IRA man Paddy McAdorey, who was shot dead by troops five months later, after he killed a soldier. One of those who fled to the Republic was reportedly linked to the 1976 Kingsmills massacre of eleven Protestant workmen.

An Historical Enquiries Team report into the murders didn't unearth enough new evidence to bring charges. But it contained one fascinating footnote: investigators found no evidence that women played any part in luring the soldiers to their deaths.

Martin Lindsay is a former editor of the *Belfast Telegraph* and *Sunday Life*.

An Irish Setter, a Palestinian hijacker, Derry and me
Gerald Seymour

He was a big fellow and he had a wonderful arrogant strut when on the move. I came across him first in Londonderry in the autumn of 1971. If the wind was funnelled down William Street and was coming from behind him, then the feathers of the tail and undercarriage of my second-favourite Irish Setter would be blowing out and around him.

He was a marvellous-looking dog, with the classic auburn coat, and he would be out in all weathers and regardless of the security situation on his home territory. The rain could be falling in stair rods from low leaden clouds and he would be on his late afternoon patrol, or the street could be shrouded in smoke and echoing with the discharge of rubber bullets and the shouts of hatred and anger, and he'd not miss his constitutional.

The cameraman I worked with knew that it was pretty much obligatory to work in a shot of him, if only a few seconds, into his filming. Later, back in Belfast, when the story of that day's events in the city was edited, the guys and girls who put the scenes in order would slot in a snatch of this big fellow and he'd make it into some millions of homes on the *News At Ten* transmission ...

I'd whistle softly for him sometimes but never had even so much as an acknowledgement for my introducing him to that wider audience now admiring him. I was ignored and probably regarded as an intruder on his home ground. He was magnificent, very handsome.

A year before, we'd welcomed our own Irish Setter into our home. An extravagantly spoiled and pampered puppy called Leila. She'd been bred by a chef at the Café Royal in London and was used to nothing but the best. We doted on her and could bore for the whole of the UK on Irish Setters. Our enthusiasm was real, not manufactured and sometimes helpful as it turned out.

An afternoon when there was a report of an 'incident' in the Creggan. The light starting to fail, three Brits in a car with Belfast plates, probably not entirely sensible to be there, and a crowd starting to gather, and the usual remarks and Honest Joe enquiries not falling on sympathetic ears – and nothing to suggest anything untoward had happened.

The people round the car had little affection for us and shortening tempers. I was out of the vehicle and attempting explanations and not finding any takers ... and another Irish Setter trotted round the corner with its owner, and came to greet me.

It was a mirror image of ours at home and I was down on a knee and having my face washed and congratulating the man on the quality of his dog and telling him about mine, and the whole thing was too ridiculous and hostility to us just drained away into the dusk, and we were no longer regarded with suspicion. I did wonder if my big chum from William Street had played a part is this very pretty little soul's procreation.

The price was £25 for Leila. I'd been covering a hijack story after airliners were landed in the Jordanian desert in a coordinated series of attacks by the Palestinian PFLP faction. When a civil war erupted in Amman, I shared a bathroom – safer to sleep there when the whizz-bangs were pinging through the bedroom area – with a reporter who had a setter at home and praised its lunatic beauty.

Back home after the war had fizzled, my newscaster colleague Peter Snow wrote a book on the story of those days in the Middle East, and generously paid me £25 for helping him with eyewitness parts of the story.

The book was published as *Leila's Hijack War*, and our pup was inevitably Leila. Leila Khaled was one of the PFLP's wannabe hijackers but had failed to take over an El Al flight, and had been overpowered by Israeli sky marshals.

A couple of years later, one of our cameramen had a bad experience. Late at night, out and investigating a major explosion in the Lower Falls, a gang pinned him down and a firearm was held against his head. They released him when he shouted out that I was his reporter, but still in the Europa Hotel with a guest.

The message that I should have been with him was relayed to me. Early the next morning, I was out with him in the narrow streets and looking for someone with 'authority' to speak to. We were fiercely proud of our independence from sectarian elements and intelligence-gathering organisations. I met a man and we spoke quietly among the hung-out and drying washing in a terrace yard, and I tried to emphasise the need for our crews to move freely and not be assaulted.

Eventually, very politely, he said: 'Your problem, Mr Seymour, is that you'll never understand what our struggle is about.'

I disagreed and told him: 'What, me not understand, and with an Irish Setter at home, and it's named after a Palestinian hijacker?'

He looked bemused – but we had a tentative handshake, and something of a guarantee, and I told him some more about my dog at home, and we had no more difficulties in that district.

I covered Bloody Sunday and both my cameraman and I kept a look out for our William Street friend, but he did not show. I assumed he was shut inside for the day. When we did see him those many times it seemed to reassure us that, with him at least, some sanity prevailed.

Gerald Seymour was an ITN correspondent who reported extensively on Northern Ireland before becoming a bestselling author. His book *Harry's Game* was one of the first novels based on the Troubles.

The crews of old
Robin Walsh

The Bogside, Derry, 30 January 1972.
Bloody Sunday – members of the Parachute Regiment shoot dead thirteen civilians. Cameraman: Cyril Cave; sound recordist: Jim Deeney. Lasting image: priest waving a white handkerchief as a wounded civilian is carried away.

Oxford Street Bus Station, Belfast, 21 July 1972.
Bloody Friday – six people are killed as part of a Provincial IRA bombing blitz of Belfast which costs nine lives. Cameraman: Patsy Hill. Lasting image: body parts being put in plastic bags.

Milltown Cemetery, Belfast, 19 March 1988.
Loyalist terrorist Michael Stone attacks mourners and murders three people. Cameraman: Peter Cooper; sound recordist: Karl Walker. Lasting image: a man firing shots and throwing grenades as people cower behind gravestones.

This is the stuff of television news, the medium whose lifeblood is the moving picture – brought to the screen not by the instantly recognisable reporter, but by the anonymous cameraman.

In all three instances – as in countless others down the decades – there was much that was simply taken for granted.

There was courage. Cave could not have stayed hidden behind a protective wall as the army bullets whistled by and managed to capture that image of Father Edward Daly any more than Cooper could have kept his camera behind the headstone as Stone approached with his lethal weapons. And although his life was not in danger, it took no little fortitude on Hill's part to capture the images that showed the real consequences of terrorism.

There was, as time went by, the virtual acceptance on the part of the camera crews that the abnormal was normal. No war-zone training. Limited protective clothing. No stress counselling on return to base – job done, where to next?

There was the equipment – particularly in the case of Cave and Hill: heavier and more visible with its umbilical cord that inextricably linked cameraman and sound recordist, a far cry from today's lightweight gear that allows mobility and independence.

And again with Cave and Hill, there was the rush to beat the on-air deadline, often as hair-raising as the taking of the pictures. The pre-video days of film demanded a return to the office and the time-consuming wait for the pictures to emerge from the processing machine. Cave's record for the seventy-mile drive from the Bogside to Ormeau Avenue in Belfast in the days of limited motorway was under the hour.

The life of the pre-Troubles news camera crews was to be found elsewhere in regional broadcasting – the varied round of assignments that painted a picture of their communities on the nightly news magazines. From the early days of the '50s to the late '60s it was, by and large, the normal fare of provincial news.

From October 1968 all was to change and the local crews found themselves covering an international news story shoulder to shoulder with the battle-hardened outfits from the networks, fresh from the trouble spots of the world. There were new tricks to be learned, and quickly.

Most were about survival. Rioters saw the camera as another enemy – when to produce it and where to shoot from were to become fine judgements. The choice of crew car distinguished the streetwise from the naive: the former drove a two-door car, knowing it was of little use to hijackers on the prowl for transport for their next bombing expedition.

Then the editorial conundrum of what to shoot and what not to shoot. Essentially they shot all they could, rightly leaving the delicate judgement of what to transmit in the hands of programme editors back at base. Yet, very quickly they were to display a sensitivity in spite of the pressure: 'pulling out' from the covered body or pool of blood rather than dramatically 'zooming in', and the same camera editing when dealing with the distraught burying their dead. It was a subtle message.

Unlike the 'visiting firemen' from London and beyond, the locals found themselves in an unrelenting grind, covering a community that was their own, tearing itself apart. Cameraman Dick Macmillan and sound recordist Brian Willis were on the way to an assignment in Derry on 31 July 1972 when they heard an explosion and saw the rising smoke as they neared the village of Claudy.

The scene they encountered was indescribable – nine people lay dead as a result of the IRA's no-warning bombs. The Paisleyite *Protestant Telegraph* accused the BBC of having advance notice of the bombing, such was the immediacy of the pictures. Little did they know that Macmillan had stumbled across the body of a young relative who had perished in the atrocity. When informed, the newspaper still refused to withdraw this gross slur.

Those of us now long retired continue to marvel at the work of today's camera crews. Some of the problems and pressures of old may have gone but in their stead have come new ones.

The digital and satellite age, combined with twenty-four-hour rolling news has heralded the era of the never-ending deadline. The appetite for pictures has never been more voracious nor the competition fiercer.

The capacity to transmit live pictures from just about anywhere has put additional editorial burdens on the shoulders of picture takers. The death toll in the trouble spots of the world indicates that they are literally in the firing line to an extent rarely before experienced.

The pressure on programme editors has never been greater in a relentless news-gathering process that includes everyone with a home video or mobile phone.

But within the Northern Ireland context it was the crews of old for whom I shall have everlasting admiration. They learned as they went along because the awfulness of the Troubles was new. The legacy of those who have now retired – or who, like Patsy Hill and Dick Macmillan, have sadly passed away – is to be found in the excellence of the new breed.

Robin Walsh was controller of BBC NI. He previously worked as news editor of Ulster Television and BBC NI, and as editor of BBC Television's *Nine O'Clock News*.

Bloody Sunday
Peter Taylor

Appropriately I write this in Derry/Londonderry in a hotel room overlooking the Bogside, forty-six years after British paratroopers shot dead thirteen civil rights marchers on that bright crisp afternoon in 1972. Beneath the rooftops, the memorial is still there but the flowers that marked the places where the victims fell are long gone. That day, and the experience of the days that followed, are still seared in my memory.

It was to be my first ever trip to any part of Ireland. I was a green young reporter for Thames Television's *This Week* programme, sent to cover the aftermath of the killings. I didn't even know where Derry – or was it Londonderry? – was. The team had planned to cover the anti-internment march that Sunday, anticipating likely trouble following the clash the previous weekend between protestors and the Paras on the beach below Magilligan internment camp, a few miles up the coast from Derry.

It was clear there were likely to be similar clashes during the planned demonstration the following Sunday. We had hoped to cover the march extensively with three camera crews: one with the marchers, one with police and army, and one with a licence to roam wherever events led. It was not to be.

The militant trade union, the Association of Cinematograph, Television and Allied Technicians (ACTT) wouldn't allow the crews to go because Thames Television's management refused to pay the amount of 'danger money' the union demanded. Had we not been prevented from taking three crews to cover the march, the filmic record of Bloody Sunday, that landmark day in the evolution of the Troubles, would probably have been significantly different.

I remember sitting in the bedroom in my London flat that freezing cold Sunday afternoon and being shocked as I heard the news of what had happened in Derry coming through on the radio. I immediately phoned the editor of *This Week* and, with a hastily assembled crew, rushed to Heathrow to join the queue of journalists all desperate to get to Derry as quickly as possible. It was a huge story and it was to get even bigger.

I arrived in the city just before midnight that Sunday evening and checked into a B&B, nervous that an IRA sniper might pick me off as I got ready for bed. I did say I was a green young reporter. I was a naive one as well.

The following morning I nervously ventured into the Bogside. You could

almost touch the silence. There was not a soul around. It was an eerie experience. There were pools of blood on the ground where many of the victims had fallen. Fresh flowers too now marked the scenes of the killings. The Bogside is a small and tight-knit community. I knew I had to find eyewitnesses and the only way I could do that was by knocking on doors as there was no one around. Again I did this with some trepidation, fearful of the reception a Brit was likely to get knocking on the doors of those who would have known many of the dead. I could not have been more wrong. Doors were opened and I was welcomed, watered with endless cups of tea and fed with sandwiches, cakes and Blue Riband chocolate biscuits. People said they were grateful that I had come from London to try and find out what happened and record what they had seen. They were only too willing to talk. It was their side of the story.

Several families directed me to a flat on the first floor of Glenfada Park that overlooked the rubble barricade where William Nash, John Young and Michael McDaid were shot dead. The occupant was a former British soldier from Wales, Jack Chapman, who had witnessed at first hand the killings around the makeshift barricade below his balcony. He told me that no shots had been fired at the Paras and the protestors had been shot dead in cold blood. Given his background, his testimony seemed about as unbiased as I was likely to find. I filmed an interview with him on the balcony that had given him a grandstand view.

I stayed in Derry for three days filming interviews for a *This Week* programme due for transmission the following Thursday evening. I interviewed the commander of the IRA's Derry Brigade, who remained anonymous. Martin McGuinness was soon to succeed him. The commander was clearly nervous and I waited whilst he rang the IRA's General Headquarters Staff (GHQ) in Dublin to get the okay to go on the record. In the interview he told me that the IRA (the Provisional IRA, that is) had no weapons in the Bogside that day as its volunteers had been ordered to remove them to the Creggan estate on the hill above.

I filmed the procession of mourners who made their way to the church atop the Creggan where the thirteen coffins were lying. I remember standing next to the SDLP's John Hume, who pointed out one of the young men in the procession. 'There's someone you should talk to,' he said. 'His name is Martin McGuinness.'

I followed his advice and met McGuinness for the first time at the disused gasworks that the IRA frequented at the time, at the edge of the Bogside, out of sight of the British Army stationed on the city walls above. He was impressive, with a natural charm that belied the steel that lay behind it. When he said that he would rather be washing the car and mowing the lawn on a Sunday than doing what he was doing, I hesitated to ask him what that was and felt slightly guilty that I tended to believe him.

I carried on talking to McGuinness, on and off the record, for the continuing years of the conflict until his premature death in March 2017. In those exchanges, I saw both the charm and the steel; the steel evident in that unnerving, intimidating stare. I attended his funeral as I had attended Ian Paisley's memorial service three years earlier. The 'Chuckle Brothers' – the sobriquet the media chose to describe the remarkable relationship between the two inveterate former enemies – were now gone.

And what of the film due for transmission the Thursday after Bloody Sunday? Thames TV was understandably nervous given that the Conservative government of the day had just announced a judicial inquiry under Lord Widgery, an inquiry subsequently dismissed in most quarters as a whitewash. Thames' controller of features, Jeremy Isaacs, courageously circumvented the potential legal problem by signing off a *This Week* called 'Two Sides of the Story' in which two unedited ten-minute reels of film – clapper boards included (those were the pre-tape days of magazines of film) – were juxtaposed. One reel was my interview with Jack Chapman; the other an unedited reel of interviews with the Paras recorded by my colleague Peter Williams. Thames' justification for broadcasting the programme was that it reflected two diametrically opposed accounts of what happened, with neither account being edited, as was apparent from the clapper boards visible at the beginning of each roll of film.

Viewers were left to make up their own minds as to whom they believed. When Lord Widgery's successor, Lord Saville, finally completed his subsequent inquiry, lasting twelve years and costing almost £200 million, he concluded that many soldiers had 'knowingly put forward false stories in order to seek to justify their firing'. Eyewitnesses like Jack Chapman were vindicated. The soldiers' accounts were not. That was Lord Saville's judgement on 'Two Sides of the Story'.

And the effect of Bloody Sunday on me? At the time I felt guilty on two counts: that 'my' soldiers seemed to have shot dead unarmed and innocent civil rights marchers; and that I was totally ignorant about the conflict in Ireland, having no understanding of the conflict or of why it had arisen – let alone what the solution might be. I spent the next four decades and more trying to find out.

Peter Taylor has reported on terrorism and political violence throughout the world for the BBC and ITV for over forty-five years, and has written eight books on the subject. His work includes many groundbreaking documentaries on Northern Ireland.

'Get that Irish bitch off the air or someone else will'
Gloria Hunniford

Scores of people were lying on the street screaming in pain, terror and confusion by the time I arrived at the scene of the IRA bomb attack on the Abercorn restaurant in the centre of Belfast on that Saturday afternoon in March 1972. I'd seen some terrible things before but the Abercorn was the worst disaster I had encountered during my time reporting for the BBC in Northern Ireland.

I couldn't count how many times I had to report on the atrocities of the day back then. The call would come to me: 'There's been an explosion in Belfast. Get down there and cover it.' And so I did.

The bomb at the Abercorn was a relatively small explosive but it had been planted under a seat in the very crowded restaurant. A fire had broken out too and many people were terribly badly burnt over their entire bodies. I shuddered when I heard that two young women had been killed. Another 139 people were maimed or seriously injured. Many of the injured lost their legs or arms; others lost their sight when they were hit in the face by shards of glass.

One television reporter was so overcome that he broke down on camera, trying to cover it up by saying that he was out of breath from running up the stairs. It was the first time that I'd witnessed the aftermath of a bomb at such close quarters and I was absolutely horrified.

I saw the partially burnt driving licence of one of the women who was killed and all around me were handbags with their contents spilling out over the road; teddy bears with charred faces – people's everyday lives broken and tossed aside by the force of the blast.

The Abercorn report was the first one I had ever filed to England to a national audience for the *Today* programme on BBC Radio 4 and that scene in Cornmarket has remained with me throughout the years.

I really felt the futility of the conflict that day – women and children who had become victims, simply because they happened to be out shopping on a Saturday afternoon.

I was close to another bomb in Belfast several years later. It was the mid-70s by then and I was just about to go on air for a radio programme I was presenting when we were told a car bomb been placed at the base of the BBC studios, and was set to go off in minutes.

I decided to stay rather than evacuate the building – a bit of the 'show-must-go-on' spirit – but the sense of nervousness was overwhelming. Quite suddenly the blast erupted and the solid building shook like jelly and it was almost impossible to see or breathe. Decades of dust clouded the studio. But we were live on air and I had no choice but to describe what was happening to the aghast listeners.

In 1983, after going to work in England, I was frighteningly close to a devastating bomb near Harrods in London. I'd taken my thirteen-year-old son Michael to the famous Knightsbridge store as there was a specific game he was after, and I let him explore the toy room while I went to the china department.

At 1.30 p.m. a car bomb exploded in a nearby side street killing three police officers on their way to investigate it and three civilians. Everyone was instructed to file out via a certain exit. Everyone did so in an eerie silence but inside I was hysterical not knowing where Michael was.

Outside the scene was chaotic; some of the injured were staggering around with rumours rife that there was another bomb elsewhere. All I could do was struggle back to my car, which was parked nearby, and pray that Michael would come and find me there. It was as if time stood still, except my heart was racing with panic. Thank God Michael turned up minutes later, although to me it felt like hours.

In London too I received a warning that my name was on a death list after another double-bomb attack. I was presenting my own show on Radio 2 in July 1982 when the two bombs exploded in Hyde Park and Regent's Park, killing eleven people and seven horses. I was live on air and was linking to the horrific news bulletins with little else under discussion. However, unknown to me, complaints started coming in with threats along the lines of 'Get that Irish bitch off the air or someone else will.'

I was told about the death threat as my live programme finished. I was suddenly very conscious of many men in suits who turned out to be BBC security personnel. I wasn't allowed to drive myself home that day – the upside was that I was forever allowed to park in the BBC's inner sanctum.

It wasn't the first death threat.

In 1969 my fellow broadcaster Sean Rafferty and I started to record a show together for the British Forces Broadcasting Service (BFBS) with the title *Ulster Calling*. The idea was to keep families on the military bases in Germany in touch with soldiers in Northern Ireland.

On one occasion Sean and I were visiting army back-up units and families in Germany. As we were leaving to go to the airport, we were mysteriously called in to see the brigadier at his home. Sean and I wondered what was happening. After we had got past the pleasantries the brigadier said he felt he should tell us that we had both been placed on an IRA hit list. He added that he would understand if we wanted to give the programme up.

Sean and I looked at each other.

But as we had been doing the show for seven years we decided there was no point in stopping and we carried on.

Gloria Hunniford is a television presenter. When she worked in Belfast, she was a news reporter for BBC Radio Ulster and hosted UTV's nightly hour-long *Good Evening Ulster* programme.

Uncle Ted
Deric Henderson

It came with a rap on my bedroom door in the summer of 1972. My mother looked in. She sounded in control, and then told me: 'Ted has been shot.'

She had just returned from Derry where her younger brother lay critically injured and on a life-support machine in a private ward at Altnagelvin Hospital. It was the middle of the night, and the family quickly adjourned to sit in silence in the front living room of our home in Omagh.

Ted Megahey had been in the front seat in the third of four Land Rovers heading in a convoy towards the Irish border to relieve regular soldiers on checkpoint duty on the Buncrana Road. He had been wearing a beret as part of his Ulster Defence Regiment uniform, holding a self-loading rifle with the barrel pointing upwards, and according to one of the men with him, he was remarking about the fading skyline of the distant hills of Donegal.

'Isn't that lovely?' he asked.

Suddenly the window of the passenger door shattered, sending shards and splinters of glass on top of him, the driver and the two men in the rear. The driver managed to stop fifty yards further on. Ted was still upright, leaning slightly to his right, but unconscious when they reached inside to carry him out, and by the time he was rested by the roadside they could hear his laboured breathing, and see he had been shot in the back of the head.

He was bleeding badly and somebody radioed for an ambulance.

He died three days later on 9 June, the 396th victim of the Troubles.

Uncle Ted was aged forty-five and lived with his parents on the family farm at Leganvey House outside the village of Drumquin, ten miles from Omagh. His father, Edward, a Protestant from Crumlin, County Antrim, was a retired RUC officer who began his policing career with the Royal Irish Constabulary in Carrick-on-Shannon, County Leitrim, and who went on to marry a woman from Portglenone. They had four daughters and two sons.

None of the grandchildren knew until that Sunday afternoon of the funeral that our grandmother, Mary Jane McCloskey, was once a Catholic. A group of strangers, her relatives, had arrived in the farmyard. Several hundred people walked the three miles behind undertaker Ian Duncan's hearse for the service at the local Church of Ireland on the far side of the village, where my grandmother had become a faithful, and very active, member of the parish.

It was a desperately sad occasion. There were a lot of tears, handshakes and commiserations, and it must have taken the best part of two hours before the last of the mourners had departed to leave the family to stand by themselves, and read the cards attached to dozens of floral tributes. The message on the wreath left by his parents read, 'Resting where no shadows fall.'

His plot, just yards from the church entrance, was the first to be dug at Lower Langfield. He was among a group of parishioners who had helped clear away trees and shrubbery to make way for the new graveyard.

Uncle Ted worked as a panel beater for the bus company, the Ulster Transport Authority, in Omagh. He was balding and retained handsome features, and although a lady from Castlederg had serious designs on him, he never married.

He kept himself in great shape. He was a useful boxer by all accounts, but outside the ring he could be just as quick with his temper and his fists. He was never one for standing back. He was no saint, but he was very well liked within a close circle of friends.

He was a fast driver – especially at the wheel of an old black Austin A40, which once or twice ended up in ditches on the main Omagh–Drumquin road – and he later became the owner of a second-hand Jaguar with an English registration number, which attracted admiring glances. He was as proud as punch when he first pulled up outside our home in his gleaming new light-blue car.

I remember him wearing the dark green blazer with the crest of Omagh Academicals, and sipping water at the rugby club's then unofficial HQ, the front bar of the town's Royal Arms Hotel, pretending he had never lost his taste for vodka and lemonade. He once had a drink problem, but by that stage he hadn't touched alcohol in years. That's the way he was.

He was a man who had a lot of catching up to do, and in the years before he died he travelled far and wide, sometimes on bus excursions to various parts of continental Europe. My late mother loved him to bits. She used to make him sandwiches filled with Branston pickle, and apart from his brother Deric, she probably found it more difficult than anyone else within the family to come to terms with the circumstances of his death. It was an awful time.

And yet it might never have happened. The night he was shot, he was standing in for a friend. Somebody called the house to see if he was available, and within an hour or so he was linking up with other members of E Company, 6th Battalion UDR, based outside Newtownstewart, before being detailed to go to Derry.

There was a briefing session at Fort George, a Ministry of Defence site close to the banks of the River Foyle, and then they headed off to take over from soldiers belonging to the 2nd Battalion of the Royal Green Jackets. The checkpoint was in open countryside with just one house about fifty yards away.

The traffic had been fairly heavy, but nobody heard or saw anything suspicious to give rise to alarm. The regulars were waiting to be replaced, and the first of the Land Rovers was preparing to come to a halt when a single shot rang out. Just one. Somebody noticed a flash, and one of the soldiers believed it may have come from the area of the house. But he couldn't be sure.

He later said, 'I then formed the opinion that what I heard was the echo bouncing off the walls of the house.'

The IRA claimed responsibility for the shooting the day after Uncle Ted was buried. Large parts of the city on the slopes on the western side of the Foyle were effectively no-go areas for police and troops, with many of the roads blocked by makeshift barricades. They could be viewed from the upper floors of the hospital where we took turns to look out while maintaining a vigil of sorts, but in our heart of hearts we all knew it was only a matter of time.

I don't remember who told me late that Friday afternoon that my uncle had died, but I do recall the distress and the heartache, and a grieving process that seemed to go on forever. There was bitterness as well.

My grandfather was a formidable man who would reminisce from time to time about his policing days in Cookstown, Plumbridge, Carrickmore and his final posting to Drumquin. But he had moved on, retired, and bought the farm from a brother of the man, Felix Kearney, who wrote a famous ballad with the lines: 'Drumquin, you're not a city, but all the world to me ...'

My grandfather got on well with his neighbours. He worked unbelievably hard, took great pride in his cattle and his land, and every one of us looked up to him. He always commanded our full attention.

However, unlike his wife – a great woman in the kitchen, who collected antiques, especially clocks, and who was never happier than when playing cards with her local GP and helping out at the church – he wasn't one for showing signs of emotion.

But like us all back then, he was completely broken. Devastation doesn't even come close to describing how we all felt. It still reverberates to this day.

There are a couple of memorial stones. One of them is on the church wall at Langfield where the extended family gather every Remembrance Sunday for the annual service and the laying of poppies, and another at a local Orange Hall. Uncle Ted was a member of the Orange Order. The inscription on his headstone at Lower Langfield reads, 'Weep not for me, but courage take. Love one another for my sake.'

My parents and grandparents, as well as an aunt who returned from Canada, are now buried in that graveyard, but rarely does a week pass when I don't think of Uncle Ted, and what happened that night all those years ago.

Were the murderers in the room?
Robert Fisk

The first body I saw in Northern Ireland was neatly laid out in a coffin made of oak. John Brown lay inside it in the front room. A big box it was, with gold handles and satin padding.

Cecil Rock, his father-in-law, was meeting visitors at the door of the tiny terraced house that June morning in 1972, alongside what we called the 'peace line', and above the body hung the banners of the Ulster Defence Association, all red hands and crowns and endless stitched versions of '*Quis separabit*'. Protestant paramilitaries chose to use the motto of Anglo-Irish regiments, government officials and at least one cardinal. 'Who shall separate us?' Well, indeed.

There were a lot of silent young UDA men sitting along the back wall of the front room, also holding banners. They all wore brown fatigues. A few sported sunglasses. John Brown was a volunteer but he had died on his way home to the Springmartin housing estate four days earlier, late at night.

His face, like that of all dead men, appeared unreal but it was covered in scars and great black bruises. Before he was shot in the head, John Brown had been beaten up. I recall that Cecil lifted a dead hand from the coffin to show me that his son-in-law's fingers had been broken.

'It could not have been anyone but the IRA,' he said. 'They are just animals. How could they do it? He hurt no one and he was on his way home to his wife and son.' Cecil said that Protestants and Catholics would never come together to find a new future together.

I was very uneasy, standing in that front room. Like all violence in Belfast at the time, it had a simple narrative. A Protestant murdered by Catholics – four men had stopped him just twenty yards from his front door, beaten him, kicked him, broken his fingers and shot him. Presumably in that order.

But I was troubled by the solemn, sullen young men at the back of the room. There were always feuds among the Belfast paramilitaries, and I was suddenly possessed of the idea that John Brown might have been murdered by his old comrades. Perhaps the bleak young men in shades just behind me knew something about it. Were the murderers in the room?

I spent almost five years in Northern Ireland for the London *Times*. And then more than four decades in the Middle East, mostly for the London *Independent*.

That June of 1972, a subeditor in London thought up an ingenious – and shallow and, of course, canny – headline to my story that night. 'John Brown's (beaten) body,' it said.

The Northern Ireland war in those days was a small-scale affair in world history. I'd see more dead; occasionally, I would actually see someone die.

In Andersonstown one morning, I'd been talking to a Catholic family on the estate – a bright, sunny day, kids shouting, me saying goodbye on the scrubby front lawn. Then there was gunfire, which sounded to me like matchsticks snapping, and an army 'Pig' came racing down the road and a British soldier toppled out the back, his self-loading rifle banging on to the tarmac. I lay on the grass and looked up and saw, perhaps for only four or five seconds, a youth with immensely long hair crouching behind a dustbin and shooting with what looked like a Thompson sub-machine gun.

The whole thing took only a few seconds longer than it took you to read that last sentence. Then the young man had gone and so had the army 'Pig' with the dead man hauled inside. That was it. If death was an institution, it came brutally and often suddenly – I'm not sure if John Brown's path to eternity was so mercifully quick – and, for us reporters, it was another day done and dusted, make the deadline at 6 p.m., update an hour later.

I found that when some of my own acquaintances were killed – not many, for this was a small war – I would write 'died' over their names in my contacts book, as if they had made an exit at the end of a play. Their theatrical role was over.

We journalists, I fear, often regarded those we wrote about as somehow removed from the lives we ourselves led. I remember, in Beirut in 1976, hearing of Máire Drumm's death. She was shot in her bed at the Mater Hospital in Belfast after an eye operation, and shot again as she crawled across the floor of the ward seeking salvation.

She had given me coffee at her home many times and even met my editor from London, a British Territorial officer whom she nonetheless treated with great respect; and then she invited the local IRA Provisionals to her home to say goodbye to me when I was about to leave for the dangers of the Middle East. And what did I write when I read she'd been murdered? I opened my old contacts book and found 'Drumm, Máire' and wrote 'DIED' in biro over her name.

By then I was watching death on a more titanic scale, lives as full of meaning as any in Belfast, equally betrayed by politics and history, but destroyed in such number that the tragedy of Belfast and Derry seemed irrelevant, preposterous, the fag-end of an old novel that was no longer worth reading.

I would subconsciously thank Northern Ireland for teaching me to stand up to people with power. I was threatened by the UVF and the Official IRA – in a single joint visitation to my office at the Europa Hotel – and I was constantly harassed and abused and lied to by the British Army. Choosing to print and be damned – and refusing intimidation is a choice – was a fine lesson to take with me to the Middle East when I had to challenge far more powerful governments and mendacious lobby groups and much more murderous individuals.

But there are moments that must make you weep unless you have a heart of stone, and that prove that all wars – the Middle East or Belfast – are about human suffering on an epic scale of sorrow. There was a young woman in Beirut who drank poison on a clifftop during the Lebanese civil war, facing the sun setting over the Mediterranean, because her son had been kidnapped and she could not bear his loss. And there was the inquest in Northern Ireland in which it was recorded that an Ulster Defence Regiment soldier had been shot in front of his wife, who told him – as he lay on the ground before her – that he must not die. And his last words to her were, 'No, I will never leave you.'

Robert Fisk is Middle East correspondent for the *Independent* and has lived in the Arab world for forty-two years. He was Belfast correspondent for *The Times* from 1992 to 1995.

The little boy who witnessed an attempt on a neighbour's life
Ian Woods

I noticed the car when it first passed my house. It had three men inside. It was only when it drove by the house again shortly afterwards, that I thought it was unusual. Cars were still rare enough on our council estate that we could play football and other games without having to pause very often for passing traffic.

On this occasion in July 1972 I was in the front garden, mucking about with my cousins. Maybe we were playing marbles, as we often did, but I can't remember for sure, because something more memorable was about to happen.

The car came round the corner a third time and it stopped outside number 3. I lived in number 7. Two men jumped out. At least one had a handgun and they also carried a petrol can. They ran to the front door and forced their way in. There was the sound of gunfire from inside. Then the men ran out, jumped into the car and the driver sped away. Within a few moments smoke started emerging from the house. I banged on our front door to tell my mum that something had happened at the McGladderys' house.

Daniel McGladdery had been a unionist senator in the old Stormont parliament. As a young lad I had a vague sense that he was important, but in later life I discovered he was a former trade union leader who became deputy leader of the senate, and then worked in the prime minister's office under Lord Brookeborough and then Captain Terence O'Neill.

He survived this assassination attempt. He ran into the back garden and somehow the bullets missed. The intruders contented themselves with splashing petrol around the house and setting fire to it. The home was badly damaged, but the fire brigade arrived in time to save it. It was repaired, and Mr McGladdery and his wife carried on living there, though their front door was made more secure.

It was a comparatively minor incident in the bloody history of the Troubles, but it was a big deal in my life at the time. Police and soldiers descended on the neighbourhood. A couple of TV cameras turned up to film the aftermath. Even then I was desperate to be on TV and wanted to volunteer my eyewitness account. I was dissuaded by family and friends who warned of dire consequences if I went public. 'You'll get shot in a reprisal attack.' Such was the vocabulary of the time. And anyway, the reporters might not have trusted the account of an eight-year-old boy.

I spent my entire childhood in Cliftondene, a council estate just off the Oldpark Road in North Belfast. The broadcaster Eamonn Holmes was a neighbour.

I can vividly remember flames rising from dozens of burning houses in nearby Ardoyne, and conversations with kids my age about whether or not there was going to be a civil war. We repeated phrases we'd heard from TV or parents, without really understanding what was going on. For a time, when sectarian violence in Ardoyne threatened to spill over into our area, my father used to fill the bath and position buckets of water around the house in case we should ever get firebombed.

I once witnessed a bomber carrying his device into a nearby shop. I thought that the way he was carrying the box looked suspicious, and told my mum. She laughed it off and we got on the bus and went into town. When we returned, the shop had been reduced to rubble. Like I said, who'd believe a kid's version of events?

I couldn't wait to leave Northern Ireland when I was eighteen. It was 1982 and the Troubles were all I'd ever really known. I escaped lightly. Nobody I knew had been killed, but an English university seemed a far more attractive option than staying in Belfast and going to Queen's or Coleraine. Once I left I quickly embarked on a career in journalism, and often met English reporters who knew my home city better than I did. Newsrooms used Ulster as a training ground for young journalists, and it became a place where reporters made their reputations.

By contrast I covered conflicts all over the world without ever working in Northern Ireland. In the past decade I've rediscovered the country, visiting family, and for the first time, reporting on it. On one visit I was walking up the steps of Stormont, sheltering from driving rain under an umbrella, only to be halted by a melee at my feet as security guards wrestled with the notorious loyalist terrorist Michael Stone who was attempting to kill Sinn Féin leaders Gerry Adams and Martin McGuinness inside Parliament Buildings.

At least I knew who he was and could enlighten the Sky News audience about his background. More recently I've filmed inside the ruins of Crumlin Road court with men who were once convicted there.

The journalist in me wishes I had experienced more of the Troubles. But I'm more relieved that none of my family or friends were among the victims.

Ian Woods is a Sky News correspondent. He was born in Belfast.

The Bloody Friday survivors who inspired me
Alf McCreary

Journalists who covered the Troubles have many memories of tension, trauma and death. I vividly recall reporting on the funerals after Bloody Sunday, the aftermath of the Kingsmills atrocity near my native village of Bessbrook, and the Enniskillen Cenotaph bombing – all of which will be with me as long as I live.

However one of the most frightening, and in the long term most troubling, atrocities was the Bloody Friday bombing of 21 July 1972 when the Provisional IRA exploded more than twenty bombs within a mile radius of Belfast city centre, and all within seventy-five minutes.

There were gruesome scenes at the Oxford Street Bus Station where six people died – two soldiers and four civilians. The carnage was so bad that rescue workers had to brush parts of dismembered bodies into bags. What made it worse was the fact that the television stations broadcast the disturbing pictures.

Three other people died at a row of shops on the Cavehill Road, including fourteen-year-old Stephen Parker. As well as the nine who died in various parts of the city, another 130 people were injured, and some of them badly.

The Belfast Brigade of the Provisional IRA later accepted responsibility, and claimed that warnings had been given to the Samaritans and to the media. Few, if any, people believed them. It was an act of gross savagery to detonate twenty-two bombs in the middle of a shopping day in summer with so many people in the city.

I heard the first bomb go off not far from the offices of the *Belfast Telegraph* in Royal Avenue where I was working as a staff leader-writer and feature writer.

We had been used to bombs and bomb-scares, and this bomb sounded no different. Then the explosions kept coming at regular intervals – boom, boom, boom. Though we did not find out the exact locations until later, it was a very worrying situation.

In those days the *Telegraph* was an evening paper, and while the news staff worked away to gather as much information as they could about the bombs and the aftermath for the next day, there was nothing I could do as a leader-writer on that sombre afternoon.

The same applied to our chief political reporter John Wallace, so – with permission from the editor – we joined crowds of other people rushing out of the city on York Street.

I cannot remember how I got my car, or where it had been parked, but as John and I moved along the road we were aware of the large number of people around us. I also noticed the traders boarding up their front windows – yet again.

When we reached my house at Carnmoney, some miles north of the city, my wife Hilary made tea for John and me as we watched the ghastly drama unfold on television. When Hilary brought in the tea, she began to cry at the awful spectacle of the remains of human bodies being lifted and scraped off the pavement at Oxford Street.

I wondered why she was crying because at that stage I was living in a parallel universe inhabited by many journalists watching or covering a dreadful story such as Bloody Friday. I was in a kind of overdrive, picking up details, listening to statements, and all the time gathering information that I knew I might need to write up for a commentary the next day. It was only much later that the awfulness of the human tragedy began to sink in.

Not long after the Bloody Friday bombings I wrote *Survivors*, which was probably the first book to recount the human suffering at the heart of the Troubles.

I remember meeting a lovely man called Billy Magowan whose wife, Vera, suffered severe brain damage in the Cavehill Road explosion. For weeks she lay in the intensive care unit in the Royal Victoria Hospital with shrapnel in her head.

She returned home, but life for Billy and Vera was never the same again. Vera was still able to walk and talk, but with great difficulty. The once vivacious businesswoman became confined mainly to her own home.

Billy said, 'One day it hit me, what we would have to face together, and the tears started to flow. We are still very close, but so much of my time is taken up with looking after Vera. Sometimes I'm up two or three times a night trying to help her. On Sunday afternoons I go to bed to catch up on my sleep. Can you imagine what it is like being up in the middle of the night with Vera in pain and knowing that neither you nor the doctors are able do anything for her, and her asking you "Why do I have to suffer in this way? What did I do wrong?"'

I wrote those words some forty-five years ago when I interviewed Billy and Vera for *Survivors*, and as I re-type them today they still have a powerful, sombre and searing effect that has not lessened down the years.

More recently I was reminded of another victim of Bloody Friday when the *Belfast Telegraph* asked me to write the obituary of the Reverend Joseph Parker, whose fourteen-year-old son Stephen died in the bombing.

Joe Parker was then the chaplain to the Missions to Seamen, and he had the awful task of identifying Stephen in the mortuary. He could only recognise his son by his one remaining hand, his trouser belt and by a box of boys' 'trick matches' in his pocket. And then he had to break the devastating news to the rest of the family.

For three years Joe Parker ran virtually a one-man peace campaign, which involved, among other things, an all-night vigil outside Belfast City Hall.

He founded an organisation called Witness for Peace, and later he and his family emigrated to Canada, where he became the chaplain to the Missions to Seamen in Vancouver.

He worked very successfully there until his retirement in 1993. He died in Canada at the age of 89. Another son, Roger, told me for the obituary that his father had made a return visit to Northern Ireland, and was pleased by the Good Friday Agreement, which – he believed – was the culmination of the groundwork for reconciliation that had been laid by many other groups down the years, including Witness for Peace.

Today I choose to take the positive attitude and underline that in Joe Parker's life some light had come out of the darkness of Bloody Friday, but it is hard to remember any good from the bomb that destroyed the lives of the innocent couple Billy and Vera Magowan, and many others.

As I get older I become very saddened when I think of these things, and I wonder what all the suffering really achieved in the end. I can only hope and pray that it will never happen here again.

Alf McCreary is an author and award-winning journalist who was, for many years, a staff feature and editorial writer for the *Belfast Telegraph*. He is now freelance and also religion correspondent for the *Telegraph*.

The day the army missed the IRA's top commander
Chris Ryder

As civil disorder engulfed Northern Ireland after 1968, it was left to the media to interpret the blood-soaked developments. With unionism diametrically opposed to republicanism, there was plenty to write about as I joined *The Sunday Times* early in 1972. Apart from the economy, the paper stated there was no more important topic than Ulster on the British political agenda.

The recently opened Europa Hotel quickly became home and office for the reporters deployed to Belfast. We were resident there not due to its luxury but because it had a modern telephone in every room and a telex in the reception. Another bonus was that the porter's desk was in constant touch with the citywide network of taxi cabs with radios who proved to be a useful source of breaking news. Before long, some taxi men were earning top money from the big news organisations.

With the Troubles, as they were now universally known, older republican voices fanned the embers of earlier conflicts with the aim of finally achieving a united Ireland. A new generation quickly joined them, bringing a new ruthlessness to fulfil the long-cherished dream. There was a similar mobilisation on the unionist side, with angry militant leaders robustly opposed to even the tiniest concession to the united-Irelanders.

The security forces were, of course, constantly seeking to capture these self-appointed, unelected, reckless 'warlords', who directed gun and bomb attacks, indiscriminately killing or maiming anyone who crossed their paths.

So persuading these elusive individuals to justify their competing causes was a task fraught with difficulty. You couldn't just ring them up to ask for an interview. Other channels had to be used as their priority was to conceal their whereabouts to avoid arrest.

During the autumn of 1972, as the violence intensified, a contact in Belfast told me to be in the Royal Dublin Hotel by lunchtime the next day. About mid-afternoon, a young man sidled up beside me in the lounge and explained we had to go to the bar of the Gresham Hotel, just across O'Connell Street, and wait for the all-clear.

I was aware we were being watched and, although I couldn't see them, I knew that once they were sure we weren't being followed, I'd get my interview. My escort went to a public phone bay in the foyer and after a brief conversation gave me the thumbs up. We were to go to the nearby Anchor Hotel, a modest Georgian-style boarding house whose faded decor echoed grander days.

I took a seat and moments later Dáithí Ó Conaill and Ruairí Ó Brádaigh, two of the most influential IRA leaders, joined me. But almost as soon as they sat down there was the unmistakable thump of an explosion, strong enough to send its after-tremors rippling along O'Connell Street. The graceful old Anchor shook to it roots but my guests were gone, slipped away into the night. (I learned later two explosions in nearby Sackville Street killed two city bus drivers.) When I returned to the Royal Dublin a message had been left with my room key at the reception. Another meeting soon, it promised.

Some days afterwards, I was in the bar at the Europa when one of the porters handed me a message advising me to expect a visitor at 4 p.m. Right on time, a smartly dressed young woman told me I was to get a black taxi to Andersonstown.

When I got to the black taxi rank in Castle Street a man put his finger across his lips and gestured me to take a seat in a nearby vehicle. Minutes later, my silent co-passenger tapped the taxi driver's shoulder and he pulled left and stopped. We got out, crossed the road and entered a double-fronted Victorian detached house. The front doors were opened by a young man, who directed me into a large lounge.

The door opened again and two men came in: Jimmy Drumm, a lifelong republican who was a highly influential figure in the Provisionals. His companion I recognised as Seamus Twomey, the leader of the IRA in Belfast.

After some small talk, Twomey laid out the IRA's unchanging demands for a ceasefire and a grandiose British statement of intent to withdraw from Ireland. He said I could report in the coming weekend's *Sunday Times* that there would be a general ceasefire over Christmas and the New Year to facilitate the start of negotiations.

As Twomey finished talking, there was a commotion in the hallway and one of the 'minders' shouted: 'It's the Brits.' The clatter of military boots could be heard going upstairs and there was the noise of rooms being robustly searched.

I was certain that somehow the soldiers had learned of Twomey's presence and were now going to make a prize capture. Bizarrely neither of the fugitives seemed concerned. Drumm merely leaned over and increased the TV sound.

The shouts of the soldiers eased and an officer and two squaddies from the Gordon Highlanders then pushed into the lounge. After a cursory glance around, the officer apologised for disturbing us. I was astonished that none of us was asked for any proof of identity. I reckoned they had come in to check it really was Twomey and were going to detain him once he left the building.

When the patrol departed, the two IRA leaders swiftly left. I was told to remain behind and to go back into the city by black taxi. For years, I've dined out on the story about how the army had Twomey, one of their most wanted fugitives, under their very noses but didn't seem to recognise him.

The promised ceasefire spluttered into life for a brief period but the unyielding IRA demands strangled it at birth. As IRA violence intensified new loyalist groups emerged to wage war against them, not least by matching their propaganda.

Soon afterwards I was offered an interview. My intermediary told me to stand outside the Europa a few nights later and I would be picked up. Sure enough a large van arrived with a driver wearing sunglasses. I was then manhandled into it as a balaclava was forced over my head and a pair of sunglasses taped over my eyes.

After the twists and turns of the journey, I was now fairly sure that we were in the Shankill Road area and likely going to a pub I knew well. My hunch was confirmed when my mask was lifted. We were actually in the snug of the bar.

The brigadiers read their intractable statement without raising their masks but the episode reached a farcical level when the hatch between the pub and snug was thrown open. 'Yous'uns want a drink?' asked the barman. Then he noticed me and his face lit up. 'What about you Big Chris?'

The perils of undercover journalism and faux-theatre, I thought, as a tray with a cluster of foaming pints of Guinness arrived through the hatch.

Chris Ryder worked for *The Sunday Times* and *Daily Telegraph*.

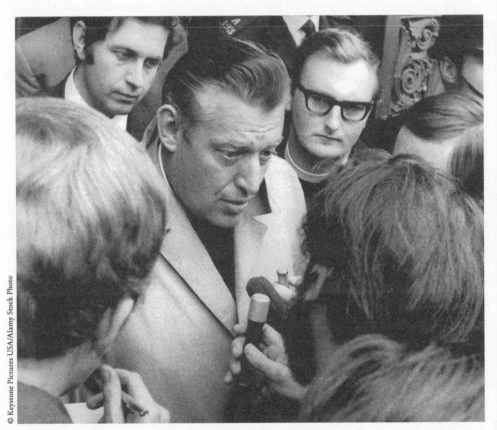

The Rev. Ian Paisley, 1971.

When Edward Heath branded Paisley 'a disloyalist'
Gordon Burns

In 1973 I was in my fourth year of presenting the nightly half-hour news programme, *UTV Reports*. This time was arguably the most violent period of the Troubles and a difficult and challenging time for all reporters and news presenters. But thanks to its brilliant, brave and innovative editor, Robin Walsh, *UTV Reports* was by far the most watched news programme in Northern Ireland.

The political focus at the end of March that year was on the new, first and highly controversial power-sharing Assembly the British government was imposing on Northern Ireland. It was to be elected by proportional representation and the executive had to include members of the SDLP and Alliance parties. This caused outrage amongst the unionist community. The fiercely loyalist Vanguard movement, led by former Stormont Home Affairs Minister William Craig, and the relatively new DUP, led by the Rev. Ian Paisley, declared they would wreck the Assembly.

But the main unionist party, the UUP, agreed to take part with the proviso that the control of security, including the RUC police force, returned from direct rule to the new Assembly. Their leader, and certain to be the Assembly's first minister, was former Northern Ireland Prime Minister Brian Faulkner who warned he and his party would walk away if control of security was not returned.

The British government was about to publish a white paper on the proposed new Assembly with a two-day Westminster debate to take place on 28 and 29 March.

Robin Walsh decided our programme must come live from London on those two days, so, after presenting the evening programme from Havelock House on the 27th, I headed to Aldergrove airport to catch the late flight. As I dashed to the departure gate a tannoy announcement blared: 'Would Mr Gordon Burns please go immediately to the nearest phone.'

On the other end of that phone was Robin. With an economy of words he said sharply, 'Change of plan, tomorrow, 10 Downing Street, interview Prime Minister Edward Heath.'

I used some choice words to tell him to stop messing me about and asked what he really wanted. He insisted he wasn't joking – it was to be an exclusive interview.

My head was reeling. British prime ministers didn't give interviews to local television and certainly not about the minefield that was Northern Ireland. This was astonishing, groundbreaking and of huge importance, a massive coup for UTV. I sat up most of the night in my London hotel room planning my interview in semi-shock.

I arrived next morning at 10 Downing Street, stomach churning and knees knocking. I went up the famous staircase lined with pictures of former prime ministers and entered the lounge. Eventually Mr Heath shuffled through the door. He was cold, distant and barely uttered more than a grunt to the crew and me as we prepared to do the half-hour interview. Little did I know at that moment what a huge impact this interview was about to have across the UK and the Republic of Ireland.

The explosive moment came three-quarters of the way through. I reminded the prime minister that handing back control of security was of vital importance to unionists and asked him if that would happen. His answer was blunt: 'We have no plans to do that ... and as long as British forces remain engaged in Northern Ireland the responsibility is going to rest at Westminster. That's where it ought to be.'

This was a shattering response for all unionists but worse was to follow.

Mr Heath warned the people of Northern Ireland that, until they worked together and gave the Assembly a chance, he foresaw no institutions in the country.

I responded by reminding him that the loyalists had already threatened they would make the country ungovernable if they didn't get what they wanted. At that the prime minister flew into a rage. His face went bright red with fury and he blasted, 'You keep using the word loyalist. I don't know if you have any idea how much offence it gives to the rest of the United Kingdom. To describe them as loyalists is completely untrue. There are no more disloyal people in the United Kingdom than people who take that attitude and to many like myself over here it gives the utmost offence. They are in fact disloyal.'

There I was, a young man aged about thirty, still fairly inexperienced, being shouted at by the prime minister, with his face ever reddening in anger, accusing me of causing the 'utmost offence' to the rest of the UK and him. It was a scary and highly challenging moment. But I remain ever proud of keeping my cool, on the outside at least, and coming back with my next question.

'So you are saying the Vanguard group and the coalition led by Mr William Craig and the Rev. Ian Paisley are disloyal?'

I could see the sudden panic on his face. He knew immediately he couldn't label the Rev. Paisley and William Craig and their mass of followers disloyal – they were the very people who constantly waved the Union Jack, sang 'God Save the Queen' at every opportunity and pledged total loyalty to the Crown.

He knew the damage he had already caused with that outburst and he was into damage limitation. He gave the only response he could, being careful not to point the finger directly at Paisley and Craig. He literally spluttered the words: 'I'm saying that any people who take the attitude you have described are disloyal and have no right to describe themselves as loyalists.'

I wound the interview up. I knew immediately we had a massive scoop on our hands. The prime minister had pulled the rug out from under the unionists by saying unequivocally that security was staying in the hands of Westminster and by labelling tens of thousands of loyalists as disloyal.

The interview in its entirety ran on *UTV Reports* that night and the proverbial duly hit the fan. The station was inundated with calls from angry loyalists. An ITV *News at Ten* team permanently based at Havelock House throughout the Troubles leapt on it for their evening national news. Everyone wanted clips or the transcript.

Next morning it was front page news nationally as well as locally.

'Disloyalists – Heath Raps Wreckers' screamed the *Daily Mirror* headline.

The unionist-supporting Belfast *News Letter* wrote, 'The Loyalists of Ulster have suffered much from the terror of the IRA and the treachery of Downing Street but they have found nothing more hurtful than the venom which Mr Heath spewed in their direction in his TV interview.'

And the *Irish Times*, under a leading article headlined 'Cold Blast', said: 'In a UTV interview with Gordon Burns he [Heath] showed a coldness and distaste for some loyalist attitudes which was chilling even to many who are not of that ilk.'

They carried the whole interview verbatim so important did they rate it.

There was uproar on the floor of the House of Commons that day with Heath coming under fire from the unionists. A group of Labour MPs hit out at him for talking to UTV before the House of Commons. The Vanguard movement fired off a telegram of protest to the Queen.

The fallout from that interview raged for many weeks and played a significant part in the politics of that time. As one who has interviewed eight successive British prime ministers, from Heath to Cameron, my 1973 encounter with Heath remains to this day the one I am most proud of.

Gordon Burns began his TV career with UTV at the outset of the Troubles before moving to Manchester. A former presenter of *The Krypton Factor*, he also hosted nightly news programmes for the BBC and Granada TV.

How Paisley turned the jeers to cheers for me
Conor O'Clery

Before I took up the post of northern editor of the *Irish Times* in 1973, my editor Douglas Gageby told me to spare no expense in getting acquainted with the main political figures, especially the unionists, as so little was known in Dublin about who these men were – and they were all men – and what they were about.

He said I should establish good relations with them through the usual medium of lunch or dinner. So now, when I think back to my experiences of the early years of the Troubles, I recall not just the close shaves – like when a bomb exploded near our office in Fanum House on Great Victoria Street seconds after I passed – but of civil lunches with hardy unionists like John Taylor.

Two years earlier I had been a Queen's University student demonstrating against the then home affairs minister, with gun-toting RUC men in between. Now I found myself separated from Mr Taylor by only a starched tablecloth and the Europa Hotel's best cutlery.

In the 1970s the unionist community disintegrated under the pressure of events and formed factions with different leaders, so the expense account got a bit stretched. There existed at different times the Official Unionist Party, the Democratic Unionist Party, the Vanguard Unionist Party, the pledged unionists, the unpledged unionists, the pro-Assembly unionists, the anti-Sunningdale Unionists, the United Ulster Unionists and so on.

Practically the only luminary on that side of the house whom I didn't get to wine and dine was the DUP leader, the Reverend Ian Paisley. He didn't wine at all, and he definitely didn't dine with individual journalists from the southern newspapers. Most of these outfits merged at one time into the United Ulster Unionist Coalition to fight a general election, and when this grouping held an election rally in Dunmurry, a town south of Belfast, I went along to compile a report.

At the time there was a lot of hostility towards the southern media on the unionist side, and Dr Paisley was known to incite his followers to disrespect reporters, sometimes physically. So I planned to loiter at the back without taking out my notebook, and just listen to the proceedings.

Peter Martin of the *Cork Examiner* came with me. We were challenged at the door and on being identified as newspapermen we were escorted to a row of empty chairs right in the front. We were told these were the press seats. There was no escape. No other reporter showed up. We could almost feel the hostility from some young hotheads on the back of our necks.

When the hall was full, the coalition's leaders came on stage and sat on a row of chairs facing the hall. They nodded almost imperceptibly at us from the stage – to wave would perhaps imply a too-cosy relationship with the press – except for Ian Paisley who scowled in my direction.

When the Big Man got up to speak he glared down at me, then announced, 'Good people, I wish to draw your attention to someone in this hall tonight. There is, sitting in the front row –' pause for effect – 'a reporter from the *Irish Times*.' He elongated the vowels of the word *Times* with menacing effect. There was a hissing sound from behind me, someone kicked the back of my chair and I got a thump on the shoulder. I thought to myself, this is not going to end well.

'Good people,' continued Paisley. 'I have one question to ask.' He paused again for dramatic effect. I shrank in my chair. 'Where is the BBC? Where is Ulster Television? Where is the *News Letter*? Where is the *Belfast Telegraph*? I say fair play to the man from the *Irish Times* for coming here to listen to what we have to say.'

A cheer went up, I was slapped on the shoulder and someone behind me, perhaps the same stalwart who had given me a thump, cried out, 'Fair play to ye!'

I did get to dine with Paisley. In 1979, after boycotting the European Economic Council as it then was, mainly because it resulted from the Treaty of *Rome*, the DUP leader accepted an invitation to bring a party delegation on a fact-finding mission to Brussels. I had a good relationship with his deputy, Peter Robinson, and he secured permission for me to come along so that I could write about what sort of a reception they received, and generally get a sense of the occasion, with the proviso that I respected confidentiality where required. We were wined and dined by the commission – at least I was, as the rest drank only orange juice.

I recall in particular a meeting with the agriculture commissioner, at which a DUP delegate, Douglas (Dougie) Hutchinson, who had an orchard in County Armagh, asked about the level of subventions to fruit farmers in the North compared to that in the South. When hearing that apple growers in the Republic received a greater amount of European money per holding, he thought for a moment and then said to Paisley, 'We're living on the wrong side of the border.' Paisley turned to me. 'Don't you print that,' he thundered. I never did, until now.

I would have a number of civil conversations with Dr Paisley over the years, but he was never anything but uncivil at press conferences, when he liked to verbally beat up individual reporters, even the ones with whom he had just been having a bit of banter off camera.

My last encounter with him was at the centenary dinner for Queen's University in Belfast in 2008. As we emerged from the dining hall he recognised me and asked, 'Are you still creating mischief?'

'I am,' I replied.

'Good man yourself,' he said, and gave a great laugh.

Conor O'Clery worked for the *Irish Times* for over thirty years, in Belfast, London, Moscow, Washington DC, New York and Beijing.

My night with a loyalist drag queen and the 'beast from hell'
Sam Smyth

The editor splashed 'Inside the UDA clubs' as a '*Sunday World* exclusive' on the front page of Ireland's first colour newspaper.

As a rookie reporter in 1975, I saw the assignment as a calculated risk but now, more than forty years later, reckless vanity would be a more accurate assessment.

We planned to do the story on loyalist clubs on Belfast's Shankill Road when it was a virtual no-go area for the security forces and where the Ulster Defence Association (UDA) ruled like an occupying army.

The driver assigned to us by the UDA that Saturday evening was their press officer, Sammy Duddy, who moonlighted as a drag artist and wore fishnet stockings in his cabaret act. Duddy was a close associate of Davy Payne, a serial killer known by the nickname 'Psychopath' on the Shankill Road where his control as UDA commander ran from door to door.

Payne met photographer Liam O'Connor and me in a city-centre hotel. Peering over his purple spectacles, Payne said ominously that we should not tell anyone we were from a Dublin newspaper. He instructed the photographer (a Dublin-born Catholic) to call himself 'Billy Connor' and on no account to speak in his 'Irish brogue'. As a 'Sammy', raised a Methodist in Belfast with a distinctive local accent, I would not be an obvious interloper.

Duddy drove his family saloon Ford, Payne sat beside him in the front and Liam O'Connor and I were in the back seat. We went to a couple of small pubs and clubs run by the UDA and after Duddy and Payne vouched for us, we spoke to customers and took photographs.

The third club we visited was different. Two men with bulging muscles and an intimidating presence stood outside a metal cage shielding the door, and when Payne nodded they ushered us inside. Men stood drinking at the bar, women sat nearby on fold-up chairs while musicians played on a tiny stage.

Payne was very respectful to the young man behind the bar as he introduced us. The barman was about thirty years old, and his shirt and hair were soaked in sweat as he was celebrating his release from internment. Payne said the recently released internee was disappointed to be accused of just nine murders;

he had actually killed sixteen people.

The barman spilled his glass of vodka turning to Liam O'Connor when he was taking photographs and said, 'I want to talk to you,' but women were clapping and demanding that the celebrating former internee sing. He took the microphone and launched into a raucous ballad in which 'Fenian blood' was a hook line in the chorus. He kept gesturing for us to come up to him.

Those drinkers around the club who were suspicious of us had become openly hostile. I humoured them until an aggressive drunk asked why the photographer didn't speak when spoken to. 'Billy' has an excruciating stammer, I explained. We urgently searched for Davy Payne; he had disappeared.

The perpetually perky Sammy Duddy looked worried: he realised the former internee outranked him in street cred and whispered to us, 'Get the fuck out of here.'

The former internee was still gesturing to us to join him on stage while we eased our way to the door. Duddy negotiated our departure with the doormen. Our drag artist driver was elated and animated on the journey back to the hotel where he had picked us up earlier (we were canny enough to stay in a different hotel).

The pictures and copy were splashed in the paper and we were reassured by the weasel words of colleagues: that the ends justified the means.

Wiser and more experienced reporters and former neighbours in Belfast later asked if I had a death wish; they said that my visit to the loyalist clubs was vainglorious and stupid.

I never met Davy Payne or Sammy Duddy again.

The twice-married drag artist (his stage name was 'Samantha') cut an eccentric dash and he made me laugh. A founder member of the UDA, Duddy wore lurid purple lipstick and more mascara than Dusty Springfield, often on stage. He also swore that he never played a military role in the paramilitary organisation of which he was such a valued senior member.

Duddy and his pet dog, a chihuahua called Bambi, were inseparable until a rival UDA faction fired shots into his home off the Shankill Road. Duddy escaped without injury but in a bizarre twist, Bambi took a fatal bullet. Duddy died of natural causes, aged sixty-two, in 2007.

Davy Payne lived up to his nickname and fearsome reputation. A former British paratrooper, he commanded the UDA on the Shankill and also led the local unit of the Ulster Freedom Fighters (UFF), a cover name for UDA death squads that randomly abducted, tortured and murdered Catholic men and women.

Payne was a sadist reputed to have killed more than thirty people. I did not know as I drove around Belfast with him on that tour of UDA clubs that one of his victims was a friend of mine. Payne, I was later assured, was a leader of the squad that abducted, tortured, mutilated and murdered Senator Paddy Wilson, aged thirty-nine, a founder and first general secretary of the SDLP.

I knew Paddy Wilson from my childhood. His wife Bridie and my mother worked for a bespoke tailor in Belfast, and she and Paddy were regular visitors to my family home. Before his death, I often had a drink with him in McGlade's pub behind the *Belfast Telegraph*.

Davy Payne died, aged fifty-three, of natural causes in 2003 and I'll leave the last word to an obituary in the *Irish Times* written by Kevin Myers: 'He was a uniquely qualified evil man, and if I could have done anything to hasten his end, frankly, I would have. Payne was a beast from hell, and the sooner he was returned to his native homeland, the better.'

Sam Smyth is a columnist with the *Irish Mail on Sunday*. He previously worked at the *Irish Independent* and *Sunday World*.

An almost fatal knockout

Henry McDonald

When I was blown up I was watching *It's a Knockout*.

Seconds after one of the European nations played their 'Joker' there was an almighty boom, an invisible force propelled my father and me across the front living room and the panes of glass from the windows scattered in slivers and fragments all over our bodies.

My dad had dived on top on me as we crashed on to the floor and even above the seething, hissing, ringing tones in my ear caused by the explosion, there was still the audible voice of a hyperventilating Stuart Hall roaring with laughter on the TV commentary: 'Ha ha ha, look at the Belgians, just look at the Belgians.'

It was the summer of 1975 and we were targeted in the car bomb attack because our home in 1 Eliza Street was right up beside Mooney's Bar in the Market area of Belfast city centre. This was the time of the pub bombings and shootings – when sectarian attacks were mounted on punters frequenting bars all over Northern Ireland, but particularly in my home city.

Growing up beside Mooney's, which stretched around the corner of Cromac and Eliza Streets, was both idyllic and dangerous. My sister Cathy and I used to love running up the long stairs to the kitchen above the bar and lounge where Mrs Mooney used to make the most delicious, finely-cut, mouth-watering salad sandwiches wrapped in greaseproof paper – a real treat for lunch on school days. There were Saturday afternoons of orange mineral, potato crisps, Dr Who and the Daleks while watching the marvel of colour TV in the lounge bar as my parents chatted over pints to relatives and friends. Yet there was also the ever-present threat of being killed, even while out playing football or swinging around the lamp post facing Murdock's horse stables across the road.

A few months before the blue Cortina exploded outside our door I had been shooting penalties into a net created from chalk around the wooden door of Mooney's keg house to the left of the lounge bar entrance. Then the real shooting started! It was a Friday afternoon, with my friend Billy and I re-enacting the penalty the West German team scored in the '74 World Cup final the previous summer. I noticed a white Cortina with orange puffed-up pillows in the back seat cruising up and down Cromac Street a few times. I thought nothing of it until, on about the third journey back up Cromac, the window wound down and a black pipe-like object stuck out. Then there was fire emitting from it as the man pulling the trigger of what we were later told was a Sterling sub-machine gun raked the area around the front of the pub and our 'penalty box' with gunfire. Being seasoned 'war babies' we adhered to the drill our parents taught us – Billy and I dived on to our bellies as the bullets whizzed above our heads. Neither of us were injured.

Nor were my father and I badly hurt by the bomb just a couple of months later that shook our house and smashed up everything bar the television that continued to replay images from continental Europe of EU citizens dressing up and playing silly games in what they called *Jeux Sans Frontières*. Later that night the police who arrived to search around the house, along with a British Army patrol, told my dad that the Ulster Volunteer Force was probably responsible for placing the car bomb outside our front window, and that the aim had probably been to catch some of Mooney's punters on their way for a Friday night tipple in the explosion. Fortunately the only casualties were my father and me, and our injuries were minimal.

Fast forward eighteen years to 1993 – I am sitting in a dank, dingy 'office' on the Shankill Road in what used to be a fish and chip shop known as The Eagle. It is the headquarters of the UVF in their Shankill heartland at a time when Northern Ireland, just like in 1975, is perilously close to outright civil war.

I am there to interview the UVF Brigade Staff in my first-ever encounter with the oldest illegal loyalist armed movement on the island. It is partly to write an article for the *Evening Press* in Dublin, prompted by information I have received from an ex-Official IRA figure who informs me that there is a serious debate inside the UVF about calling a ceasefire … even before the Provisional IRA is prepared to do so. However, I am also there to establish some connections as the brilliant veteran journalist Jim Cusack and I are considering writing a history book about the loyalist terror group.

This is a nervous and uncertain period to be on the Shankill Road inside the HQ of the UVF. It is only a few weeks after the IRA atrocity at Frizzell's fish shop down the road and both the UVF and UDA are engaged in a bloody revenge spree of blatant sectarian assassination that includes Catholic victims ranging from council workers to taxi drivers. To say I did not feel totally safe in this environment would have been my personal understatement of 1993!

As I climb the stairs to meet and possibly interview the UVF leadership I am gripped by fear and apprehension. So much so that when I sit down around a table facing men with granite faces and sour expressions, their arms folded, I try pathetically to break the ice.

I tell them who I am, who I work for and then remind them that had their bomb makers been as efficient as, say, the Provisional IRA, then I would not be here today. At that moment I had recalled an aside I heard the policeman almost whisper to my father a few hours after our almost fatal knockout back in '75. The UVF bomb maker had placed the explosive device the wrong way inside the hijacked blue car, resulting in the blast from the explosion shooting up vertically into the air – limiting the shockwave that had rippled into our house breaking glass and temporarily deafening my father and me.

The UVF leaders look perplexed when I relay this to them and so I have to explain that I am only still on the planet thanks to the partial ineptitude of the 'team' that left the blue Cortina at our door. One of them replies with a snigger: 'Sorry, son, it was nothing personal.'

Another, however, has no time for golden-oldie Troubles stories. He wants to talk about what the IRA and Sinn Féin are up to, and whether the rumours that the Provisionals are edging towards a ceasefire are true. I tell him that I believe it is true and that I have sources who are insisting to me that, even despite the slaughter at Frizzell's and the subsequent carnage at Greysteel, the Provo leadership are inching towards calling off their 'war'.

Emboldened, I continue by asking this man, who has a walrus moustache and is smoking a pipe, a question – what is his message to the PIRA/Sinn Féin leadership? He takes a puff on the pipe, blows out a jet of smoke into the air and says: 'Tell them directly – you stop, we stop. Simple as that.'

It is only later when I am talking to the old OIRA source, who was in Long Kesh in the early 1970s at the same time, that I discover who this pipe smoker amongst the members of the UVF Brigade Staff is. His name? David Ervine.

Henry McDonald has been reporting the Northern Ireland story since the mid-1980s, and was the *Guardian* and the *Observer*'s Ireland correspondent for more than two decades. He also worked in the Middle East and Europe as a reporter.

The broken spectacles that trapped a Miami Showband killer

Ivan McMichael

On 31 July 1975 the Miami Showband were returning to Dublin after playing in the Castle Ballroom, Banbridge, County Down, when their minibus was stopped by a UVF gang posing as a British Army patrol.

Two members of the loyalist gang – Wesley Somerville and Harris Boyle – were killed when the bomb they were loading into the band's minibus exploded prematurely. The terrorists had planned for it to explode on the band's journey south, to make it look as though they were members of the IRA.

Other members of the gang then opened fire on the five bandsmen who had earlier been ordered out and lined up. Fran O'Toole, 29; Brian McCoy, 33; and Tony Geraghty, 23, were shot dead. Stephen Travers was seriously wounded while Des McAlea escaped with minor injuries.

Two members of the murder gang – James McDowell and Thomas Crozier – stood trial for the murders at Belfast City Commission [the forerunner of the crown court] in October 1976. The trial was before the judge alone – a so-called Diplock court, brought in to counter intimidation of jurors. I reported on the case.

A stifled gasp of disbelief, clearly audible in the tense, packed courtroom, is a memory that remains with me after all these years. The show of emotion was in response to the record sentences handed down by the trial judge, Lord Justice Edward Jones. The thirty-five-year terms were the longest ever imposed in a murder case in Northern Ireland.

Lord Justice Jones told the pair, 'You went with others to kill … the result was a massacre. People who acted as you did must be made an example of. Such atrocities must be stopped.'

That I reported the trial at all is a tale in itself. At the time criminal trials in Belfast were generally held in the now near-derelict Crumlin Road Courthouse. But the Miami case was switched to the high court in Chichester Street, officially titled the Royal Courts of Justice but rarely referred to as such.

The high court was my 'beat' for many years, and I covered mainly civil hearings – judicial reviews, compensation claims and the like. The only criminal cases I came across were the none-too-frequent cases in the court of appeal, presided over by two or three judges.

So for me it was a rare experience as I took my seat in the press box of court number one at the far end of the marble-walled great hall of the impressive high court building.

Liam McCollum, QC, now a retired Lord Justice of Appeal, led the prosecution team and raised an alarming spectacle in his opening submission. It was a sad and shocking thing to relate, he said, that at least two of the men who stopped the showband's van – the defendants Crozier and McDowell – were wearing the uniform of the UDR and at the time were NCOs in the regiment. 'But that night their purpose had been anything but the proper and lawful exercise of the functions of that regiment,' declared McCollum.

My other abiding memory of that long-ago trial is the vital piece of detective work that was key to the outcome of the trial. In the mayhem following the 'own goal' explosion, which was quickly followed by merciless gunfire, McDowell's spectacles were ripped from his face and smashed into tiny particles. A few slivers of the broken specs were recovered at the scene and detectives then began trolling through optical prescriptions in dozens of opticians all over mid-Ulster. They checked over one hundred thousand before their painstaking work paid off – they established that McDowell was one of only seven people in the area with the same optical lenses. One by one the others were eliminated and McDowell was arrested.

As a footnote to the truly horrific events of that summer night in 1975, I think it is worth recording the words of survivor Stephen Travers, who in 2016 established the Truth and Reconciliation Platform to give people from all sides the opportunity to tell their stories from the Troubles. In 2007 Mr Travers, along with Neil Fetherstonhaugh, wrote a book entitled *The Miami Showband Massacre: A survivor's search for the truth*. In the prologue he makes a remarkable statement about the men who slaughtered his friends and tried to kill him. 'I've prayed at my bedside for those men every night before going to sleep. I see them as the victims of the atrocity, too. I want to make sense of it all and show a curious world how those, who might ultimately reveal themselves as just ordinary people under extraordinary circumstances, can arrive at such a position.'

Ivan McMichael was a reporter at the high court in Belfast. He previously worked for the *Sunday Express*, *Belfast Telegraph* and *Tyrone Constitution*.

The beginning of 1976
Paul Clark

In January 1976, I was distracted. I was twenty-two, and I had recently met Carol, who had just become my girlfriend.

While this was a fresh chapter in my own life, the new year began as the old one had ended – with more murder. The '70s were a horrid time. The year 1976 turned out to have the second-highest number of casualties during the Troubles.

At the time, I was working as a radio reporter for *Good Morning Ulster* on the BBC. On Sunday evening, 4 January, I was in Gilford, covering the murders of Barry, Declan and Joe O'Dowd – all members of the same family.

The next evening I was in the *GMU* office, on the third floor of Broadcasting House, when word came through on the television news that there had been an attack on a minibus that was carrying workmen home from a factory in South Armagh.

The shooting had happened near the village of Kingsmills. As a radio reporter, I travelled light. I lifted my Uher reel-to-reel tape recorder – which was actually quite bulky compared to today's devices – made sure I had enough tape and batteries, and drove alone, into the night, down to South Armagh. You have to remember that this was a time before satnav and mobile phones. Once you hit the road, you really were on your own.

In those days, the security situation was so bad that soldiers had primacy – not the police. With rough directions, and no knowledge of the local roads, I eventually reached the army cordon.

Soldiers corralled all of us journalists, and ordered us to wait. I was the cub reporter. I certainly did not have the experience of my more senior colleagues from newspapers, radio and television. They had been covering the Troubles for years and were 'seasoned hacks'.

We spent the time comparing notes and talking about the latest spiral of atrocities while smoking cigarettes – me included.

Once the bodies had been removed, and the immediate area around the minibus made secure, we were escorted up the road on foot to the vehicle. Though it was a dark, the scene of the attack had been bathed in light; the power provided by a generator. It was clear to see what had happened.

While the cameramen (they were all men in those days) and photographers were taking their pictures, I could examine the scene myself, describing it by talking into my tape recorder. I could see the holes in the side of the red van, where the bullets had pierced the metal. The back door was open, so I was able to look inside. I could see where the bullets had ripped through the seating.

Two images live with me from that night. The first is an empty quarter-bottle of whiskey that was lying on the road. I believe it had been used for milk for the flask of tea. The second was half a set of false teeth. Though they didn't particularly register at the time, those images have never left me.

I spent that night in Bessbrook where nobody wanted to talk to me. But I remember going to a number of houses where people had gathered. Nobody agreed to be interviewed. And, quite frankly, who could blame them? I remember silence, broken, occasionally, by women sobbing. Largely, it was subdued, not wailing.

In the end, the only person I did talk to was the local Church of Ireland rector, the Rev. Albert E. Crawford.

Then, it was a rush back to Belfast, to edit my package for *Good Morning Ulster*. I was travelling a little too fast, and picked up a speeding ticket en route. The police were still about.

Years later, I heard more news about the events of that night.

I already knew that on the previous night, the Reavey family had been attacked. Brothers Brian and John Reavey died that night; a third brother, Anthony, died less than a month later. Three members of the O'Dowd family had been murdered too. All were Catholics.

One day later, John Bryans, Robert Chambers, Reginald Chapman, Walter Chapman, Robert Freeburn, Joseph Lemmon, John McConville, James McWhirter, Robert Walker, Kenneth Worton and Alan Black – all Protestants – were returning home from work with Richard Hughes, the only Catholic among these men.

Their minibus was stopped, and the men were lined up outside. They were asked one question. 'Which one's the Catholic?'

Given the events of the previous night, they all thought that Richard Hughes was the intended target. As they stood with their hands against the bus, the two men on either side of Richard Hughes would not allow him to identify himself. He couldn't raise his hand.

Once again: 'Which one's the Catholic?' And, again, his Protestant colleagues held his hand down.

Eventually, he was identified and told to 'clear off'. That's when the shooting started. His colleagues were murdered where they stood, facing the van, shot in the back. Alan Black – who was severely injured in the attack – was the only other survivor.

On the tenth anniversary of Kingsmills, BBC Northern Ireland produced a special programme, which was broadcast on the network. It was presented by the late Austin Hunter, and produced by Rob Morrison, who, years later, would become my boss at UTV.

When the Catholic survivor, Richard Hughes, died of natural causes many years later, I volunteered to cover his funeral in Bessbrook. It was unashamedly cross-community. Here was a man who had carried the burden of that night for the rest of his life. And he had done so with great dignity. His passing also provided a certain amount of closure for me.

To this day I have a conscience about my own feelings about Kingsmills on that fateful night. As I wrote at the beginning, I was distracted by my new relationship, which would open a new chapter in my life – Carol and I married years later; and we are still married. And here I was reporting on lives which had been ended in the most heinous of ways, at the side of a country road in Armagh. It was a real paradox.

But, Kingsmills, and the weekend events that led up to that atrocity, still lurk in the shadows. Over forty years later, they have never gone away.

Paul Clark is a presenter with UTV. He previously worked for BBC Northern Ireland and the *Irish News*.

'Why does there have to be bad people in the world? My daddy was good.'

Denis Murray

It was the thirtieth murder that year, and it was only mid-March. Just another day in the Troubles in the 1970s. For this particular year as a whole, it was an average of one death every three days.

Perhaps the greatest tragedy is that nearly all of the victims have gone unremarked and unremembered by the vast majority of people, mourned only by their families and those close to them.

The year was 1977; the day, Thursday 17 March. Daniel Carville was thirty-five years old, married to Sheila, and the father of five children, aged three to ten. He and his wife had been planning to go out that night for a St Patrick's Day celebration. He was driving from the family home in Ardoyne across to the Springfield Road to collect a relative, and took the route most people would have – across Cambrai Street and the Shankill Road to the Springfield Road.

There were security ramps at the junction of Cambrai Street and the Shankill, for which Mr Carville had to slow down, almost to a stop. Gunmen approached, and shot him dead. Loyalists murdering a Catholic for the simple reason of his religion.

Mr Carville's ten-year-old son, Frankie, was in the front passenger seat, and his dad, on seeing the killers, had thrown himself on top of the boy, saving Frankie's life, even as he lost his own.

Next morning, the *Belfast Telegraph* news editor told me to go out with a photographer and try to get an interview with the boy. This was an unusual mission to be given as I was only just reaching full reporter status after my journalism training period of two years or so. Normally, such a job would have been given to one of the much more experienced (and frankly, better) reporters.

So off we went to the family home in Ardoyne where I interviewed Sheila, now a widow. 'I just can't take it in,' she said. 'I haven't a clue why they picked on him, as he never bothered with anything like that. All he did was work and come home.'

Mrs Carville told us Frankie was staying on the Springfield Road, and there we met his aunt. In the back room, Frankie was playing happily with his cousins. Now, I knew something about this. My father had died when I was five, and I knew first-hand that kids are tough, and resilient. Playing seemed an excellent way to cope.

I talked to Frankie in the front room, with his aunt present, and he told me what happened.

'Daddy shouted "Duck" and he threw me down on the seat. He threw himself across me. Then the window screen all cracked up.'

Frankie was really upset during this, so I kept it as short as possible. He'd climbed out of the driver's side when the shooting stopped, and people came running. 'A woman took me in to her house to see about my leg which was cut.'

An act of compassion that was in sharp contradiction to the murder.

Frankie went back to playing, when I realised I had forgotten to ask him something. His aunt told him the man from the paper wanted another word. 'What, again?' came a sad little voice.

I told the aunt we'd leave it at that. She told me one thing Frankie had said the night before: 'Why does there have to be bad people in the world? My daddy was good.' This became the headline in that evening's paper.

Back in the office, one of the news editors said, 'You look depressed, you mustn't have got the interview,' to which I replied that I looked that way because I HAD got the interview. As I typed up the report, I realised that now a series of reporters would be heading for Frankie's aunt's house. The *Daily Mail, Daily Mirror*, UTV, and God-knows-who-else. And I'd been thinking, what the hell had I been doing in that house? All I could hear was that 'What, again?'

Frankie wasn't the last grieving relative I spoke with, and it was by no means the last time I wondered, 'What the hell am I doing in this house?'

But it was something reporters did, and perhaps at the end of the day, it was all we could do – tell people's stories. When Susan McKay's book *Bear in Mind These Dead* came out, the late Paddy O'Flaherty of the BBC interviewed some of the people who'd contributed to it at the book launch, and asked them why they were telling their stories now. 'Because nobody asked me before,' came the reply. I hope telling us journos their stories helped those who did talk to us.

Frankie's interview and the story of his daddy had one lasting effect. When I became the BBC's Ireland Correspondent, I insisted that every murder must be reported by the network news, no matter how much the British (chiefly English) audience didn't want to hear about the Troubles.

Because one of the greatest tragedies of the Troubles was all those forgotten deaths, so many of them. We in the media, and in Northern Ireland generally, are great at remembering the 'big' tragedies, events in which there were multiple deaths. But the 'little' individual tragedies are no less tragic. I used to hate doing anniversary pieces on the 'big' events – every day of the year is a Troubles anniversary.

And every St Patrick's Day I think about Mr Daniel Carville, and Frankie, a wee boy every bit as brave as his daddy.

Denis Murray was Ireland correspondent for the BBC. He previously worked for RTÉ and the *Belfast Telegraph*.

Hidden in the ashes – my terrible reminder of La Mon
Wendy Austin

It was one of many mornings in 1978 when the news was a painful listen. Twelve innocent people, seven of them women, were killed in a fireball at La Mon House Hotel on the outskirts of Belfast as they enjoyed a night out. Thirty more were injured, many of them scarred for life.

The incendiary bomb, one of the most lethal the IRA had assembled, was attached to cans filled with a mixture of petrol and sugar designed to stick to whatever or whomever it hit. It was like home-made napalm, and the results were more like what we'd seen in Vietnam than Northern Ireland.

I'd been working at the BBC for just two years, and as a very junior reporter had no expectation of covering the day's main news. But my marking from the morning meeting was to follow a man who was a legend in his own field, Brendan McCann, then a staff photographer at the *Irish Independent*. He had deservedly won the NI Press Photographer of the Year the previous night, and we wanted to see how he went about his business.

He went to La Mon.

We set off in another legendary TV cameraman's car. Patsy Hill was at the wheel of his Volvo with his sound recordist, Eamonn Doyle, in the passenger seat, and Brendan and me in the back. We were talking about his win at the awards ceremony the previous night when we caught sight of the destruction at La Mon and how horrible it was. It was hard to contemplate such a dreadful tragedy.

By the time we pulled up at La Mon, the hotel was a blackened shell. Some walls were still standing. Other areas were reduced to a low pile of still-smouldering ash. There had been 450 people in the hotel when the bomb went off. It was left hanging from a meat hook on the security grille of the Peacock Room window. The victims were all Protestants and included members of the Irish Collie Club, and the Northern Ireland Junior Motor Cycle Club. Both clubs had been enjoying a dinner and prize-giving in there – it was difficult to see how anybody could have survived.

The fire brigade was at La Mon in minutes, but the officer in charge, Alec Withers, said that, even had they been in the car park, they couldn't have done more. Withers said he had never seen a bomb with that effect before – 'not one that spread a fireball with such rapid intensity. The only thing I could liken it to would be somewhere like Vietnam where someone had used a flamethrower or napalm.'

Later those survivors would tell their stories of that night. Lily McDowell talked of the fireball – 'The bomb went off and it came like a ball of fire from the bottom of the room right up the centre,' she told UTV's Ivan Little ten years later. 'It just looked like a huge ball ... a big orange ball.'

Lyn Coulter, another survivor, said that pandemonium ensued as anyone who could get out tried to get out. She said she watched the flames dancing on the function room's dance floor before running for the door, after she had seen her friend: 'she was just charred – there was nothing there'.

Lily McDowell's husband, Billy, who was guiding her out through the flames lost her when he took off his jacket to throw it over the head of a woman whose hair was on fire. He couldn't find Lily again. She says it was God Himself who got her out after she had said the Lord's Prayer and asked Him to look after Billy and their sons. Someone pulled her out by the leg. When she arrived at the burns unit of the Ulster Hospital, mercifully nearby, she was found to be the most seriously injured of the survivors – both physically and mentally. With 50 per cent third-degree burns to her face, neck and body, she endured years of painful skin grafts and several nervous breakdowns.

Brendan got his cameras ready. Patsy and Eamonn got the gear out of the car and we walked towards the hotel door, which had remained without any walls. It seemed strange that we were allowed to pick our way through a crime scene. But those were different times. Brendan took photographs. Patsy filmed him and the scene around us, which included police and fire officers.

Treading carefully, we made our way round the remains of the hotel. Suddenly Patsy stopped.

'What's that?' he asked. He bent down, brushed the ash away and picked up a small shining object.

It was the silver collie dog from the top of one of the trophies.

Later on the day of the bombing the IRA admitted responsibility for the bombing and apologised for the inadequate warning – only nine minutes. They said a nearby telephone box wasn't working.

In the aftermath of the attack, twenty-five people were arrested, including Gerry Adams, who was released from custody in July 1978, and who became president of Sinn Féin two months later. In September 1981 Belfast man

Robert Murphy was given twelve life sentences for the manslaughter of those who died. Murphy was freed from prison on licence in 1995.

La Mon was a family business – Wesley Huddleston and his wife, Isobel, went on to reopen in the old farmhouse, which was relatively unscathed. As she said at the time, there were too many jobs depending on them, including their own, for them to close. They kept the name that had come from that original historic farmhouse. Now, forty years later, it is an prizewinning four-star hotel and spa, still on the same site nestled in the Castlereagh Hills.

Wendy Austin works for BBC NI. She previously worked for the *Belfast Telegraph* and Downtown Radio.

Lord Mountbatten with members of his family on his thirty-foot boat, *Shadow V*, at Mullaghmore, County Sligo, in the Republic of Ireland, circa 1975. It was during a similar trip in 1979 that Mountbatten, Nicholas Knatchbull, Paul Maxwell and Lady Patricia Brabourne were killed by an IRA bomb planted on the craft.

The day the IRA killed Lord Mountbatten, two teenagers, an elderly woman and eighteen soldiers
Nicholas Witchell

It started with a telephone tip-off: a call stating that there'd been an explosion in the town of Mullaghmore in County Sligo which, the caller stated, was the holiday home of Earl Mountbatten, a cousin of the Queen. The date was 27 August 1979. It was a bank holiday Monday. I was a junior journalist in the BBC's Belfast newsroom.

I took that call. It was just before lunchtime. I followed the normal procedure. I telephoned the Garda press office, which was then based at Dublin Castle. I told them it was the BBC in Belfast calling and asked if they had any information about a reported explosion in Mullaghmore.

I was kept holding on for many minutes. And then I could hear the Garda press officer returning to the phone and picking it up. I heard him say to a colleague, 'I've got the BBC here. It's okay to tell them then?'

Moments later he told me that an explosion had occurred aboard a small boat owned by Lord Mounbatten and that he was dead. He told me that two other people had been killed: Lord Mountbatten's grandson Nicholas Knatchbull, aged fourteen, and Paul Maxwell, a fifteen-year-old boy from Enniskillen, who was in Mullaghmore for the summer and who'd been acting as a member of crew.

I scribbled down the details. I remember forming the words 'Mountbatten dead' in my notebook. There was no time to reflect. The voice from Dublin Castle was moving on, describing in clinical, impassive terms the violent death of a member of the extended family of the Queen.

The details were passed to the BBC's newsrooms in London. There was a delay, as I recall, of about forty minutes and then the bank holiday edition of the sports programme *Grandstand* was interrupted. The continuity announcer said they were crossing to the newsroom for a newsflash.

The bare details were given, which, by then, had been confirmed by British sources. The newsreader handed back to the *Grandstand* studio and a shocked sports presenter who was left to observe that it was difficult to think about sport after news such as that.

In those days there was always a network news reporter from London based in Belfast. They came on rotation. The network reporter in Belfast that day was a man called Prakash Mirchandani. He was Indian. The death of Lord Mountbatten had a very particular significance to people across the Indian subcontinent. He'd been the man who, as India's last viceroy, had brought British rule to an end and prepared India for its independence.

Prakash set off immediately for Mullaghmore with one of BBC Northern Ireland's most determined and distinguished news cameramen, Cyril Cave. Cyril always drove fast, but never as fast as he drove that afternoon. The round trip from Belfast to Mullaghmore is 250 miles. They got there, secured the footage of the splintered remains of the Mountbatten boat, *Shadow V,* being brought ashore and interviews with local witnesses, and were back in Belfast in time for Prakash to file his report for the BBC evening news.

My role was to continue feeding information through to London and to broadcast on BBC Radio Ulster. And then, in the middle of the afternoon, I had a call from someone I knew in the Republican Press Centre on the Falls Road. They wanted to meet. They specified a road junction. I drove up to the appointed place, pulled over and this man got into the passenger seat. Little was said. Instead he reached into his mouth and removed a small scrap of paper wrapped in cling film.

He unwrapped and read out the message on the scrap of paper. It was the statement from the Provisional IRA stating that they were responsible for the explosion that had killed Lord Mountbatten. I took down the details. He got out of the car and was gone.

The language of the statement was a cynical attempt to justify the murder of a seventy-nine-year-old whose only connection to Ireland had been his enjoyment of the hospitality it had afforded him during his many holidays at the family home in Mullaghmore. There was no reference to the deaths of the two teenagers or the critical injuries suffered by the eighty-three-year-old Dowager Lady Brabourne, from which she died the following day.

Back in the BBC newsroom the details of the IRA statement were passed to London and broadcast.

And then, in the late afternoon, word started to come of an explosion on the border between Northern Ireland and the Republic: the location was given as Warrenpoint. Calls in this instance were to the army press office in Lisburn. It was apparent very quickly that this was a major incident with a significant number of casualties.

It took some hours for the full picture to emerge: how a remote control bomb had been detonated as a British Army convoy had driven past Narrow Water Castle. Six soldiers from the Parachute Regiment were killed. More than half an hour later, as reinforcements and rescuers had gathered at the scene, a second bomb had been detonated in a gatehouse on the opposite side of the road. Twelve soldiers died in that explosion, including the commanding officer of the Queen's Own Highlanders.

It was 27 August 1979, the day the IRA murdered a member of the royal family, eighteen British soldiers, two young teenage boys and an elderly woman.

Nicholas Witchell is royal correspondent for the BBC. He previously worked for BBC Northern Ireland.

Gunned down at a football match
Eddie McIlwaine

'It's a superb afternoon for the match,' said policeman David Purse as we chatted briefly at the main gates of Seaview football stadium that terrible January day in 1980. The 43-year-old Royal Ulster Constabulary part-time reservist was on duty with a foot patrol in North Belfast where Seaview, the home of Crusaders FC, is situated, and I was on my way to the press box to report on the Crues v. Portadown match in the Irish League. I nodded in agreement about the weather and predicted the result would be a draw.

If I had suspected that murder was lurking just around the corner, our conversation might have been more profound and I might have saved David's life with a warning. Hindsight is a wonderful thing.

It was a game that never reached a result. Around ninety minutes after our conversation, good cop Purse lay dying on the grass just inside the ground, with a fatal wound in his head, inflicted by one of five bullets fired into his body by a passing IRA unit.

I heard the crack of the gunfire around the eightieth minute of play and as spectators dived for cover, I prayed no one had died. Confusion reigned around Seaview that Saturday, 12 January, 38 years ago, as word filtered around the crowd that Purse, a father of three from Glengormley, and married to Ann, had become the latest victim of the violence.

I need hardly say it wasn't a perfect afternoon for football as fear and grief and anger took over the ground. The match was abandoned. I remember the late Walter McFarland, a Crusaders player, grabbing my arm soon after the brutal killing and pleading: 'Tell me it's a nightmare and didn't really happen.'

Harry Davidson, who was at the match and who is now the secretary at Seaview, said, 'The gunman who fired the fatal shots crept up behind the policeman as he stood just inside the gates. I don't mind admitting that I shed mighty tears when the awful news reached me. Football was forgotten as spectators mingled around not knowing what to do.'

David had been asked by his sergeant to return to the main gates ten minutes before the match ended to open them up for fans going home. It was just after he did so and turned away that he was shot.

Another journalist – the late Gordon Hanna, who had been sharing the press box with me – and I were swamped by calls from newspapers from around the UK for information. That was the day I set out to write a report of a football match and ended up dictating the facts about murder most foul down the telephone line to the *Belfast Telegraph*.

I can reveal now that I was so sickened by the murder that I didn't go back to a football match for five seasons. Then one Saturday the *Telegraph* sports editor, the late Malcolm Brodie, persuaded me to think again. So I resumed my Saturday afternoon visits to the press boxes.

But although I've been a spectator on the Seaview terraces from time to time I've never gone back to the ground as a reporter. I'm not afraid to admit that I still get bad dreams about that afternoon.

That Crusaders v. Portadown encounter was never replayed. The 2–0 scoreline in favour of the home team was allowed to stand.

There is a memorial on a wall at Tennent Street police station to David's memory. When out of uniform he worked as a maintenance fitter at a factory at Mallusk, on the northern outskirts of Belfast.

But there will be a more permanent memorial when the Crusaders museum opens. It is now being designed and planned by two loyal regulars at Seaview: retired journalist Colin McAlpin and retired policeman Trevor Goodall, who knew Purse well. He had been talking with him at half-time.

No one has ever been arrested or convicted for the murder. The case was investigated by the Historical Enquiries Team of the PSNI in 2007.

Talking to David's son, David Jnr, who was a 14-year-old pupil at Ballyclare High School when his father was murdered, I could detect no bitterness in his voice about the killing.

'If the man who pulled the trigger was captured now after all these years I wouldn't want to slap him about the head if we came face to face,' he says. 'But I would tell him that my father was a child of God – the same God the killer will have to face one day.

'He and the rest of his terrorist gang will not escape the Almighty's courtroom. He is the judge of all the earth and I will leave it with Him.'

David Jnr emphasised that the horror of that day never caused him to lose his Christian faith and he is now the senior pastor at the Whitewell Metropolitan Tabernacle, which his dad helped to set up back in 1957 when it was called the Church of God.

Eddie McIlwaine is a retired reporter and columnist who worked for the *Belfast Telegraph* and *Daily Mirror*.

The Rev. Robert Bradford pictured with his wife, Norah, after his victory in the 1974 General Election.

The murder of my neighbour, Robert Bradford MP
Ed Curran

The Troubles touched virtually everyone of my generation in Northern Ireland. Violence knew no barriers of creed or class. Just to be in the wrong place at the wrong time could be fatal.

The violence was also reflected in my journalist contacts diary. Every so often I would strike off a name and telephone number as contactable no longer, the consequence of another shooting, another murder, another individual's life cut short by a gunman on their doorstep.

On Saturday 14 November 1981 the violence moved even closer to home and I found myself the first journalist on the scene of a neighbour's murder. Living and working in Belfast in the 1970s and '80s was like taking part in a lottery of life and death. Public figures had police bodyguards. Everyone entering the city centre was searched. Security roadblocks manned by soldiers and police officers caused long and exasperating traffic delays. Even if a person were not deliberately targeted by one terror group or another, there was always the danger of no-warning bombs killing or injuring bystanders. Daring to socialise in what few of the city's restaurants, hotels and bars remained open for business was just as risky. Yet what was abnormal eventually became the norm. No matter how oppressive and disruptive the security precautions, they were seen as a necessary part of life's daily tapestry across Northern Ireland.

I lived in South Belfast, in a leafy avenue off the Malone Road, a middle-class neighbourhood remote from the tough and teeming streets of the west, north and east of the city where sectarian terror was at its most virulent.

Yet nowhere and no one was immune from the gunmen or bombers. Living directly opposite my home was one of Northern Ireland's leading barristers. His involvement in terrorist-related cases was enough to make him a potential target. His garage was converted into a base for a round-the-clock police guard. When his children and mine played in the garden after school, they were watched over by a police officer with a Sten gun at the ready.

An even more high-profile figure than the barrister lived close by – the Member of Parliament for South Belfast. The Rev. Robert Bradford spent much of his time at Westminster, returning home at weekends during which he held his Saturday morning surgery in a community centre about two miles away. His wife, Norah, and their only child, Claire, were friendly neighbours, the latter a tomboyish seven-year-old who could more than hold her own with my son, Jonathan, who was a year older.

Though the outspoken political and religious opinions of Mr Bradford made headlines regularly in the *Belfast Telegraph*, where I was deputy editor, we rarely spoke. At best, we would nod politely at one another when he passed my house on his customary Sunday afternoon walk, accompanied always by his plain-clothes police bodyguard.

The MP's hard-line unionist views were a far cry from the moderate, middle-of-the-road editorial viewpoint of the *Belfast Telegraph*. Though Norah and Claire were friendly with my family, the MP preferred to keep his distance.

In his youth Robert Bradford had a promising soccer career. He was offered a trial by Sheffield Wednesday but he didn't make the top-level grade in England and instead played for two clubs in the Irish League.

He was ordained as a Methodist minister and immersed himself in the politics of unionism, his outspoken and uncompromising views gaining notice and votes in an increasingly polarised society. His reward was victory in South Belfast in the 1974 general election. Fearlessly, he demanded tougher security measures against the IRA, criticised the Catholic church and condemned the power-sharing arrangements between unionists and nationalists, which swiftly collapsed.

While his hard-line brand of unionism added to his popularity amongst Belfast's Protestant community, he became a marked man for the IRA. Little wonder then that he needed a police guard, like so many other politicians and public figures in Northern Ireland at the height of the Troubles. Undeterred by threats and warnings that his life was in danger, Bradford went about his MP's work in South Belfast – until that fateful November day in 1981.

As usual, I had driven Jonathan to his Saturday morning school sports. Returning home, I found our babysitter, who had stayed overnight, standing on the front doorstep. She looked distressed and agitated.

'Mr Bradford's been shot,' she screamed at me. Her mother had just phoned from her home beside the community centre where the MP had been meeting his constituents.

I dropped off my son, called the *Belfast Telegraph* news desk and set off for the centre, knowing only too well that if Robert Bradford had been attacked, there would be serious and far-reaching consequences.

It was close to noon when I arrived at the community centre in the southern Belfast suburb of Finaghy. Local residents were milling around outside. I realised I was the first journalist there and I remember thinking that the many police and soldiers arriving at the scene were too late to protect him or to save his life.

Three gunmen, members of the Provisional IRA, had arrived at the community centre less than an hour earlier. Disguised as workmen and wearing painters' overalls, the 'tools' they carried were guns. Most likely they had come from, and escaped to, West Belfast, the large Catholic district barely a mile away, which was a stronghold of the IRA.

They shot dead the community centre caretaker, twenty-nine-year-old Kenneth Campbell, and forced a police bodyguard at gunpoint to lie on the floor. Then they confronted Mr Bradford. He stood no chance at point-blank range. He was shot in the eye, chest, neck and ear, and died instantly. The police guard fired after the attackers but they escaped and have never been apprehended.

I reported on the cold-blooded murder of my neighbour in time to make the front-page headlines in that evening's *Belfast Telegraph*. After phoning through my report, and being relieved by other reporters from the paper, I drove home. As I did so, I passed by the MP's house. I knew that inside were his young wife and daughter who could not have known at that moment the full horror of what I had just encountered.

The death of Robert Bradford, forty years old, husband and father as well as Westminster MP, made headlines around the world. 1981 was the year of the IRA hunger strikes in Northern Ireland's Maze prison. Ten republican prisoners had fasted to death as the British prime minister, Margaret Thatcher, had refused to accede to their demands. The MP's murder added greatly to the tensions already running high between the unionist and nationalist communities.

On the eve of the MP's funeral, the narrow lane outside my home was lined with the cars of mourners paying their respects to his widow. Northern Ireland was in renewed turmoil. Politicians across Britain and Ireland condemned the killing as an attack on democracy. The IRA issued a brief statement claiming responsibility and blaming Bradford as 'one of the key people responsible for winding up the loyalist paramilitary sectarian machine'.

Unionist anger spilt over into a day of protest called to coincide with his funeral. The Rev. Ian Paisley addressed a rally at Belfast City Hall, his firebrand speech demanding tougher security measures against the IRA. The British secretary of state for Northern Ireland, James Prior, was jeered and jostled at the funeral service in an East Belfast church. Worst of all, Protestant paramilitary groups retaliated ruthlessly. Within four days, they had shot dead three young Catholic men. Northern Ireland would remain locked in tit-for-tat terror for another decade and more before signs of peace began to emerge.

The murder of a Westminster MP met with strong condemnation around the world. The Irish taoiseach, Garret FitzGerald, said: 'The killing of an elected representative of the people calls for particular condemnation in the strongest possible terms. The IRA has shown again its utter contempt for human life and for the democratic process.'

When I returned home from the *Belfast Telegraph* in the late afternoon on the day of the funeral, I found Claire Bradford playing as she often did with my son, Jonathan. They were chasing one another up and down the stairs and from room to room, boisterously and noisily preoccupied with each other's company. I was trying to watch the early evening national news, the headlines dominated by the funeral of Claire's father.

In that moment there seemed a brutally cruel irony between the image of a little girl enjoying her playtime and the television pictures I was witnessing.

Oblivious to it all, Claire and Jonathan played on, shouting and scampering around the house. Their childhood innocence belied the terrible loss that Robert Bradford's daughter would have to live with for the rest of her life, like so many other children whose parents became victims of the Troubles of Ulster.

Ed Curran is a former editor of the *Belfast Telegraph* and *Sunday Life*.

'Daddy won't get up' – murder under a Christmas tree
Kate Adie

How close do you get to a story?

The Troubles were the greatest test. I once reported a story in Belfast, omitting the only witness to a murder, and with no mention of the whereabouts of the body, in the poignant shadow of a twinkling Christmas tree.

I found the city curiously familiar – a declining shipyard industry, rows of neat terraced houses, a Catholic/Protestant divide; like my home town of Sunderland, but all in a thirty-year time-slip. Shops and restaurants and pubs completely closed on Sundays, and churches thronged with women wearing neat hats and hairstyles, and their children in mini-adult Sunday-best clothes. The women might have been prominent in the congregations, but were almost invisible in politics. I was addressed as 'a wee girl'.

This was not quite 'mainland' Britain – a forbidden phrase, I soon discovered, along with a list of other 'provocative' words – Provos, the Irish, Derry, Six Counties, Éire. And absolutely not civil war.

Along with this verbal minefield, any reporter had to contend with a city that differed from many other journalist hotspots of the times. It wasn't anything like the contemporary tribal conflicts in Angola, Somalia and Ethiopia, the aerial bombing by Russians in Afghanistan, or the Iran/Iraq war, all with battlefields and strategies. This was 'the Troubles' and the greatest danger to a reporter was not physical, but getting the story wrong.

On a Sunday evening, our newsroom was tipped off about a shooting in West Belfast, in a street already known for numerous incidents, and where there were many empty houses.

Protestants had once lived there in considerable numbers, but had been gradually forced out by threats and the occasional arson attack. Driving there with my crew was the familiar routine of slowing down at traffic lights, but not stopping, in case we might find ourselves unwillingly 'lending' the vehicle to unknown men.

The occasional British Army wagon and the grey lumbering police vans prowled the streets, guns ready. The road went up westwards, and looked eerily empty.

As journalists, most of us stuck to finding the facts we could see and hear. As 'visiting' journalists from London newsrooms we had the near-impossible task of discovering the finer details of even the smallest incident.

Neighbours, bystanders were circumspect or often silent – and with good reason. As for the motives behind any explosion, shooting or murder – most of us were left with only the broad picture of sectarian violence. Trying to pinpoint why someone had been singled out for retribution, why a particular building had suddenly gone up in flames, or why a shop was reduced to a pile of glass and bricks was knowledge that was kept deep within a community. We might speculate, but might add fuel to the fire should we be wrong.

Not that we weren't tolerated, even welcomed. With the odd exception, we were treated as a necessary nuisance, and often given tea and kindness. But not information.

The BBC tended to be regarded by Protestants as traitors to the unionist cause, the Catholics saw us as enemies of republicanism. Both appeared to have decided years previously that this made for a (sort of) even playing field, and as all felt the need to watch the TV news, we were a necessary evil.

'Getting it wrong' is of course always a present danger. But in Northern Ireland, it felt less forgivable. There was no language barrier to misunderstanding; civil society's rules, the legal process, the political structure were all our own.

Our local colleagues were endlessly helpful, but would sometimes shake their heads ruefully when we probed for more information. Everything was too close to home, literally. They lived, worked, looked out for their families within this society. We were just visitors.

Not all of my colleagues from London landed at Aldergrove with enthusiasm. Some of them loathed coming, and made no secret of their disdain for their regional counterparts – and for what they considered a grubby, impenetrable, tribal saga. Though only once did I hear a seasoned Belfast subeditor turn on a confident young spark from London in front of everyone with 'we know you despise us, but kindly keep your opinions for your smart friends in Chelsea'.

Matters were complicated by the fact that the TV news bulletins in Northern Ireland had just about everyone watching the two main channels every night. Viewers wanted to know what was happening, however bad or depressing the events. They wanted information, and to know that what was happening around them mattered. However, the opposite pertained for broadcasts to the 'mainland' audience.

Several years into the Troubles, there was hard and precise evidence that if the words 'In Northern Ireland tonight' led the *Nine O'Clock News* bulletin, the audience immediately dropped by 20 per cent. Dislike, indifference, bafflement all played their part.

As I got out of the car on the Ligoniel Road, I realised that our tip-off had for once got us very early to the scene. The street was semi-derelict, and a little knot of people, two women and an elderly man, were on the pavement outside a terraced house. Army vehicles could be seen creeping down the far end of the road, on the lookout. The neighbours pointed silently to the dimly lit hall. I went inside and then into the front room, where a small boy of seven or eight was standing in front of the fireplace. 'Me daddy', he said to me. 'Me daddy won't get up.'

A man's body lay awkwardly under the Christmas tree. There was a small bullet hole in the window. A commotion at the door, and a young soldier stood in the living-room doorway, staring horrified at the scene. And then asking me, 'You'll deal with the lad, will you?'

I felt useless, an intruder, the wrong person – and went to the two women outside and asked them to take the little boy out and look after him.

I'm a reporter, and I like to get to the heart of the story. But we can all get too near.

Later I wrote a script, cut to pictures of the house from the road outside, the little hole in the window, and the gentle coloured glow of the Christmas tree. The two women had whispered that the boy's mother was a nurse on night shift, her family the only Protestants left in the street.

Today's reporting would most likely include the intimate details of the tragedy, and the reporter's reaction. I omitted the scene inside, and the boy's words. In reporting the Troubles, I felt the audience near, a lesson learned. My own emotion was irrelevant, and the bare facts of a little boy losing his father in front of him, his mother coming home to this, were enough.

Reporters need objectivity, but need to judge how much detail they give. And when the political and social difficulties are hard to explain, and fear lies at the door of many homes, and motives are shrouded at the heart of a conflict, we cannot speculate. Simple facts are the best we can offer, unclouded by our own views.

A lesson learned from the Troubles.

Kate Adie was chief news correspondent for BBC News, during which time she became well known for reporting from war zones around the world. She is now a freelance broadcaster.

The dirty little secret and the tears of a cub reporter
Bill Neely

I met a man in my first weeks as a journalist whom I've never forgotten. William Rutherford was a senior surgeon at Belfast's Royal Victoria Hospital. It was 1981, at the height of the hunger strikes when ten republican prisoners died and the area around the hospital was in furious turmoil.

I'd grown up amid the Troubles but now I was meeting people deep inside the conflict. Within days, I went from seeing the body of a hunger striker who'd starved himself to death to meeting Rutherford, a man dedicated to preserving life. What has stayed with me, more than the gun battles and the riots, the funerals and the fears of those years, was the humanity and humility of this man. He had simultaneously treated an IRA gunman and the British soldier the gunman had tried to kill. He'd seen every form of horrific injury a bomb and a bullet can do to a body.

But what moved him to the point of tears was recalling the children he'd lost in the operating theatre. That, he said, was the toughest part of his work. Losing a child to violence, then telling a mother or father the devastating news, turned those dark days much darker for Rutherford.

And there were so many dark days, when I thought the thin layer that separated Northern Ireland from even more brutal conflicts like Bosnia would be ripped away. The massacre at Darkley, when gunmen crossed an unspoken moral red line by attacking a church service. The week when three IRA members were shot dead in Gibraltar, their joint funeral later ambushed by a loyalist gunman whose attack was caught on camera; just as cameras caught the full horror of the funeral days later of one of the victims when two soldiers were attacked and murdered. After these, and a handful of other killings, we all felt anything could happen. The murders of the corporals seemed no different to me than the disgusting 'necklace killings' of South Africa, when victims were burned alive by mobs setting fire to tyres around their necks.

But amid all this, the dirty little secret of journalism was that it was exciting to suddenly find yourself covering mayhem and murder. The sound of a nearby explosion had everyone in the BBC's Belfast newsroom, and Radio Foyle where I also worked, reaching for a phone to the police or a coat to rush out the door, on the way perhaps bumping into Martin Bell, Kate Adie or

Peter Taylor, giants of journalism for a cub reporter like me.

Nothing took away the horror of a murder scene, but for years it was an adrenalin rush to get there fast and file a report just minutes or hours later.

It was only after about a year in the job that it hit me. It was December 1982, and I'd been covering the massacre at the Droppin Well pub in Ballykelly where INLA bombers killed seventeen people, eleven of them soldiers. On the last of five days and nights on the story, I went back to my hotel room, sat on the bed and suddenly began crying uncontrollably. Everything I'd held in came pouring out. It was the first time I realised that covering conflict can come with a price; a small one, often barely detectable, but one that eventually emerges, in anger, tears, alcohol or worse.

Often it was the small but heartbreaking details of atrocities that stuck in my mind. The milkman shot dead on his float in South Belfast, his blood mixing with the milk from smashed bottles on the ground. The hideously dehumanised hooded bodies, bound and dumped on border roads after accusations of treachery and days of torture. The gloriously sunny Saturday afternoon in Newry in July 1986: I can still see two of the three dead policemen, who'd been relaxing just a couple of hours beforehand with ice creams, slumped in their blue Ford Cortina, where they'd been shot by gunmen, at least one of whom wore a butcher's apron.

We all learned to develop an eye for the detail that might add life to the story of each death, before the ritual condemnations and tired clichés of the politicians, and the chilling justifications of murder by the gunmen and bombers. And I remember one other small detail of my first years as a reporter. Before the internet gave us Google and Wikipedia, journalists at the BBC in Belfast would hurry to the newspaper cuttings room, run by June Gamble, where the reports of every killing were compiled and filed. There I often shuddered at the sight of the empty files on the table, numbered but not yet named, for those still alive who would be the next victims of our dirty little war.

Bill Neely is chief global correspondent for NBC News. He previously worked for BBC Northern Ireland, Sky News and ITN.

Taking flight with Margaret Thatcher
Deric Henderson

It was never personal, but I always dreaded the sight of her when she visited Northern Ireland. Her impending arrival was usually signalled the night before by a familiar voice on the telephone from Stormont Castle, whispering instructions and warning me to tell no one.

'Could you be you-know-where, at the usual time. Security have your details.'

She was pleasant enough, businesslike, and in all the years we travelled together on those noisy, cold and uncomfortable helicopters, she always met me with a knowing smile and a nod of acknowledgement without addressing me by name.

She was generally the first of the delegation who had just arrived by private plane from London to climb the steps of the big Westland Wessex sitting waiting at RAF Aldergrove, fifteen miles north of Belfast. It was the usual pre-dawn rendezvous point, and back then – at a time when the protocols were not as rigid – Downing Street believed it convenient to have a seat reserved for a representative of the Press Association.

This was a privileged media position that I took up every so often over the best part of a decade, enabling more or less unrestricted access to a woman who could be fussy about the company she kept, but I never accepted with any degree of enthusiasm because of the fear of a terrorist bid to blow us out of the sky.

It was always a hairy ride and yet it didn't seem to faze Margaret Thatcher on her regular trips to a troubled land where friends were few and far between, especially in the aftermath of the 1981 republican hunger strike, and when she sent unionists into a tailspin after signing up to the 1985 Anglo-Irish Agreement.

The IRA came close to killing her when they bombed the Grand Hotel in Brighton in revenge for the ten deaths at the Maze Prison, and the loyalist and Protestant community never forgave her for agreeing a deal a year later that allowed the Republic's government to have a say for the first time in the constitutional affairs of Northern Ireland.

The passenger list included her smartly dressed private secretary, Charles Powell; the government press secretary, Bernard Ingham, a gruff Yorkshireman with heavy eyebrows; two Special Branch detectives; the current Northern Ireland secretary of state; his press secretary, David Gilliland; and a lady working from a notebook with a portable typewriter balanced on her knees. She was a member of the staff based in an office overlooking the lawns at the back of number 10, who were affectionately nicknamed 'The Garden Room Girls'.

Thatcher's husband, Denis, never the most communicative individual, accompanied her from time to time, usually at Christmas, when the seasonal objective was to rally the troops, and reaffirm her government's commitment to finding some sort of political solution.

Everybody was strapped in. She, Powell and the security people in adjoining seats were then issued with headsets in an attempt to drown out the racket from the turbine-powered engines and rotor blades. She wore hers upside down, so as not to spoil her heavily-lacquered hairstyle. It allowed her to listen in on the crackling radio exchanges between the two-man crew at the controls up front.

She sat, occasionally cat napping and apparently oblivious to the threat of a missile or gun attack, without a care in the world. Or so it seemed.

There was always a second Wessex that stayed close. These helicopters were normally used for troop-carrying missions and this second one was also fairly crowded and included a member of the Parachute Regiment in combat fatigues, wearing his maroon beret with the regimental badge. He was a small man with sharp features, and at every location he rarely left her side. He never smiled or spoke, his shifting eyes taking in all around him.

One of the doors of Mrs Thatcher's helicopter always stayed open to facilitate a soldier with his finger on the trigger of a belt-fed, heavy-calibre machine gun placed on top of a tripod, and the barrel pointing downwards.

I hated every terrifying minute of our time in the air. The apprehension and anxiety never eased, especially during what turned out to be her final visit.

It was Friday 16 November 1990. The high winds and driving rain made for a bumpy ride. As usual, the first engagement was in the west. By the time we headed towards Enniskillen, visibility had improved and we skimmed the treetops of the Clogher Valley, the helicopter staying as low as possible to lessen the chances of taking a hit.

Mrs Thatcher was facing a leadership challenge. She had a lot on her mind, but her closest advisors were more concerned about her physical wellbeing, as well as their own safety. After landing, a relieved Ingham called me aside and remarked just loud enough for his boss to hear, 'That's the first time I've ever flown underground.'

Powell added, 'We even heard the cattle ducking.'

The ever-attentive Powell in his double-breasted pinstripe suit, usually carrying a folder, was always on hand. Flying by helicopter in Northern Ireland was never an experience he particularly enjoyed either. Twice he had to lodge dry-cleaning-expenses claims after drops of hydraulic oil from somewhere inside the Wessex smeared his lapels. Denis also complained when he discovered a stain on his tweed jacket following a trip to South Armagh.

The chief constable at the time was Sir John Hermon, who went to inordinate lengths to make sure she would not be harmed on his watch, especially after the Brighton bombing. The day following that attack, I was summoned to West Belfast to take delivery of the statement confirming the IRA's involvement, and that included words directed at the prime minister: 'Remember, we only have to be lucky once. You have to lucky always.'

The man who handed me that piece of typewritten paper – lavender coloured, as I recall – is still around. We meet from time to time, occasionally over coffee, but that secret encounter just off the Falls Road all those years ago isn't mentioned, and strangely the police and Downing Street have never discussed it with me either.

Hermon's relationship with the prime minister could be tense, but she stood by him through some difficult times, especially when he was under serious pressure over claims that his men had a shoot-to-kill policy against suspected republicans.

Her engagements with the media could also be fraught. In the months leading up to the death of the IRA hunger striker Bobby Sands, the interviews were stressful and awkward. She was not an easy subject, especially face to face, and I recall sitting with her in a room at Parliament Buildings, Stormont, where she stayed silent for few minutes to try and compose herself after a vicious exchange with the broadcast journalist, Eamonn Mallie. She found him, and his combative style, difficult to handle.

She was always civil with me. That day at Enniskillen, when she was facing a battle with Michael Heseltine to stay in charge, she told me, 'I'll win and I'll win well.' A week later John Major had taken over and, within days, made his first visit to Northern Ireland. I remember him clambering up a narrow ladder at a hilltop army spy-post near Newry, County Down, before gathering himself to take in the views of the hostile South Armagh landscape. He was by himself, and had the faraway look of a man who wished he was anywhere but overlooking the main Belfast–Dublin road.

Mrs Thatcher seemed to thrive on her visits, especially when she met with soldiers and their commanders. Some were unashamedly in awe of her. She could be thoughtful and charming when visiting wounded soldiers at Musgrave Park Hospital, Belfast, or gracious and comforting while commiserating with widows and families of terrorist victims.

She was visibly upset while attending a church service in the aftermath of the IRA's Remembrance Day bombing in Enniskillen in November 1987, but I also witnessed her agitation when she once faced some hard questions on a trip to the Lisanalley army barracks in Omagh, County Tyrone.

Five Northern Ireland secretaries of state worked with her: Humphrey Atkins, Jim Prior, Douglas Hurd, Tom King and Peter Brooke, who was by far the nicest, if not the most effective. I never heard her raise her voice in front of any of them, not even when she was confronted by Prior – with whom she'd always had a tense relationship – at Christmas in 1982. He had launched an initiative for a constitutional convention in an attempt to get the politicians on all sides to sit down together. We were at Aldergrove, where a room had been set aside for her to deliver a prepared statement to the TV cameras in time for the teatime news bulletins.

Some of the Downing Street staff were beginning to show signs of weariness, and I had a wife and two young sons waiting patiently at home, preparing for Santa's arrival.

Mrs Thatcher liked a stiff Scotch whisky (Bell's) at the end of every Northern Ireland visit, but before she could raise the tumbler after emerging from the makeshift television studio, Prior thundered at her, 'How could you? How could you? How could you go through with that and not talk about the convention? I can't believe you did that.' He could not contain himself.

She fired him a withering look of such intensity, nobody who was there that night dared respond. As Prior turned to leave, Ingham looked at me as if to say, presumably you won't be reporting that. Eventually the prime minister's husband broke the silence to enquire if she had enough soda water.

'Yes, Denis,' she replied. 'I'll just take another dash if you don't mind. A small dash will do.'

The Maze jailbreak
Anne Cadwallader

The first tentative reports of a breakout from the Maze jail barely caused any bored heads to rise from the Sunday newspapers that September 1983 in BBC Belfast. So it inevitably fell to the newcomer, the eager beaver, to cheerily offer to hit the road.

Driving my ancient Fiat westwards down the M1 towards Lisburn, I began to notice an unusually large number of blue flashing lights on the roads under the motorway and choppers overhead.

Could the report possibly be true? Nah. Still, press on and take a look.

The traffic worsened to gridlock and, as eager beavers do, I took a few legal liberties and mounted the central reservation before cheekily crossing two lanes and exiting by the Lisburn slip road.

My then boyfriend was an aficionado of horse racing so I knew the back roads to the Maze racecourse close to the jail. When stopped by various British soldiers, I was waved through. Perhaps my clipped English accent and British car registration helped.

Then, before you could say 'Jack Robinson', I found myself at the prison's main gates, desperate by now to establish what had happened.

A cop in a pale green shirt spoke those few words so beloved of reporters everywhere: 'I shouldn't be telling you this ...' followed by a claim that nineteen prisoners had broken out.

Even more desperate to verify the facts now I'd heard this amazing claim, I approached another cop – this one wearing a white shirt, which indicated his seniority – and he repeated those blessed words: 'I shouldn't be telling you this, but thirty-eight prisoners have escaped.'

It was time to hit the phone – but in those far-off days there were no mobiles. I marched up to the front door of the nearest house – a white bungalow from memory – and asked to use theirs.

By now, the newsroom vaguely knew there was something in those first reports. A shrill but relieved voice answered the phone.

'Are you absolutely sure? Thirty-eight?'

'A policeman told me.'

So I went on to the 6 p.m. Radio 4 news to tell an astonished world that thirty-eight inmates had broken free from what was supposedly the most secure prison in Europe. I knew that, if I was wrong, it meant a very premature end to my career as a radio journalist. But I wasn't.

Outside the comfort of the white bungalow, there was near panic going on with bomb scares reported and the sound of guns firing in the distance. Soldiers and police were running everywhere.

What next? 'You'll stay right where you are,' came the answer. 'And file every hour – no matter what.'

By now, a 'cordon of steel' – as the cliché has it – had been 'thrown up' around the jail and, if I had left, I certainly would not have got back in. My heart sank. My beloved sister, Jane, had arrived late the previous night on a visit from Barcelona. We had waited months to see each other. What could I do though? I had to stay where I was.

I based myself at a crossroads where soldiers and police were nervously fingering their weapons, and started knocking on doors to try and get eyewitness accounts.

The evening wore on. I filed, as requested, every sixty minutes. There were some good accounts of fleeing cars, their doors still open, with prisoners hanging out.

A taxi came to pick up the recorded tapes. Editing had to be done back at base.

There was a panicky, almost hysterical, atmosphere about. Even the cops couldn't believe what had happened. The atmosphere changed dramatically, however, when the news filtered through that a prison officer had died of a heart attack.

As luck would have it, I was wearing a standard (then) reporter's mackintosh, pale enough to be seen in the dying light. I walked around all night with my hands in the air, hoping no one would take a potshot. I startled some troops, hidden in rows of Brussels sprouts in the fields between the jail and the River Lagan. They were lying, faces blacked-up, in the mud. Luckily, the soldiers kept their nerve.

I ran out of the quarter-inch reel-to-reel tape we used in those days and phoned the office.

'If you're sending out a taxi, you might as well bring a hot-water bottle, toothpaste and toothbrush.' I chanced my arm. A taxi duly arrived carrying the blank tapes and required domestic accoutrements, the driver handing them to me over the metal barricade before disappearing again.

I have since spoken to some of those thirty-eight Maze escapers and they've told me how, hidden beneath floorboards or in cars travelling south, they heard my reports and were almost as startled as everyone else was at what they had pulled off.

As the cold night wore on, I knocked on a door nearby for some hot water for the bottle to keep myself warm. I wasn't asked inside.

When the world woke up that Monday morning, I was on bulletins wall-to-wall, losing track of how many live interviews I did, how many 'voicers' into the BBC World Service as well as into Radios 1 to 4. The rest of the day passed in a daze and the following night. I was finally allowed to return home, almost dead with fatigue. Everywhere there were checkpoints, miles of queuing traffic.

The adrenalin rushing through my system wouldn't let me sleep more than four hours and I reported for work as soon as I could. Jane had, long ago, departed back to Spain.

News bulletins were full of reports of security operations intended to prevent the escapers making it south to the Republic. The headlines all spoke about 'the largest-ever north–south security operation ever seen' that was taking place along the border.

I wonder what that looks like, I thought. Are they sharing out the hundreds of border roads between the RUC and Gardai? Or are they each manning every road? Are they dug into the fields? Where are the helicopters focussing? Forkhill or the Monaghan road?

I asked my producer to send me out to take a look. What I discovered? Well, that's another story.

Anne Cadwallader was a newspaper and broadcast journalist in Ireland for over thirty years.

The massacre at Darkley – and the nature of certainty
Michael Cairns

Death visited so often and so randomly in the early 1980s that those of us covering its aftermath found ourselves working to a macabre template aimed at securing facts and interviews from witnesses and those who had known the dead. As a reporter at the phenomenally successful Downtown Radio, I was constantly on the road, getting to murder scenes, or trying to reflect the pain of bereaved relatives whose doors I would have to knock.

One Monday morning in 1983 the road led to the village of Darkley and to an encounter that made me throw away the template.

Darkley Pentecostal Hall, known as the Mountain Lodge, was one of many independent places of worship found scattered across the rural landscape of Northern Ireland. In Wales they might be termed chapels, in other parts mission halls – their main purpose was to allow people to gather to sing hymns and hear interpretations of the bible. And unlike the more reserved Protestant churches – such as Presbyterians or Church of Ireland – they were places where people openly made declarations of wanting to be or having been 'saved' or 'born again' in line with the core message of the New Testament.

The Mountain Lodge was built of wood and sat on an isolated country road on a hill in South Armagh, near the town of Keady. The ground there is poor, with much of it given over to forestry because of its wet nature. Lower down the slopes sheep and beef cattle farming is possible, and the small congregation had its roots in this or associated jobs and businesses. It also drew evangelicals from outside the area who had heard of the speaking power of the flock's pastor, Robert Bain. On Sunday 20 November 1983 the congregation followed its normal pattern of having a service in the morning and then a second in the evening. People began arriving at around 5.40 p.m. By 6.30 three of them were dead, and nine were badly wounded.

Members of the republican terror group the INLA had singled out the Mountain Lodge as a sectarian target to send a sick message to loyalists. It has been suggested that they intended to open fire on the entire congregation in the hall with the aim of killing as many as possible, but when they approached the porch area they found three church elders at or just inside the door ready to hand out hymn sheets.

The three elders, David Wilson, Harold Brown and Victor Cunningham were caught in the first fusillade. Mr Brown and Mr Cunningham died instantly but despite being fatally wounded, David Wilson was able to open the inside door of the hall, shout warnings and make his way to the far end of the small building before falling dead. He had closed the door behind him and the gunmen now resorted to circling the hall, firing indiscriminately through the wooden walls. Another nine people were wounded.

My colleague Mervyn Jess did an exceptional job covering the shooting, including getting hold of a tape recording of the service in which the shots and screams were heard. Next morning I was sent to try and get interviews with those who knew the dead.

The horrific nature of the attack on innocents galvanised the religious denominations and political leaderships into public demonstrations of condemnation. The leaders of the five main churches announced they were going to Darkley to visit the bereaved – a rare act of public solidarity designed to say enough is enough. My logistical challenge was to find the homes of the three murdered men scattered across the South Armagh countryside, and to be there at the same time as the church leaders.

In relation to the Brown family I succeeded in the first part but not in the second – I found myself standing in their farmyard after everyone else had gone. I was deeply embarrassed. But then the first of a number of extraordinary actions from this community enveloped me.

Harold Brown's wife, Elizabeth, came out and said she was very sorry that I had missed the church leaders and thanked me for coming to their home. I said I was sorry to have added to the intrusion to which she replied, 'If you are late, you are late for a reason which God has decided. You have come a long way – would you like to come in?'

I was now torn between knowing I was even more likely to miss the church leaders if I stayed and the unexpected warmth of this invitation. Having got photographs of the church leaders, the press pack had moved on from this house and hadn't spoken to the family. Now here I was, talking with the widow who had witnessed her husband cut down some eighteen hours earlier. Would this lead to me, the reporter, getting an interview? Would I live with myself if I turned down her offer of tea to catch up with the church leaders?

And so I went in. It was a typical Ulster farmhouse, dark because of small windows, and decorated with ornaments and family photos. The Browns had three school-age boys and they sat quietly talking to each other. The adults, however, were less subdued and as I introduced myself they told me I was welcome and enquired as to where I came from. As she delivered the tea to me I said to Elizabeth Brown that she really shouldn't worry about me at a time of such grief for her. 'But we're not grieving, son,' she replied. 'We are rejoicing that Harold is with the Redeemer right now. You see Harold was ready to be with the Lord as all the people were in that hall.' Then she smiled and said, 'You see, I know where he is right now.'

As I was preparing to leave I had to ask the question as tactfully as possible – would anyone want to do an interview on tape? The answer was no, they would be too embarrassed. Disappointed, I turned to the door. Then someone said, 'You tell our story, tell people what you have seen. That is the reason you were late today. Nothing happens without a reason.'

I would see the Browns one more time at the funeral in Armaghbreague Church. The young boys, dressed in matching grey sports coats, were understandably in bits as their father's coffin was put in the earth. But around them, their mother and other people sang loudly of the glory offered to those who believe.

I found this sense of joy and optimism verging on the overwhelming at the second funeral I attended: the burial of thirty-nine-year-old Victor Cunningham at an isolated graveyard south of Armagh city. The sun was bright but perhaps due to the nature of the landscape, moisture and the cold air had led to a haze forming that blurred the sun's effect.

As the coffin was brought to the graveside the only sound to be heard came from rooks perched in the surrounding trees. Two figures stood close to the grave. Victor's wife, Edna, was in a Lincoln-green outfit and the other woman was in maroon. Both wore hats, in keeping with the Baptist and gospel hall tradition.

They stood, arms raised, singing with a passion of certainty that gospel hall standard, 'In the sweet by and by we shall meet on that beautiful shore'.

The Troubles were frequently – but wrongly – described as a conflict over religion. Ultimately what they were about was the taking of life. For some, religion defined their tribe, giving them a justification to hate; for some it gave them a reason to forgive.

But for those I reported on at Darkley, forgiveness and hate were irrelevant because they had something remarkable. They had certainty. And that was truly extraordinary to witness.

Michael Cairns works at BBC Northern Ireland where he has held senior editorial roles. After leaving Downtown Radio in 1987 he joined the BBC in England.

IRA war against border Protestants
John Devine

The old man sobbed uncontrollably for over ten minutes, occasionally wailing. Broken, beyond words. Stripped of all dignity. Unforgettable.

He had been recounting for me how his inheriting son, who worked part-time on the farm, had been murdered just two weeks after it had been signed over to him. To use the parlance of the day, what I was researching was really 'the murder of Prods on the border'. The words 'ethnic cleansing' had not yet entered the lexicon of everyday usage.

Irish border Protestants believed that the IRA plan was to have fewer of them and more Catholic landowners there, and a more porous frontier.

Church of Ireland Bishop of Clogher Gordon McMullan told me that he would prefer not to talk about the issue lest he subscribe to a self-fulfilling prophecy.

Fear still ruled the borderlands even though it was some time since there had been a land-linked murder, something the bishop then accepted, abandoning his vow of silence.

Nearly everyone that was to die so that 'the Field' might be claimed had already died. From Tynan, County Armagh, all along the Blackwater river to Caledon in County Tyrone, many empty and boarded-up farm houses stood as mute sentinels to a naked attempted land grab that was to have been achieved by murderous attrition.

This was also true along the Fermanagh border where to survive some farmers had fled to Scotland, and others took to living in towns from which they worked their farms.

Often when working the land, or tending animals, the womenfolk would ride tractor shotgun for their menfolk. But not all the men had women. The bachelors were easy pickings for the assassins. And not all women either were exempt from being murdered.

The IRA miscalculated. Protestant resilience was more obdurate than it had anticipated and mysterious Protestant finance arrangements seemed to magically underwrite all efforts to ensure that the threatened farms did not fall into 'the wrong hands'.

The man, whose son had been slain, welcomed me into his narrow, oblong kitchen, which had parallel seating facing either side. Across from us sat his wife, daughter and my guide, who was known to the family and who was responsible for the introduction.

The two older sons, the man said, had careers and had no interest in farming. The daughter, who sat with us, had just become employed in the county town. No mention was made of what she wanted.

'I made an arrangement in town with the family solicitor to have the documents for the handover of the farm completed,' he said. On the appointed day he went to town, completed the deal and 'officially retired'.

Hardly two weeks had passed when early one morning two men dressed in boiler suits came into the farmyard, unseen.

The mother heard the shots and found her son slumped over the tractor steering wheel. Dead. She saw the killers disappear across the field behind the house, heading for the border and in no great hurry.

Now the man began sobbing, tears running down his cheeks, breathing heavily and unevenly. We all sat staring at each other and him, for what seemed like forever. Until he stopped no one spoke.

Eventually, haltingly, resuming his narrative he said that the only person he had told about the handover was his Catholic neighbour, whom he had known for years and would trust with his life. They had relied on each other for cooperation over the years, especially in times of hardship and emergency. Their families grew up together.

'Perhaps over the dinner table,' he said, 'my friend, as part of normal daily chat, mentioned that I had signed over the farm. It had never crossed my mind before that not all his family would have his views, or his loyalty. I just assumed that when I spoke to him things would go no further. I now know that not to be true. I know also I can never confide in him again.'

John Devine was northern editor of the *Irish Independent*. He previously worked for the *Irish Times* and *Ulster Herald*.

Death on my doorstep
Richard Kay

Sunday, 8 April 1984 had dawned with bright sunshine. The promise of spring was in the air as Tom Travers, his wife, Joan, and their twenty-two-year-old daughter Mary set off from home in a leafy suburb of south Belfast for the short walk to church. They were well on time for midday Mass at nearby St Brigid's, where the family were popular and frequent members of the congregation.

On the three previous Sundays, Mr Travers had attended Mass at the same church, not far from where I lived.

Such a detail would hardly matter to most people but Tom Travers was a magistrate, a public servant who saw it as nothing less than his duty to serve his community. But it was a duty that came at a terrible price for it made him a 'legitimate target' for the IRA because of his role in the hated British judicial system.

Routine creates a pattern; his visits to St Brigid's had been logged, his comings and goings recorded. By the time Mass was over a trap had been sprung, an ambush set and in moments the Travers's lives were to change for ever.

After saying their devotions, the family stayed to chat to friends outside the church for fifteen minutes before retracing their steps for home and the promise of Sunday lunch.

The prelude to murder began with a woman in white walking a Pomeranian dog. She was the lookout.

As the Travers family passed the entrance to a tennis club two men, one stout in a grey suit, the other younger in brown, leapt out from behind some bushes. Both were armed with handguns and from point-blank range they fired round after round at the family.

Mr Travers was shot six times yet somehow survived. His slim, dark-haired daughter Mary, two terms into the job of her dreams as a primary school teacher, was hit once through the spine, killing her almost instantly.

At the time it was thought she had been trying to shield her father from the terrorists' bullets. It was certainly the kind of selfless action that her friends said a young woman who abhorred violence would do.

But for a jammed gun Mrs Travers would almost certainly have been dead too.

Later Tom Travers described those terrifying seconds. 'Mary lay dying on her mum's breast, her gentle heart pouring its pure blood on to a dusty street in Belfast. The murderer's gun, which was pointed at my wife's head, misfired twice. Another gunman shot me six times. As he prepared to fire the first shot I saw the look of hatred on his face, a face I will never forget.'

The same handgun had been used with deadly effect to murder another member of the judiciary, Judge William Doyle, after he had left the same Catholic chapel a year earlier.

Even in a city hardened to mass murder, where one terrorist outrage was matched by the degeneracy of another, the killing of Mary Travers plumbed the very depths of inhumanity.

There had been many other ghastly atrocities during my three years reporting from Belfast: the shooting of worshippers at prayer in a gospel hall, a headmaster cut down in a hail of bullets in front of his class, and soldiers blown to pieces while off duty at a pub social night. For each and every one of those lives lost there were countless more left to grieve: sons without fathers, wives without husbands, and in Belfast that April day, a mother without a daughter.

To Gerry Adams and the apologists of Sinn Féin, the IRA struggle was one of 'humanity, dignity, humour and vitality'. In reality it was one of cruelty, brutality and cold-hearted wickedness. There was nothing noble in the slaughter of Mary Travers and there was certainly nothing brave.

That it should remain nearly thirty-five years later such a powerful memory was perhaps because it happened on my doorstep but also because the murder scene was so far removed from the killing fields of East and West Belfast.

Tree-lined Windsor Avenue where the Travers' family lived was peopled by solid, middle-class folk. Thomas Andrews, the designer of the *Titanic* and who perished on its maiden voyage in 1912 after assisting many into lifeboats, had been a resident. Here Protestant and Catholic live side by side with no wall to divide them as there are to separate loyalist and republican enclaves in other parts of the city.

The family's route to church that spring morning took them past the manicured courts of the Windsor Lawn Tennis Club, a beacon of genteel respectability for almost a century and where the Troubles rarely intruded.

When I moved from London to Belfast in 1982 it was in a quiet residential street parallel to Windsor Avenue that I settled. With the Queen's University campus nearby and student accommodation all round it felt reassuringly familiar in an unfamiliar city.

An alleyway ran between the back of my flat and Windsor Avenue. On sunny days I sometimes sat there. Had I done so that day I might have seen the men who had turned their guns on the softest of soft targets fleeing for their waiting getaway car and the welcoming embrace of the nationalist Twinbrook estate of West Belfast.

We don't need to ask what kind of men they were. We all knew. They were men for whom assassination at close quarters of a young woman was no more than a regrettable inconvenience, skilfully supported by the likes of Adams, for whom the ends always justify the means.

How ironic that while their intended victim, unarmed Tom Travers who refused a bodyguard, would survive, the girl they left bleeding to death was a teacher at a school in Twinbrook's neighbouring republican stronghold of Andersonstown.

The Ulster violence had seen so many funerals, desolate each and every one, but the Requiem Mass for Mary Travers was profoundly moving. It was at the very church Mary and her father had attended before they were shot. Across town Holy Child Primary School closed its doors and sent six of Mary's pupils from class 3a to her funeral with poignant messages of love and loss.

The children were as devoted to her as she was to them. With a good degree from Queen's and a teacher training certificate from Belfast's St Mary's College, Mary had embarked on a career brimming with promise and dedication.

She loved music, played the harp, helped with the school choir and supervised recorder classes. A life of opportunity stretched ahead.

Her death was one more senseless murder.

Richard Kay is editor-at-large and columnist for the *Daily Mail*. He was the paper's Belfast correspondent from 1982 to 1985.

'We'll get you next time, Campbell'
Jim Campbell

As I sat at my desk in an upstairs room, reading a newspaper and relaxing after the evening meal, I glanced out the window and noted that a car was driving slowly past my North Belfast home. A few minutes later I noticed the same car again drive slowly past my gate but assumed it was looking for one of the neighbouring houses.

However, I jotted down the car's number on the paper I was reading. In Belfast in May 1984, at the height of a tit-for-tat shooting war, you couldn't be too careful.

Downstairs my wife, Grace, my son and my two daughters were watching television. The doorbell rang and my wife came part way up the stairs to tell me there were two men at the door asking for me. She whispered that she didn't like the look of them but as I worked from home and had all sorts of people calling she crossed the hall back into the lounge. The door was ajar and as I drew it open I saw two young men aged about twenty standing in the porch.

The younger of the two, who seemed nervous and uptight, asked, 'Are you Jim Campbell?'

Even as I said I was he pulled his right hand from behind his back and pointed a gun straight at me. I still had my hand on the door and tried to slam it shut but I wasn't fast enough.

I heard several shots and felt the bullets ripping into my stomach, driving me back against the stairway, and felt myself slide down on to the floor. The gunman stepped in and tried to fire another shot at my head but the gun seemed to jam. Through the open door I saw the gunman and his older accomplice run to the gate, jump into a waiting car and speed off. It was the same car I had earlier seen cruising slowly past the house.

As I lay in the hall I noticed the ejected shells from the pistol scattered on the hall floor. They shone brightly as if they were brand new and I remember thinking in a dazed sort of way that the gunman must have had them in his pocket and nervously rubbed them a few times before loading them into the pistol shortly before the hit.

As I lay gripping the wounds in my stomach I could hear the panic all round me as my family realised what had happened. My wife comforted me;

my son ran outside and saw the car speeding away towards a nearby loyalist enclave at Ballysillan, and then rushed in and rang an ambulance. My two daughters were in a state of shock.

One of the first to arrive on the scene was a policeman who lived two doors away, followed by two friends living nearby who had heard the shots. An ambulance arrived very quickly and I was put on a stretcher. The journey to the Mater Hospital took only a matter of minutes but I felt every bump in the road surface. As I lay there I felt a blackness filling my head. It seemed to slip slowly from the back of my head towards the front, as if someone was pulling a hood down over my face, and I was convinced that if it got any lower I would die.

I remember being put on a trolley and rushed along a corridor. My arm was over the side of the trolley and I felt it bang off a wall as I was hurriedly pushed round a corner. Someone running alongside the trolley was cutting off my sweater, and then the darkness seemed to completely cover my head and I lost consciousness.

I was told later I was technically dead at that point. But what saved my life was the fact that a top surgeon, a leading anaesthetist and a full operating team had just finished another operation when they were alerted that I was on my way, and they were waiting in the operating theatre to start immediately working to save my life.

When I came round many hours later I was still drugged, breathing through an oxygen mask and had several tubes going into my body. My wife was at my bedside but she was the only one allowed near me in the intensive care unit. I was hallucinating off and on because of the drugs I was being given, and a lot of my stomach and intestines were so riddled by the bullets they had to be removed, but I was alive.

I spent some time in hospital with a police guard outside the door and even when I was allowed home, I was confined to bed for some weeks.

By that time journalistic colleagues had ferreted out the full story of the attempt to kill me. I had been writing a series of articles about a loyalist murder gang led by a notorious UVF sectarian hit man, Robin Jackson, nicknamed The Jackal. He had been linked to dozens of killings in the so-called mid-Ulster 'Murder Triangle', and he wanted me silenced. Another UVF murder gang , based in North and West Belfast and known as the Shankill Butchers, agreed to carry out the attack.

When I survived the murder attempt at my home, a three-foot-high graffiti message was daubed at the entrance to the M1 motorway near a loyalist area, warning, 'We'll get you next time Campbell.'

They didn't get me but another loyalist murder gang, a splinter group from the UVF known as the LVF, and led originally by Billy 'King Rat' Wright, shot dead my deputy and close friend, Martin O'Hagan, in September 2001.

Ironically, Wright was himself shot dead by republicans, and Robin Jackson died of cancer claiming to the end he'd been poisoned by British Intelligence because they thought he was about to betray the fact that he'd been one of their agents when carrying out sectarian murders.

Life as a journalist during that era of the Troubles in Northern Ireland was dodgy at times.

Before the attempt on my life I'd been kidnapped by the Provisional IRA who mistakenly believed I was a British agent. On another occasion I was picked up by British soldiers in West Belfast and beaten so badly that some of my ribs were broken. They thought I worked for the Provisional IRA.

Bad as those incidents were, the one thing I remember most about working during the Troubles is being shot at the doorway of my home on 18 May 1984. I still have a bullet lodged in my spine to remind me of it.

Jim Campbell was northern editor of the *Sunday World*. He previously worked for the *Sunday News* and was, for many years, the Reuters correspondent in Northern Ireland.

Martin McGuinness in 1986
Justine McCarthy

The night before the interview, two men came to collect me. The rendezvous was a terraced house in Derry where I was told to sit and wait while the occupants ate their dinner from their laps, gathered around the 'Free State' RTÉ television news, which they seemed to despise. The men who came for me didn't bother with introductions. We drove to a dingy flat where they drew the curtains and inserted a cassette into a tape recorder. 'A Nation Once Again' and songs about armoured cars and tanks and guns played as they plied me with questions.

What puzzled them was that my newspaper, the thunderously anti-Sinn Féin/IRA *Irish Independent*, would want to interview Martin McGuinness. I waffled about his influence in his home city and his growing national profile. I dared not mention how the mere mention of his name could strike terror into armies.

Earlier that day, I had crossed the border at a quiet, rural checkpoint. A young English soldier, buoyed by the rare glimpse of human life, thought he'd flex his flirtation skills. I thought not. When he reached the mandatory question about the purpose of my visit to the North and I replied I was going to interview Martin McGuinness, I might as well have said 'there's a bomb in the boot' such was the alacrity of his dash to the security hut.

The next day, McGuinness, thirty-six, and reputed to be the IRA's chief-of-staff – though he claimed to not have been even a member since 1974 – was waiting upstairs in the Republican Information Centre in the Bogside. He had been released from custody twenty-four hours earlier, after being arrested for non-payment of an £80 fine for assaulting an RUC officer. On the short car ride from the Brandywell that morning, he had been stopped twice: once by a solider wanting to know where he was going; the other time by a local resident asking McGuinness to fix his water problem.

It was the end of September 1986. Derry, where the Troubles began, still showed the ravages of its principal role with its rubble and its barricades. McGuinness recalled being shot at by soldiers during the Battle of the Bogside in 1969 while people around him were killed. 'It was more luck than anything else that I escaped.'

He had gone on the run at twenty-one, the day internment was introduced.

By Bloody Sunday, when fourteen civil rights protestors were killed by soldiers, he was second-in-command of the Derry IRA. I asked him if he carried a gun and he said no, because he couldn't risk a twelve-year jail sentence. Despite frequent death threats, he depended on the vigilance of his neighbours who, he said, were 'very security conscious'. The neighbours had helped out in other ways too as he had not had a salaried job for five years.

Above on the hill, the Catholic cathedral looked down upon the Bogside; its bishop, Edward Daly, forever etched in the iconography of Bloody Sunday, waving his white hanky to bring the wounded to safety. A few weeks prior to our interview, Daly had delivered a headline-grabbing Sunday sermon warning Catholics who condoned terrorism they were effectively excommunicating themselves. It triggered a tense stand-off between the church and the Provos.

The boyish-looking McGuinness, a 'moral contortionist', as the Dungannon priest Father Denis Faul called him, could have passed for an altar boy with his blond curls and regular Mass-going. But his words would have disqualified him from altar service. This was two years after the IRA had blown up a Brighton hotel packed with Britain's cabinet, attending the annual Tory party conference. McGuinness was making no apologies.

'I don't like to see anyone killed,' he said, 'but, if Margaret Thatcher had died at Brighton, it would have made the British less intransigent because it would have brought home to them that the IRA is not going to go away.' The IRA had taken the struggle to 'the heart of the problem,' he said, and if the British prime minister had died, there would have been 'jubilation on the Falls Road and in the Bogside.' He called Thatcher 'granite face'.

He said he had no respect for Garret FitzGerald, either, after the former taoiseach co-signed the Anglo-Irish Agreement with Thatcher in November 1985. Reunification would never be achieved, he said, by 'adopting the policies of [John] Hume, FitzGerald and [Peter] Barry'. If his words rang harsh, though, there was a hint of compromise between the lines.

He said, 'Republicans like myself have long since accepted that there can be no change without the democratic wish of the people,' and, 'we don't believe the gun or the bomb are the answer,' and, 'I don't believe that [reunification] can be done by force of arms'.

Had the tables been turned and it was the *Irish Independent* that wanted to know why McGuinness agreed to be interviewed, here was the answer. He was laying the groundwork; setting out a vision, one as liable to alienate those within his own ranks as anyone outside them.

He talked steadily and quietly, a mug of tea going cold beside him. The closest he came to betraying emotion was when he talked about his sense of identity.

'I feel as Irish as you or anybody in Cork or Kerry or Dublin and I will defend my right to be Irish against everyone and everything.'

He recalled feeling mystified as a child when he would be returning from the family's annual summer holidays on his grandmother's farm in Buncrana, County Donegal. How could it be, he wondered, that when you crossed an invisible line in the ground 'you were supposed to be in a different country, even though it looked the same'?

A year later, the IRA would kill eleven people [a twelfth victim died thirteen years later from injuries sustained that day] and injure sixty-three others with a bomb in Enniskillen on Remembrance Day. Yet here was the man some believed to be the head of the IRA saying it had been increasingly militarising its campaign and reducing the number of civilian casualties.

'The IRA themselves would say that there may have been incidents in the past when mistakes have been made, like an innocent civilian being accidentally killed.'

Agreeing to be photographed in front of the Cúchulainn monument in the city cemetery, McGuinness first made a detour, striding across the street to converse with a group of men. When he got into the car, he said, 'You see the fella with the beard,' pointing out a tall, pale man in the group. 'He's just done ten years.'

When we reached the graveyard, high on a hill overlooking Derry and the Foyle river glittering in the sunshine, he started to get out of the car, but had a sudden change of heart. 'I don't think this is such a good idea after all,' he said, indicating the sea of headstones. 'People might think I'm responsible for these.' He wasn't joking.

Like his city, Martin McGuinness was complex. And like Derry, he made history.

Two weeks after our interview, he gave his seminal speech at the Sinn Féin ard fheis in Dublin, which led to the abandonment of the party's policy of Dáil abstentionism. Two years later, Sinn Féin's president Gerry Adams began the secret talks with the SDLP leader John Hume that led to the IRA ceasefire in 1994 and the 1998 Good Friday Agreement.

Justine McCarthy is a columnist and political correspondent with *The Sunday Times*. She was previously the *Irish Independent*'s chief feature writer.

The Enniskillen Remembrance Day bombing
Denzil McDaniel

Wherever I go, if I mention that I am from Enniskillen, it's clear to me that for many people my home town is synonymous with one of Northern Ireland's darkest days. People often tell me that they remember exactly where they were on Poppy Day in 1987, such was the chilling impact of the news of the killing of twelve people who were attending a memorial service for the dead of war.

A further sixty-three people were injured, some of them grievously, when the bomb that exploded in the middle of a crowd of several hundred civilians devastated the area, both physically and emotionally.

Enniskillen is a small market town in Fermanagh, a rural county in the south-west of Northern Ireland that is close to the border with the Irish Republic. The town itself is a scenic one, built on an island between upper and lower Lough Erne, and although there was an even divide of people with differing British or Irish national identities, locals lived together harmoniously. Community relations were better than in most other towns in Northern Ireland, despite the Troubles of the 1970s and 1980s seriously impacting on communities along the border.

Enniskillen has a proud military history, having founded two British regiments: the Inniskilling Fusiliers and the Inniskilling Dragoon Guards. Local Protestants and Catholics alike were among those who served – names of both communities are on the town's impressive war memorial.

Built in 1921, the memorial has a distinctive bronze statue of a British soldier on a concrete plinth. It was a landmark in the town, and every November on Remembrance Sunday, a ceremony of laying poppy wreaths was held. By its nature there would be some military trappings, with a parade of today's soldiers alongside medal-bearing veterans, all accompanied by a brass band. But the event was more of a community and civilian one, with townspeople gathering to watch local organisations and children in school uniform or Scouts and Guides attire take part in a solemn ceremony.

The 1987 remembrance was to be no different, and like most local people I never imagined it would be the target for an attack by the Provisional IRA, even though their campaign became ever more ruthless as the Troubles wore on.

But, in the split second the device went off at 10.43 a.m., Enniskillen's name would become forever linked to a new dimension of horror.

I lived a few hundred yards away from the memorial and was at home that Sunday morning when I heard a loud thud. Looking down over the scene, there was a pall of smoke and I immediately drove to the street. The scene of pandemonium was one that I'll never forget, and as people carrying young children dashed past me, I could see in the distance the wreckage of an old building close to the memorial.

I paused for breath and felt a surreal chill as I watched men in uniform and others pull the huge chunks of rubble away with their bare hands as they tried to free people trapped under the concrete that once formed the Reading Rooms, a building that I had passed every day on my way into town. Many of the rescuers were covered in white dust from the effects of the explosion.

Like many others, I was moved back quickly for my own safety, but throughout the day the names of those who had died gradually emerged.

The scene was close to the town's Presbyterian church, and the new young minister, the Rev. David Cupples held a service that evening and emotionally told the gathering the names of six people that they'd lost.

As the international press descended in numbers on the small town, it quickly became a major story and the world watched as the community became numbed at the detail of what was emerging about the dead and injured; all Protestant and all church goers who were standing waiting for the parade, huddled in the rain against a gable wall when it crashed down on them.

As the day wore on, the names came out and in a local community, everybody knew everybody.

Three married couples perished side by side; 74-year-old Billy Mullan, a chemist in the town and his wife, Nessie, 73. Wesley and Bertha Armstrong, aged 62 and 55, died but their teenage son, Julian, survived as he had been standing between them. Popular ambulance driver, Kit Johnston, 71, and his 62-year-old wife, Jessie, were gone.

Retired painter and gospel preacher, Johnny Megaw, was 67. Alberta Quinton, known fondly as Sister Quinton, who had served in the Women's RAF, was 72 and was there to remember her comrades from war.

There were two retired policemen, Sammy Gault, 49, and Ted Armstrong, 52.

And the youngest, Marie Wilson, 20, whose last words to her father, Gordon, as he lay under the rubble were, 'Daddy, I love you very much.'

Enniskillen High School headmaster, Ronnie Hill, slipped into a coma from his injuries and never recovered, becoming the twelfth victim thirteen years later.

In the highly-charged days after the bombing, Gordon Wilson's words of forgiveness for his daughter's killers struck a chord that epitomised the spirit of the two communities coming together in Enniskillen, where Protestants and Catholics called for peace at candlelit vigils.

It was a sombre week of funerals as thousands filed silently and reverently behind coffin after coffin.

Royal visitors came to visit the injured, with Prince Charles and Princess Diana lifting their spirits. The mayor of Dublin, Carmencita Hederman, broke down in tears as she delivered books of condolence with forty-five thousand signatures. And the political ramifications were argued over.

The remembrance ceremony, which had been abandoned on 8 November 1987, was rearranged for two weeks later. This time, it was a very high-profile event with Prime Minister Margaret Thatcher attending.

Gradually, the media and visitors left, and the small town of Enniskillen was left to pick up the pieces.

Denzil McDaniel is a freelance writer. He was previously editor of the *Impartial Reporter*.

Knocking doors and intruding on grief

Noel Doran

On a cold Fermanagh morning after the worst day in her life, the woman with grief in her eyes had every reason to turn away the stranger who knocked on her front door.

I offered my apologies for disturbing her, mumbled a few inadequate words of sympathy on her loss, tried to explain my role as a journalist and prepared for the rejection that would surely follow.

However Joan Wilson did not hesitate. 'Come in,' she said. 'I will make you tea and Gordon will see you shortly.'

It was around 8 a.m. on Monday 9 November 1987. Less than twenty-four hours earlier, during a Remembrance Day ceremony at Enniskillen cenotaph, an IRA bomb had exploded without warning, killing eleven people and severely injuring dozens of others.

Among those who were buried in the rubble were Gordon Wilson and his daughter Marie, a twenty-year-old nurse.

Joan Wilson could have been there as well, but instead had to attend the morning service at Enniskillen Methodist Church where she was the organist.

She discovered that her husband and her daughter were in the Erne Hospital after the explosion. Gordon made an almost miraculous recovery, and was discharged that night, but a surgeon told Mrs Wilson that he could do no more for Marie. She died shortly afterwards, with her mother holding her hand.

The interviews that Mr Wilson gave the following day had an enormous impact, particularly when he said he would forgive those who had planted the bomb and would pray for them.

His quote – 'I bear no ill will, I bear no grudge' – went round the world and came to be regarded as a pivotal moment in the Troubles. His wife's description of their daughter, carried on the front page of that afternoon's *Belfast Telegraph*, was also poignant. 'She was so full of life and had so much to live for ... she brought cheer to everyone she knew and now she is gone.'

Visiting the family home of someone who has been caught up in a tragedy is the most difficult responsibility in journalism. The task involves a series of judgement calls, a little local knowledge, an element of luck with timing and, above all, respect for everyone concerned. It is frequently misrepresented as a callous, foot-in-the-door approach, but in my experience it was often of much wider significance during our darkest periods.

When a bombing or shooting had fatal consequences, police eventually released some basic details about the victim before moving on with their investigations.

It was left to journalists to try and explain who he or she was, why they mattered, establish as far as possible the sequence of events and, at the most basic level, put a face to a name through a photograph – known as a 'collect' – passed on in the most cruel of circumstances.

The first step was the knock at the door, never knowing whether it would be opened by an adult or a child. An intermediary was sometimes involved, but it was still impossible to say what sort of reception would follow. You had a matter of moments to apologise for the intrusion and set out a sincerely expressed case for a short discussion with someone who could represent the family.

Most put forward an amazingly coherent and generous tribute to their loved one, while others often wanted to address what they regarded as misleading or confusing claims circulating in the area. Different issues could also emerge, depending on whether loyalists, republicans, police, soldiers or unknown individuals were linked to the death.

Some relatives did not choose to speak, and I always accepted those decisions immediately, but others felt compelled to provide both their thoughts and an insight into a lost life.

While a small number talked of bitterness and revenge, others displayed rare grace under pressure – in the way that Joan Wilson epitomised. Her description of Marie still resonates.

Gordon Wilson went on to become a member of the Irish Senate and was internationally recognised for his contribution towards the cause of peace and reconciliation.

Mr Wilson died in 1995, some months after his son, Peter, was killed in a road accident. He is survived by Joan and their daughter Julie-Anne.

Noel Doran is the editor of the *Irish News* in Belfast. In 1987, he was a reporter with the *Belfast Telegraph*.

The lasting impact of the Troubles on my life
Chris Moore

It was 9 March 1971 when I turned up for my first day on duty at the *News Letter* offices in Donegall Street in Belfast – a significant event for me personally as it represented my first job as a news reporter in Northern Ireland. Until then my newspaper experience was confined to a short period of training with a daily paper in Norwich followed by a spell as editor of a small weekly paper in Belfast aimed at the teenage market.

I'd spent too many years living away, first at school in Scotland and then briefly in Norwich. As a result I had little understanding of what was happening in Northern Ireland. I was naive about the sectarian fault lines that had begun to show signs of stress during my absence. The truth is that I had no sense of the political upheaval bubbling beneath the surface.

But on 10 March, twenty-four hours into my job as a news reporter, I was left in no doubt of what was going on when the bodies of three young Scottish soldiers were found dead at the Horseshoe Bend, not far from Ligoniel in North Belfast. News reporting was about to change. In my limited experience, courts and councils were the staples of news coverage but now there were bodies and blood on the streets of Northern Ireland.

Life in Belfast changed dramatically. Bombs were going off almost on a daily basis – sometimes killing people, almost always destroying buildings and bringing a greater sense of danger to life in the city. As you walked around the city centre you had a sense you were risking your life. As you looked ahead up the street, you could not be certain that one of the parked cars did not contain a bomb that was about to go off. Belfast had officially become a dangerous place to live and work.

I remember one occasion when I was walking along Bridge Street on my way to the *News Letter*. A bomb exploded in a travel agents 150 yards ahead, shattering glass in offices and shops nearby. I felt the force of the blast pushing me back. I saw an elderly woman just to my right fall to her knees. I was unharmed and helped her up before we continued on our separate ways.

In March 1972 I had a much closer call when the *News Letter* was the target of an IRA bomb. There'd been a telephone warning and the building was in the process of being evacuated. Two policemen were examining a suspect car when it exploded. The policemen died instantly – one of them lived across the street from my home in Lisburn. Three council binmen died, as did an elderly man a month after the blast. What saved me was the metal filing cabinet in front of my desk: shards of glass flew over my head instead of entering my body.

The attacks and the killings continued on a daily basis but tactics changed as the conflict continued. Terrorists were becoming better armed and better prepared to directly target victims. And as reporters discovered, there was an insidious nature to the pattern of those targeted for assassination. This was particularly true in rural areas, where neighbours turned on neighbours, sometimes collaborating with masked gunmen in the selection of targets.

As a journalist, I found myself becoming more and more engaged with those inflicting the violent deaths on terrified communities. I met these 'faceless' men in bars, car parks and shebeens. I saw them on both sides of the sectarian/religious divide. I knew that they had taken life, or shielded and justified those who did. Our attempts at trying to make sense of the madness became madness itself.

One source I had in the seventies was the violent loyalist killer, Jim Craig. He was known as a murderer who intimidated both Catholics and Protestants, and was also involved in extortion – he divided up the spoils from the Shankill/Falls peace line with republicans. On one occasion he held me at gunpoint along with two tartan gang skinheads in a back room of a Shankill bar to await an explosion that was going to occur nearby on the Falls Road. Only the detonator went off and no one was injured. Craig was evil and, as it turns out, duplicitous. A UFF inquiry reported that he had actually helped republicans kill loyalists.

As reporters we also had republican sources. Some of these paramilitary spin doctors even attempted to engage in everyday conversations at times when they were not attempting to justify their latest murderous atrocity. They tried to talk about their own families and about normal things that happened to them. One republican described a fishing trip when he'd lost his son but hadn't noticed until the boy was found wandering alone along a river. In the next sentence, he explained why his organisation had chosen to take the life of an individual deemed expendable.

Some people cared less about what the killers had to say but more about the inhumanity they displayed by their actions. As Margaret Thatcher said, murder is murder is murder. Except when the state became involved in killings, others would retort … The issue of collusion between the paramilitaries and state security agents, such as the police or British Army, was to become a thorny subject that still troubles the British government particularly.

Collusion raised its head for me in 1989 when I revealed details of how the UDA and the UFF received or acquired information from within the security forces to enable them to target Loughlin Maginn. Details of his profile were handed over to me by the UFF after he was gunned down by that organisation in a sectarian attack. In order to try to justify the murder, the UFF provided me with what they said was intelligence of the dead man's links to the IRA. But it backfired spectacularly on the UFF because this sparked a chain of events that suggested much wider collusion between members of the security forces, police and soldiers.

By this time I had been a reporter with the BBC for ten years. I'd joined in August 1979 – and again my first day at a new job was marked by major terrorist events – the deaths at Mullaghmore, in County Sligo, of Lord Mountbatten, two teenage boys and Baroness Brabourne, killed when an IRA bomb exploded at sea on a leisure boat they were using. A few hours later two bombs near Warrenpoint in County Down killed eighteen British soldiers.

Covering such brutal deaths and the subsequent funerals was sadly all too familiar to BBC reporters like me and my late colleague Austin Hunter – and as we often discussed, we were not immune from the death and despair evoked by each act of violence. We too were human.

I can recall three occasions when I really struggled to hold back tears. One occasion was the funeral of an RUC officer in Moira when his young daughter, aged eight, I believe, cried uncontrollably as the coffin left her home. Similar pain was evident at the funeral of an IRA hunger striker in Belfast when his son too struggled with the reality that he would never again see his dad. Pain has no barriers when it comes to death and the loss of a loved one.

But there's one man who movingly exemplified the true Christian spirit of turning the other cheek.

I spent twenty-four hours working virtually nonstop to cover the Enniskillen Poppy Day killings in 1987. The morning after the explosion, which killed eleven people and wounded scores more, local man Charlie Warmington – a BBC Radio Ulster producer – arranged for me to interview Gordon Wilson. Mr Wilson's daughter Marie had died the previous day as she held his hand under the rubble at the war memorial in Enniskillen.

Charlie had already secured an interview with Mr Wilson, which was conducted by Mike Gaston and broadcast that morning on Radio Ulster. Now Mr Wilson was prepared to face a television camera to tell his story.

I asked three questions of Mr Wilson. In answering my second question he almost broke down. He managed to hold himself together and in doing so also stopped me from breaking down along with him ... and along with my crew.

Back in the office I was told to cut the piece to just over three minutes. I could find no way to cut it. I asked the news producer of the day and the news editor to watch Gordon Wilson's interview in which he forgave the men who planted the bomb that killed his daughter.

They watched in awe. And they agreed it could not be edited. I think it was close to or just over seven minutes long. It was a powerful interview because of the message of forgiveness from Gordon Wilson. It was one of the most significant moments in my career covering the Troubles.

There is one other story of the Troubles that I witnessed and that has had a lasting impact on my life. It's a story of a man called Terence McKeever. He ran an electrical engineering company that had carried out work on a number of security bases in Northern Ireland. For that reason he was abducted and shot dead by the IRA.

When I arrived at the location where Mr McKeever's body had been found, in June 1986, it was a bright, hot, sunny day. Gardaí stood fifteen yards from where his body lay in the Irish Republic. No RUC or British Army soldiers would approach until the area was declared safe from booby traps.

My film crew and I approached the body. Mr McKeever's face was partially covered by his jacket which had its arms tied behind his head to keep it in place. It was an appalling sight. There was no dignity or respect for Mr McKeever. It struck me that if the public saw this shocking image of death, it might have had an impact on support for the killers.

Throughout the afternoon, I saw a local priest arrive on three occasions with three different families who approached the remains of the dead man who had been left in such a grotesque pose on a deserted border road. They then briefly pulled the jacket aside to see the face. Each family left with the priest. This told me that three families in that area of South Armagh near Cullyhanna had loved ones missing – presumed victims of the IRA's internal security team that rooted out so-called informers and administered death to those judged guilty. As it happens, there was a booby-trap bomb in the adjacent field but Mr McKeever's father recovered the body before nightfall so his son would not be left 'lying out' all night.

Death is ugly in whatever form and for more than three decades the people who endured life during the Troubles encountered it more than three thousand times. And now we ask: to achieve what exactly?

Chris Moore has reported on the Northern Ireland conflict for more than forty years and has worked for the *News Letter* and the *Belfast Telegraph*, as well as winning major awards for his reporting with UTV and the BBC.

Mourners seek cover during Michael Stone's attack at Milltown.

Taking cover during Michael Stone's attack at Milltown

Jeanie Johnston

There were many scary moments for journalists in Northern Ireland in the 1970s, '80s and '90s. But most of them unfolded so quickly that you reacted instantly and they were over before you realised what had happened. 16 March 1988 was a little different, and as I lay flat out beside the headstone of a lady whose name I will never forget, sandwiched between cold granite and my electrician colleague, I had time to wonder just what on earth was going on in Milltown Cemetery.

Pressure had been building since the shooting dead of three IRA terrorists by British Special Forces ten days earlier in Gibraltar. In fact, it had been building since before then, but the fourteen days that started with the killing of Dan McCann, Seán Savage and Mairéad Farrell and spanned their homecoming and funerals, the Milltown Cemetery attack, the Milltown victims' funerals and the corporals' murders have been called the darkest time of the Troubles. And I wouldn't argue with that. You could practically taste the tension in the air that day as the coffins of the Gibraltar Three set out for Milltown Cemetery.

The RUC claimed they were working to defuse the situation by separating the cortèges coming north from Dublin airport, and then by stepping back from the funerals on the day. This was an unusual, even unprecedented, move – terrorist funerals in those days were accompanied by police Land Rovers, and attended by almost as many RUC officers as mourners, intent on stopping any show of paramilitary strength. The lack of police presence would later be criticised by the republicans as collusion to allow renegade loyalist Michael Stone to mount his attack, though this was strongly denied by both police and loyalists. At the time the lack of police presence just felt surreal.

I can remember the quietness as we walked to the cemetery, just the sound of footsteps and the lament of the pipes as the three hearses processed side by side, led by the pipers and followed by thousands of mourners. Funerals of this magnitude were usually characterised by unseemly jostling and jeering between mourners and police, so the peacefulness was extraordinary.

As we reached Milltown Cemetery, ranks and ranks of mourners seemed to file endlessly through the gates. The families and chief mourners had gathered around the republican plot. I was standing a little way back with my crew, busy composing a few lines of script in my head, hardly daring to believe that the funerals were passing off without incident, when the unthinkable happened.

Mairéad Farrell's coffin had just been lowered into the grave when there were several loud thumps, followed by what sounded like firecrackers going off. The first shots were mistaken by almost everyone for an IRA salute, common at such funerals. Then there was a period of uncertainty. The shots sounded unreal in the still air and people didn't know what was happening. Then we saw people streaked with blood, and reality hit. Loyalist Michael Stone had unleashed his savage attack on mourners, throwing grenades and firing shots before running down towards the M1, firing and hurling more explosives at those who began to pursue him. Television crews captured footage that would later go around the world.

With my UTV crew, I took shelter for a few moments, trying to work out where the shots were coming from. Then we began to run in Stone's direction even though we were still unsure what was happening. Everyone else was running the other way to try and escape.

As we ran we filmed people crouched behind gravestones, many of them injured and bleeding. Many more were simply too shocked and bewildered to move. Gerry Adams' voice rang out over a loudspeaker as he tried to calm the crowd. Then I saw the funeral limousines and hearses being driven at high speed out of the cemetery gates packed with injured mourners. In all, more than fifty people were wounded.

As we pushed through the crowd, the terrain of the cemetery stretching down the hill to the M1 below us presented the most incredible tableau. A barely discernible, long-haired figure in the distance was firing at the chasing pack of mourners who closed in as he reached the motorway. Eventually they seized him, pulling him to the ground. But before he could be driven away, the police arrived. Stone was arrested.

It was one of those 'did that just happen?' moments and, indeed, it was only after we returned to our offices at Havelock House that we were able to put all the pieces of the story together. The men who died were Thomas McErlean, aged 20, John Murray, aged 26, and Kevin Brady, aged 30, a member of the IRA.

The attack had further tragic consequences at Brady's funeral three days later, when two British Army corporals were dragged from their car, taken to waste ground and shot dead after inadvertently straying into the path of the funeral cortège.

Jeanie Johnston was a reporter at UTV.

Remembering Jillian Johnston
Derval Fitzsimons

Fermanagh's Boa Island is as ancient and mystic a place as can be found on the island of Ireland. The beautiful lacework of tranquil waterways and the area's rich pagan and early Christian history draw visitors from across the world, yearning for the peace and spiritual calm that it breathes.

The area was home to holy scholars and pagans whose carved deities, nestling between the trees, speak to a rich history reaching back thousands of years, and even the name Boa Island fittingly commemorates the battlegrounds of the Celtic goddess of war, Badhbh.

And yet it was here, in this quiet land sacred to the ancients, that the IRA unleashed an attack upon a young woman, an assault of such anger and ferocity that it is still as inexplicable and grotesque thirty years later as it was the night it happened.

Boa Island was Jillian Johnston's home. She knew its hedgerows and its hazel woods. It was an area that had largely gone untouched by the violence that drenched the rest of the province but all that was to change. It was 18 March 1988, a Friday night, and Jillian Johnston and her fiancé had driven the few miles into the village of Belleek for fish and chips.

Jillian lived as quiet and ordinary a life as you could imagine. Just shy of her twenty-second birthday she worked in a pharmacy and was popular with staff and customers. She was dating her high school sweetheart, Stanley Liggett. They were engaged and looking forward to a long and happy life together.

As she and Stanley sat in her daddy's car outside her family home, an IRA gunman came up unseen and pumped round after round into the car with an automatic weapon. Jillian's horrified mother, Annabella, was just yards away inside the house when she heard the shots. If you could imagine how remote this country road is, how serene and quiet it is, you could imagine how the gunfire must have ripped through the peace of that night.

Jillian Johnston died instantly. Her fiancé was badly injured. Thirty spent bullet cases were found around the car. She was hit twenty-seven times.

The IRA later admitted the killing was a mistake and said the intended victim was a member of her family who was in the UDR. But the Johnston family had no connection with the security forces and neither did her fiancé's.

To everyone living in Northern Ireland, that March was brutal. In the aftermath of violent murder, you move silently into a place between the life that was and that life that is to come. That is where we found ourselves.

I was a reporter at Downtown Radio and it was an exhilarating time to be in your early twenties, an ambitious young journalist racing with focus and determination from murder to murder. This was our story. The old guard flew in from Beirut or Luanda for the big ones but the day-to-day storytelling belonged to those of us cut from the fabric of Northern Ireland.

We were driven by two things – the race to be first and the desire to be best. In those days before the internet, Northern Ireland relied solely on its journalists to bring the victims' stories to life. We took our responsibilities seriously.

I drove down from Belfast in the hours after Jillian's death not knowing what I would find. I knew there'd been a fatal shooting but nothing more. It was dark and it was late and it was remote. The area was cordoned off when I arrived and I didn't hang about long. It was only when the details started to come through the next day that we realised this wasn't just another killing. But it was too late – the media machine had moved on as Northern Ireland grappled with new horrors. For thirty years I've ached that I did not do justice to Jillian Johnston. She could have been my sister, my friend; we were just a few years apart in age, both daughters of rural Ulster.

This unfathomably angry assault could have sparked international revolt and while it was utterly condemned, Jillian's death was buried amidst a series of events so shocking that they left the world reeling. I remember thinking that maybe under different circumstances this young woman could have changed the course of our history, yet her name has been subsumed into the bitter litany of our dead because Jillian Johnston died in the middle of a nightmare month when the purveyors of Ulster violence surpassed themselves.

The reason that her name still haunts me is because she died a shocking death in a week of shocking deaths. She was killed in the days between the now historic pillars of Milltown and Andersonstown.

Two days before she died, Michael Stone had launched his attack on mourners in Milltown Cemetery and just hours after she died, the two corporals were killed in West Belfast. The difference was that Jillian died on a Friday night, far away from the spotlight, down a remote country road in the far reaches of Fermanagh, with just her fiancé to witness her death.

The others' final moments were played out in front of the TV cameras in Belfast and the pictures were almost immediately relayed around the world.

Jillian Johnston is not, of course, a forgotten victim. She is remembered by all those who knew her as a happy girl, who never had a bad word to say about anyone. When the twenty-fifth anniversary of her death was marked, the church where she was buried was full to overflowing. She is as alive today as ever she was in the hearts of her grieving family and her friends. My enduring sadness is that her name is not also in the forefront of the minds of all of us who lived through those awful days.

Derval Fitzsimons was head of home news at ITV News and editor of Independent Radio News. She began her career in Belfast as a reporter for the *News Letter* and Downtown Radio.

Father Alec Reid administers the last rites to David Howes.

I still get flashbacks to 'the corporals' killings'
Alan Jones

'They were obviously on a suicide mission,' a mourner told me shortly after we had witnessed two men – later identified as off-duty British soldiers – driving full pelt towards the front of an IRA funeral on Belfast's Andersonstown Road. The men were dragged from their car, beaten up, bundled into a taxi, dumped on to nearby waste ground and shot.

It was one of the most horrific episodes in a chapter of violence gripping Northern Ireland at the height of the Troubles, and one that no one who witnessed it will ever forget.

I certainly won't. Saturday 19 March 1988. The first funeral of one of the mourners killed a few days earlier when loyalist Michael Stone opened fire in Milltown Cemetery as hundreds gathered for the burials of three IRA members shot dead by the SAS in Gibraltar.

Stone killed three people, and it could have been many more as he randomly opened fire, shattering the peace of a graveyard on a funeral day. It felt so unreal watching people scream in terror, run wildly away from the gunshots, crazily pointing fingers at anyone who looked as though they could be an accomplice.

The brick-shaped mobile phone my colleague Deric Henderson had hired for the day didn't work, so we ran to a nearby house to tell the story to our office, without really believing the carnage we had just witnessed.

A few days later I was back on the Andersonstown Road, walking near the front of the mourners for the funeral of Kevin Brady, one of those killed at Milltown, sensing an incredibly tense atmosphere, and noticing the complete absence of police, with the nearest military presence being an army helicopter hovering high up in the sky.

I was actually thinking about my hopes of making it back to my hotel in Belfast to watch my beloved Wales playing France in a Five Nations rugby match when the eerie silence of a funeral cortège was broken by the sound of a car in the distance. I thought initially it was just being revved up to join the back of the mourners, but a few seconds later I could see it being driven up the road, directly towards the front of the funeral procession.

Chaos, confusion and naked violence followed in the ensuing few minutes. The car stopped just short of the mourners, swung into a parking area in front of a row of shops, then reversed back on to the main road before coming to a halt.

Amid the screaming, crying and swearing, some men approached the car. One got on the roof and began wildly hitting it with what looked like a car jack, while others started dragging the soldiers out. One of the soldiers fired a shot in the air, but they were overpowered and dragged along the road and pushed over the walls of the nearby Casement Park GAA ground.

I honestly couldn't believe what I had witnessed, had absolutely no idea that the two men were soldiers, but was aware that mourners had tried to stop photographers and TV camera crews taking pictures or filming the incident. Photographers had their films ripped from cameras – this was pre-digital – hands were placed over TV cameras and reporters were threatened as the atmosphere turned ugly. The army helicopter swooped lower, the noise of its rotors heightening the sense of fear and mayhem below.

My mind was a blur but I walked as inconspicuously as I could towards a nearby leisure centre where I knew there was a public telephone so I could call my office in London. Before I got there, a black taxi emerged from the park, with its passenger pumping his arm in salute out of the window to loud cheers and the two soldiers in the back.

I made it to the leisure centre, persuaded the manager to open it up so I could use the telephone, and somehow dictated an account of what had just happened. I'm sure it made no sense, because I must have been in shock, fearing for my own safety by then, and still totally in the dark about what I had seen.

When I left the leisure centre a few minutes later, the army helicopter was still hovering nearby, and people were still crying, looking stunned or trying to get away. As I was walking around in a daze, wondering where to go, or who to speak to in order to get some sense out of the bloody scenes, I wandered on to some waste ground, where the two soldiers' bodies had been dumped. I ran away as if I was in a race, hearing the sound of police sirens coming in the opposite direction.

Information slowly emerged over the coming hours and days, but only theories about why the soldiers drove into an IRA funeral. There were rumours that they were SAS members, or that one of the soldiers was showing his newly arrived colleague what an IRA funeral looked like and inadvertently went the wrong way. I didn't believe it then, and I still don't.

An army contact told me that one of the soldiers had served in Herford in Germany and the attackers may have seen his warrant card and mistaken the word for Hereford, where the SAS is based.

What I do know is that the atmosphere in Belfast for days afterwards was frightening. A journalist colleague was chased down the street when some youths recognised him from the funeral. I used to love working in Belfast, meeting friendly, warm, decent people trying to cope with living through the horrors of the Troubles, but for once, I couldn't wait to leave.

More than thirty years later, I still get flashbacks and nightmares about the shocking cycle of violence that week in 1988. But I find it staggering that the one question everyone was asking at the time still hasn't been answered. I firmly believe someone in authority in the British military at the time knows why those two soldiers were on the Andersonstown Road. Surely it's time for the truth.

Alan Jones works as the industrial correspondent for the Press Association in London.

The Gibraltar shootings: taking on the censors
Alex Thomson

In those days it was a rare thing to see a BBC editor not in his suit (and in those days they all seemed to be men). Rarer still to see one running. Running down a corridor on a quiet Sunday afternoon and tearing into the row of small rooms that was home to *Spotlight* – BBC Northern Ireland's current affairs programme.

Wearing – I recall – a tracksuit, sweating and out of breath, Andy Colman, *Spotlight* editor, could just about get his words out to me between gasps: 'Alex – the trail? Where's the trail? Who's got the trail?'

And that is when I first knew. The first inkling of a frontal editorial storm incoming: from London, from Downing Street and from who knew where else?

My first job in journalism was as a reporter on *Spotlight*. Now it occurred to me it could be my last.

One thing was clear. The promo for the coming programme on the Gibraltar shootings was finished, edited – but it was not going to be transmitted, it seemed, as my editor stood in near-panic, demanding to know where the tape of it was.

For weeks we had been investigating the shooting dead of three Provisional IRA members in Gibraltar. Cars hired by the active service unit linked to Mairéad Farrell, Danny McCann and Seán Savage would later be found to contain 132lb of Semtex, wire, tools and a timer.

But when shot dead by the SAS they were unarmed and, said more than one eyewitness, had their hands up in surrender. Moreover, this was at the height of allegations that the British were operating death squads to kill the IRA and ask questions (or not) later.

With our thirty-minute documentary ready to go and featuring eyewitnesses and much new evidence of what had happened, we were ready to roll on that sunny Sunday afternoon in Belfast.

It's hard to exaggerate how charged the atmosphere already was. Thames TV had just broadcast *Death on the Rock*. There was intense pressure to ban that film. They went ahead. But Thames TV would lose its franchise a few years later. The struggle to withstand political censorship from the highest level of government proved, shamefully, to be not just editorial but existential for Thames.

Now, with an editor clearly under desperate pressure not to run the TV trail for our coming investigation, the same struggle was coming to the BBC.

We knew by now we had a programme that largely began where the Thames investigation ended and took the story on. Quite by chance, the two programmes dovetailed beautifully. A beauty quite lost on the British government.

As Roger Bolton, editor of the Thames TV film, later wrote: 'Relief came from an unexpected quarter ... *Spotlight* fully confirmed what we had reported and went rather further, if anything.'

Then, quite simply, the dam burst internally. Endless crisis meetings and memos ensued. Or at least I inferred from the worried looks of men in suits that there was a growing crisis.

I couldn't quite say for certain because I wasn't invited to these meetings. That seemed a little odd, as I was the person who had researched and reported, but at the time I was too busy fulfilling endless volleys of requests to check, check and quintuple-check everything in the film and many things that were not. Requests from men much older than I who looked, simply, terrified.

There was not a lot of sleep as we moved towards what would or would not be transmission day – the coming Thursday. Yet all this time as the hours passed, the wider public knew nothing. That trailer was already banned in an act of internal BBC censorship as the institutional terror set in.

Matters all came to a head when so many men in suits arrived from the BBC in London to view the film that I couldn't get near the door, still less through it and into the edit suite.

But I do vividly recall the BBC editor in Northern Ireland, John Conway, barking out, 'New witness! ... New point! ... New evidence! ...' at various points in the film. If BBC top brass were trying to take the programme down, John Conway, to his eternal credit, was standing by his team and going down fighting.

Would he prevail? In what seemed part internal turf war about London attempting – perhaps – to ban the film and Belfast having none of it, and part the wider confrontation with the government over pressure to censor the BBC, John Conway was fighting Belfast's corner.

All that week the defence secretary, the foreign secretary and much of the cabinet had insisted broadcasting our film would prejudice any subsequent inquest. Given no such inquest had yet been convened and that these same cabinet ministers were talking about how the BBC was about to appease terrorists, in parliament and all over the media, this seemed to me a somewhat hypocritical stance.

All the more so for their insistence that the SAS had been right to do what they did. Somehow the coroner wasn't a problem for them – just for journalism.

But back in the BBC in Belfast matters were not going well. After that viewing there was talk of slashing the film to ten or fifteen minutes and having a studio debate to fill the rest of the programme. There was talk of not transmitting it at all.

And I remained largely in the dark as these debates raged up to the director-general and back and I was kept well away.

So I can now, for the first time in public, break cover. Uncertain that the BBC would not cave in, I leaked whatever I knew of these internal machinations and details of the programme itself to every newspaper I could get to. If the BBC was going to kowtow to the likes of Geoffrey Howe and other cabinet ministers, I was damned if they'd be able to do it away from the glare of publicity.

The plan was highly effective and it was probably also career suicide (at the BBC). It seems strange now, but I could not have imagined how big the story would then get. Suddenly it was all over the front pages of almost every national paper.

My recollection is that the BBC arranged a hurried screening of the full, uncut film in London for journalists. Excerpts were released and I watched my BBC piece to camera used in the top story on ITN's *News at Ten*.

Externally, it had the desired effect – a film quite different from the Thames controversy had now been viewed beyond Belfast whether the BBC desired it or not.

The PR battle all but won, the film was duly broadcast – without trailers – in its planned slot, uncut, uncensored.

Curiously though, the film did not get a wider audience beyond Northern Ireland. As *Spotlight* reporters, we would routinely re-broadcast our films on *Newsnight* in those days. But somehow, not this time.

Here was a case for re-broadcasting at its full thirty minutes in a special slot, nationally, after all the days of hoo-hah. The idea of a national newspaper not running an investigation like this from a regional correspondent would be absurd, unimaginable and a blatant act of self-censorship. But it never happened. I was told at the time by a very senior BBC executive, 'Look, you've won one battle. Don't push your luck.'

My abiding impression was of BBC Northern Ireland laudably standing its ground against those from London who appeared minded to do the government's bidding and censor us.

All of this though, is nothing, nothing at all, set against the period of brutal, up close and personal bloodletting that Gibraltar seemed to somehow unleash. A bleak and dark period of a couple of weeks. It would pass and I would move on.

But where? To my first foreign assignment of my new role at *Channel 4 News* and back to Gibraltar for the inquest into the shootings. And yes, the inquest passed off with no hint of any prejudice, real or imagined. The judicial system, like journalism, proved a little more robust than the government had fondly imagined.

Alex Thomson is presenter and chief correspondent of *Channel 4 News*. He previously worked for BBC Northern Ireland.

My brushes with Margaret Thatcher and Prince Charles

Eamonn Mallie

My late friend Jim Aiken, a showbiz promoter, used to say, 'I am going to write a book about all the gobshites I have known, starting with myself.'

Across the decades I have discommoded presidents, prime ministers, leaders of the various religious denominations, the security services, members of the royal family, and especially the political parties and establishments – accountability being my guiding principle.

The arrival of a new secretary of state in Northern Ireland always came with the health warning: 'Watch Mallie.'

The late Patrick Mayhew, who learned to his cost the wisdom of the advice he was given by his mandarins, was forced to tender his resignation to Prime Minister John Major because I incontrovertibly proved the British government was secretly talking to the IRA.

Mayhew had repeatedly denied my claim about government contacts with republicans week after week until I eventually produced the smoking gun – his own document, which exposed the government's clandestine activity. Be that as it may, on his last day in Northern Ireland Mayhew revealed an admirable side.

We had assembled at the bottom of the steps of Stormont Castle, from which the former attorney general was leaving for the last time. He stepped into the green Jaguar in which he was habitually driven by the police and was whisked off at speed. Moments later the car reversed and the large bulk of the outgoing secretary of state emerged and motioned towards me, hand outstretched. He clearly accepted my treatment of him went with the turf. He was indeed a big man.

Despite my empathy with the 'left' politically, regrettably, scarcely any of the Labour viceroys despatched to lord it over us in Northern Ireland endeared themselves to me, with the possible exception of John Reid. He neatly crystallised the ugliness of violence perpetrated by paramilitary organisations, the state and the security services in the following words: 'We have just come through a murky, dirty little war here.' He got it in one sentence and the outworking of the 'murky, dirty little war' is still with us.

I found Tory secretaries of state much more intellectually substantial, people like Douglas Hurd, who would readily allow himself to be pulled aside for a quiet word if I needed clarification on a piece of information that had come my way.

One of the most disarming Conservative Party politicians to run Northern Ireland was Peter Brooke. He was nicknamed 'Babbling Brooke' by former Democratic Unionist Party leader Ian Paisley who invariably came up with a sobriquet for each new secretary of state. Douglas Hurd was known as 'Hurd the Turd'. Mr Paisley labelled the miniature Labour incumbent Roy Mason 'pint tin size Mason' – Mason was a pipe smoker of whom Paisley said, 'I never knew if he held the pipe or if the pipe held him.' Tory Tom King was branded 'Tom Cat King' and so on.

I had a natural fondness for Brooke, despite the DUP leader's acerbic description of him. I always felt he carried a historical sense of guilt for how his ancestors behaved in Ireland.

I was once asked by *Channel 4 News* to interview Mr Brooke as they were putting together a profile ahead of inter-party talks in Northern Ireland. He left me speechless when I put the following to him: 'You come across as bumbling, awkward and unsure of yourself when you speak – what do you say to that charge? He paused and said, 'Perhaps that is how I am.'

How charming and self-deprecating was that – none of the pomp and nonsense other political minnows, like Brian Mawhinney, Tom King or John Stanley, foisted upon us.

I crossed swords several times with the so-called 'Iron Lady', Margaret Thatcher.

On her first visit, during the IRA's hunger strike in 1981, she declared, 'The IRA are playing their last card.' When I went head-to-head with her in an interview on the following visit I reminded her of her previous prediction of the IRA's imminent demise. Sinn Féin had by now an MP and scores of councillors. The Conservative Party leader let her feelings about my line of questioning be known to me.

Later Deric Henderson – the Press Association Ireland editor who shadowed Thatcher when she came to Northern Ireland – revealed to me Mrs Thatcher congratulated herself for 'not losing her temper with me'. Really?

The morning of the Brighton bombing, 12 October 1984, I said a prayer of thanksgiving for the safe deliverance of Mrs Thatcher. Had the prime minister been killed I feared a lot of people, particularly in the Catholic community in Northern Ireland, might have died.

Twenty-four hours later I asked a Donegall Road woman – a Protestant who worked in our house – about the reaction in her area to the IRA attempt on Mrs Thatcher's life. She shocked me with her reply: 'Do you know, I heard some people saying it was a pity they didn't get the oul' bitch.' Working-class people, regardless of creed, hadn't forgotten the crushing of the miners by Margaret Thatcher in 1984–85.

Over the years no one ever informed me that professionally there was an effective ban on my covering of royal visits to Northern Ireland. I knew this was the case, though, and I didn't lose any sleep over it. The fear of my bosses was that I would break the protocol that prohibits the putting of questions to members of the royal family during visits.

A day or two after the Gulf War ended in 1991, Princess Diana was visiting a charity organisation in South Belfast. She did not look particularly glamorous, I felt, dressed in a wheaten-coloured two-piece suit. I was determined I would not be cowed by protocol. I chanced a harmless enough question: 'How do you feel about the ending of the Gulf War?' Fixing those large bovine eyes upon me, Diana replied, 'I am delighted, like everybody else.'

However pathetic my question, it proved to be prescient. Diana later confessed in a *Panorama* interview to having had an affair with Captain James Hewitt, who was born in Derry and who served in the Gulf War. 'Like everybody else' who had a loved one coming home, she clearly had very good reason to be 'delighted'.

The other brush I had with royalty was during a visit by Prince Charles to the RUC headquarters in Knock, Belfast.

I had violated the unofficial royal ban, and turned up armed with my microphone and an arsenal of questions. The tabloids were full of stories at the time about Charles and his private life. The usual steel barriers were in place to afford appropriate space to the member of the royal family and to keep 'the reptiles' at bay.

RTÉ cameraman Johnny Coghlan was, as was his wont, tight on my shoulder as he knew I was always likely to toss a grenade into any press situation. Prince Charles injudiciously, if not foolishly, swung left on bidding farewell to the RUC hierarchy. I pounced. 'Tell me, sir, what about all these stories about your private life in the papers?'

In those days TV sound engineers used a long boom or pole replete with a huge grey fluffy wind muff on the end. In my memory Jim McGirr of UTV always had a boom pole in his hand.

It was quite evident Prince Charles did not like my question. He took a deep breath, tossed his head skywards and rather sheepishly and foolishly asked Jim: 'What are you doing up there? Are you fishing?'

By now I was driving another arrow into Charles's ribs. 'Answer the question, please. What have you got to say about these newspaper reports?' By this point Charles had collected his thoughts and counselled, 'You must not believe everything you read in newspapers.'

At this stage the press officers from the Northern Ireland Office were clearly pondering their futures, wondering how the fox had got into the chicken coop. Needless to say, the tabloid stories and my questions to Prince Charles were borne out by history.

No knighthood for Mallie!

Despite the bleakness of the Troubles there were moments of humour too. Asked to meet an IRA source at a venue in West Belfast, my colleague Brian Rowan and I headed to a busy cafe on the Andersonstown Road.

Brian and I occupied two seats on one side of a table and the IRA representative plonked himself down in the seat opposite. Minutes later an old lady armed with a big bag barged her way into the seat beside the IRA's Mr Big, instructing him, 'Move over, son.'

We are still laughing years later about the day a woman from Andytown ordered the IRA commander to shape up!

Eamonn Mallie is a freelance journalist and commentator, who previously worked for Downtown Radio as political editor.

The killing I'll never forget
David Davin-Power

His name was Paul Moran. He was thirty-three with a young family, and his killing was the first murder I ever covered.

It was – as it turned out – the first of twenty killings in a four-week period in early 1992 that coincided with my arrival in RTÉ's Belfast office. I had to cover them all, as the station went on an unexpected strike the day I arrived. As the senior man, it fell to me to man the microphones.

But Paul Moran's murder still stays with me. The eerie stillness in Lisburn's Longstone Street. The white tape around the newsagents where he had stopped, as he generally did, to buy his morning paper; the block of flats into which his UDA killer had escaped; the pool of blood a date-stamp of evil in a nondescript Northern Ireland street.

He worked for the Lisburn Hide Company, a business alongside the railway line whose buildings reminded me of him on my journeys back to Dublin.

For a middle-class Dubliner who'd scarcely been north of the border on half a dozen occasions it was a searing few weeks. Three days later a Catholic taxi driver was targeted, then a Protestant bread-man. The next day – one of the strangest incidents of the Troubles – the murder of three men in Sinn Féin's Falls Road offices by a troubled RUC man who later took his own life; one of scores of police suicides. Then twenty-four hours later the Ormeau Road massacre of five Catholics, one a schoolboy, shot in a bookies shop by the UDA. It was becoming too much too take. The SAS killing of a four-man IRA unit in Coalisland brought this vicious interlude to a close.

But even in the darkest days, green shoots were there if you looked hard enough. The British Army GOC in the North, John Wilsey, wasn't being whimsical when he told me that 'even the Hundred Years War came to an end' (adding helpfully, though, that it took longer than a hundred years). He knew of the contacts that were helping to build the foundations of what would come to be known as the peace process.

Even Seamus Mallon's regular withering condemnations of republican and loyalist killings seemed to fall short of despair. All the while the sense was growing that even as the killing continued, something else was stirring too.

The trips to Stormont, where the shutters had been down for a decade, became more frequent as the peace talks intensified. I was learning how different Northern Ireland was from the political world I had come from. The bottomless well of distrust between the parties; the ubiquitous close protection officers shadowing every senior unionist figure; the paradox of people who regularly visited Dublin for rugby internationals regarding the Republic as alien.

Socially, too, Belfast was a world removed from my comfort zone. In college in Dublin I had been surrounded by Northerners, but in Belfast I encountered but a handful of my fellow townsmen. A night at a Free Presbyterian function held to celebrate Ian Paisley's fifty years of preaching cemented my view that this place was different.

Northern Ireland was big news then, more often than not leading the RTÉ bulletins. As rumours of a ceasefire intensified, it wasn't unusual to have up to a dozen camera crews at routine press conferences. Section 31 – banning interviews with Sinn Féin – meant RTÉ was regarded with more than usual suspicion by republicans. We were 'the spawn of Conor Cruise O'Brien', I recollect.

By the end of 1993 I was convinced that an IRA ceasefire was on the way. There was a sense of war weariness among many republicans, in contrast to the sprightly optimism of Albert Reynolds, who in the memorable words of an associate was by then 'wild for the peace'.

He was right. The night before the announcement I spoke with Gerry Adams privately in West Belfast. He told me that the message that was coming would be 'acceptable to Dublin'. That meant Albert was getting what he had held out for, a complete and unconditional cessation.

The reaction on the streets of West Belfast the next day was curious; relief tinged with a little bewilderment. This was new territory.

Eighteen months later I was enjoying a day off, heading for Murphy's butchers on the Lisburn Road. My phone rang. It was the news desk in Dublin. A message purporting to be from the IRA was being phoned in. The desk editor read it over to me as it was being transcribed. I pulled in to the kerb and told my bosses to clear the decks. This was the real thing. An hour later our man in London, Brian O'Connell, rang me to say he had heard and felt a huge explosion three miles downriver in Canary Wharf. The ceasefire was over.

It was a shock, but not a huge one. The British government had been dragging its heels on admitting Sinn Féin to political talks, and the arrival of a Fine Gael-led government in Dublin was the last straw for republicans. Indeed, some in John Bruton's cabinet at the time regarded the breakdown as a cynical ploy to undermine him in any dealings he had with Downing Street.

Whatever about that, the restoration of the ceasefire wasn't long delayed after he left office.

What had been a headlong series of events gave way to the interminable negotiations leading up to the Good Friday Agreement when Senator George Mitchell played such a key role.

And then, after the extraordinary night that saw Ian Paisley shouted down by David Ervine and his followers amid an air of frenzy outside Stormont Buildings, the talking was over. The deal was done. Within the hour the helicopters were departing Stormont. Tony Blair left to begin a long-delayed holiday; George Mitchell returned to his newborn son and Bertie Ahern departed to mourn his mother, who had died just days earlier.

For myself, I'd been broadcasting continuously for what seemed like weeks. I headed to County Clare to join my family. When we went down to the local pub I got a round of applause, not something I'm accustomed to. It was that kind of time.

Of course we had the ghastly coda of the Omagh bomb months later, but the Good Friday Agreement remains the political high-water mark for a generation. In the same pub in Clare I heard two elderly farmers discussing in terms of some erudition whether Daniel O'Connell or John Hume was the greater figure, advancing arguments for each.

Twenty years later, the elation of that time seems strange and unreachable. The political tides have ebbed and flowed, but have steadily receded year on year from the line left by the Good Friday Agreement.

That is due in part to a dearth of political leadership across the parties; figures like John Hume, Seamus Mallon, David Trimble, the late David Ervine, John Alderdice, the late Martin McGuinness and Monica McWilliams were never going to be easily replaced. But to recall them is to recall the breadth of the political spectrum that produced the deal.

Now just Sinn Féin and the DUP dominate the stage, each led by figures dramatically less substantial than those of twenty years ago.

The Agreement itself is a unique deal, painstakingly negotiated, backed by an all-island democratic majority and internationally recognised.

Nonetheless Brexit challenges the Agreement in a way that was never envisaged by those who framed it. The internal tensions caused by weak political leadership threaten a perfect storm.

But to claim it has outlived its usefulness is to betray people like the family of Paul Moran whose killing had such an impact on a rookie correspondent twenty-six years ago. They are still looking for answers, his brother insisting that in the absence of them, his death remains as raw for them as the day he died. Without the framework that the Good Friday Agreement provides, there's little chance of closure for thousands of victims like the Morans, and the real danger that an already divided society slips back towards old ways.

David Davin-Power is a broadcaster and commentator based in Dublin. He was northern editor for RTÉ between 1991 and 2001.

Sean Graham's, Ormeau Road, 1992

Ivan Little

His anguished cry is today still as heart-wrenching to listen to in the archive TV footage as it was to witness in real-life on the Ormeau Road all those years ago. Billy McManus had just sprinted up to Sean Graham's bookies after his boss told him something 'was happening' there. Billy could see the fleet of ambulances outside the tiny turf accountants on the corner of Hatfield Street and as he arrived amid the chaos and confusion, he noticed his Uncle Jim slumped on the pavement with blood pumping from bullet wounds to his stomach. Jim was able to talk, however, and told Billy to go and make sure that Billy's father, Willie, was okay but Billy couldn't get into the bookies.

'And it was then that I realised something was terribly wrong,' said Billy. 'I saw injured people like wee James Kennedy being brought out by the ambulance crews.'

Billy went over to a friend who'd been in the bookies. Ulster Television cameraman Martin Gibson captured the next harrowing moments for posterity.

'I've watched the pictures,' said Billy, 'and I can see myself asking twice "What about my daddy?" and my friend Brian says, "He's gone." Those words have stuck in my mind.'

Billy's grief-stricken wail shattered the stunned silence on the road.

I was just feet away trying to comprehend the scale of the carnage that unfolded. I had been driving up the Ormeau Road when a distressed Joyce McCartan, a woman who lived just a few doors away from UTV's Havelock House base, shouted to me that eight people had just been shot in the bookies.

Tragically that was an underestimation. In fact 12 of the 13 men in the bookies had been wounded as the 2 UFF gunmen unleashed 46 shots from a pistol and an automatic rifle in a 20-second frenzy of hate. Five of the casualties died.

I swung my car into University Avenue, little realising that the killers' getaway vehicle had driven away from that very spot only minutes earlier. My cameraman, who been due to rendezvous with me to cover another story that afternoon, was just behind me and the images he recorded were among the most painfully graphic of the Troubles.

Nowadays camera phones often capture the aftermath of an outrage but back then it was highly unusual for reporters and news crews to be on the scene of an atrocity so quickly. This was different. Shockingly different.

There was so much horror around us that it was difficult to take it all in. I saw Jim McManus with his back against the bookies' front wall. He was ashen.

The RUC were only starting to arrive and paramedics were hard pressed to cope with so many wounded men. They found it almost impossible to gain access with their stretchers through the narrow doorway. Instead they had to carry the injured away from the building on blood-soaked sheets and blankets before transferring them to stretchers.

One of the first victims to emerge from the mayhem was quite clearly only a child. I later learnt that he was James Kennedy, who was just fifteen. His father later called at UTV to ask me to stop using the pictures of his son because the family had been told James might have been breathing his last as he was wheeled past the camera.

A veritable procession of casualties followed James and dozens of panic-stricken people from the tightly-knit Lower Ormeau descended on the bookies, desperate for information about their loved ones.

Billy McManus wasn't the only one to hear the worst possible news.

Martin Magee was also seen in the TV pictures making his way through the throngs of relatives only to be informed that his eighteen-year-old twin brother, Peter, hadn't made it.

The twins' mother, Clara, was filmed as friends and relatives hustled her away from the bookies. When she was eighty-five she had to bury Martin. Friends and relatives said the forty-three-year-old father of two was another victim of the UFF gun attack, a tortured soul who could never get over the death of his twin.

Tommy Duffin had been working in the loyalist Rathcoole area when a phone call came to a house in the estate. Tommy was told his sixty-six-year-old father, Jack, whom he described as a close friend as well as a parent, had been murdered. 'I went to pieces and someone gave me a brandy to steady my nerves. When we got to the Ormeau Road the place was still frantic and people were frightened that something else was going to happen. If I hadn't been working, I would probably have been in the bookies with my father. I've never been able to go back in there since.'

A sister of another victim was in tears as she walked away after the shooting on that nightmarish Wednesday afternoon. She told me her brother, Christy Doherty, fifty-two, had only been out of the house ten minutes 'because all he wanted was his bet'.

One man who was wounded in the bookies but who didn't want to be identified told me that the shooting seemed to go on for 'ages' even though he knew it was all over in seconds. He said, 'After one of the gunmen opened up with the rifle, the other one started shooting wounded people on the ground with the pistol. There was no escape. I don't mean it to sound derogatory but it was a bit like shooting fish in a bowl and it was only by the grace of God that just five people were killed by the gunmen, who didn't utter a word.'

Another man who went into the bookies after the shooting later told how he had to brush his teeth six times to get rid of the taste of cordite that had hung heavy in the air.

For Billy McManus it took a long time for reality to register. 'I went to the morgue to identify my daddy and that was horrendous. But I think I was in shock for days. What I do remember is getting myself organised for the funeral, sorting out a black tie and shoes. It was like a bad dream.'

Billy went to live in Canada a few months after the killings. He was to spend eight years there on and off. His Uncle Jim died several years after the massacre. Billy said the seven bullet wounds he sustained 'eventually caught up with him'.

Billy had initially kept news of his father's death from his uncle, who had been standing with Willie in the bookies when the gunmen burst in. But it was the doctors who made the decision. They told Billy that Jim, who was in intensive care, wasn't strong enough to hear about Willie's passing. Jim never spoke about his ordeal before his death.

Only five people who were in the bookies are still alive today.

Billy McManus eventually returned home from Canada for good. 'Being away helped me,' he said. 'I've dealt with my demons, though Sean Graham's will never leave me. It's part of my life.'

Billy's and other Ormeau families have been campaigning for truth and justice over the murders which the UFF said were in revenge for the IRA killings in January 1992 of eight Protestant workmen at Teebane crossroads in County Tyrone, who were on their way home from a security forces' building contract.

The Ormeau families are convinced there was collusion between the RUC Special Branch and the UFF in the bookies massacre. They also said that a UDR patrol had just left after spending hours in the area.

'It's rotten,' said Billy.

The day the UVF told me, 'We bombed Dublin and Monaghan'

Ivan Little

On the afternoon of 15 July 1993 my UVF contact got in touch. Sometimes he would ring me and read out UVF statements. If I wasn't in the UTV newsroom he would preface them with pre-agreed codewords – usually the names of footballers – so that staff could check with me that the claims were authentic. Sometimes he would ask for face-to-face meetings, which invariably took place in the same quiet back street off the Shankill Road.

Usually I knew what would be on the agenda but on that afternoon I had no idea what was coming as I drove up the road.

I soon found out.

The contact got into my car and proceeded to calmly tell me that the UVF was behind the deadliest day of killings in the bloody history of the Troubles. The loyalist dispensed with the usual small talk and got straight down to business with a statement admitting that the UVF were responsible for the Dublin and Monaghan bombings, a statement that came nearly twenty years after the horrifying events.

Thirty-three people, including a pregnant woman, were killed and over three hundred injured in a blitz of barbarity on the Irish capital and on the border town of Monaghan on 17 May 1974 but even though few doubted the UVF were to blame, the terror group never claimed responsibility.

But what made them finally own up to the bombings in 1993 was a Yorkshire TV/Channel 4 documentary a week earlier that disclosed the names of some of the UVF men it alleged carried out the attacks. They were particularly stung by the fact that the programme also outlined details of the assistance given to the killers by the security forces including, it claimed, SAS soldier Robert Nairac, who was working undercover in South Armagh where he was later murdered by the IRA.

The thrust of the statement my contact read to me was to say that the Dublin and Monaghan bombing operation from its 'conception to its successful conclusion' was planned and carried out by UVF volunteers 'aided by no outside bodies'.

The statement went on: 'In contrast to the scenario painted by the programme, it would have been unnecessary and indeed undesirable to compromise our volunteers' anonimity [sic] by using clandestine security force personnel, British or otherwise, to achieve [an] objective well within our capabilities.'

On and on it went, with the UVF saying the southern bombs were similar if not identical to the devices they were using in Northern Ireland. They called the programme makers Walter Mittys and finished off by saying, 'To suggest that the UVF were not, or are not, capable of operating in the manner outlined in the programme is tempting fate to a dangerous degree.'

I broadcast the statement on the *UTV Live* programme at 6 p.m. that night and the phones started to ring with calls from journalists all over Ireland.

As I normally did, I passed the statement to the Press Association journalist Deric Henderson to circulate it to the news agency's media outlets.

But the UVF denial about collusion convinced no one. Observers said the operation was too well organised to have been the work of the UVF alone. In the past their bombs had often exploded prematurely or hadn't exploded at all. The Dublin and Monaghan bombs were in a different league.

Several years later I travelled south for the launch of a campaign – Justice for the Forgotten – by relatives of the victims of the three bombings in Dublin and the fourth in Monaghan for a public inquiry.

The news conference was held in a hotel near Leinster House, the seat of the Irish parliament. The emotion was palpable just as it had been at the launch events of other victims' groups – unionist and nationalist – in the North who wanted justice for their loved ones. It was impossible not to sympathise with the victims' families as the names of their nearest and dearest were listed. And it was also difficult not to feel that the chances of the Dublin and Monaghan families of ever getting justice were slim.

My UVF contact and many of the bombing suspects are long since dead, taking the secrets of the Dublin and Monaghan slaughter to the grave with them.

In 2011 I was in Dublin as Sinn Féin's Gerry Adams took part in a service on the thirty-seventh anniversary of the Dublin bombings beside a memorial to the victims in Talbot Street.

Another visitor to Dublin that day made history. The timing of the Queen's trip was questioned by the Justice for the Forgotten group, who didn't actually criticise the monarch's trip but called it an 'extraordinary coincidence'. Gerry Adams said he hoped the visit could, in a roundabout way, bring closure to the families.

He backed calls from the relatives for Taoiseach Enda Kenny to pressurise the British to open up intelligence files and unlock the secrets of the massacres.

The families are still waiting.

An Irish reporter in the English pack

Sean O'Neill

The Fleet Street press pack in action is a thing to behold.

A group of voracious journalists descends on a town stricken by some awful tragedy – an act of terrorism or a horrific child murder for example – and strips the place clean of information.

It is a ruthless news-gathering machine in which reporters simultaneously collaborate with and compete against each other while keeping the emotional toll of the subject at bay with the darkest humour and copious amounts of alcohol.

Locals, initially excited to be at the centre of a major event, quickly become tired of the questions, cameras and intrusion. Resentment simmers and sometimes boils over into confrontation. Then the story gets replaced at the top of the agenda with the next big headline and the news caravan moves on.

I have lost count of the number of 'pack jobs' I have been on, but some last long in the memory – the extraordinary unfolding of the investigation into the murders of Jessica Chapman and Holly Wells in Soham in the summer of 2002, and the serial killing of five women in Ipswich at the end of 2006.

And then there was that terrifying week in Northern Ireland at the end of October 1993 when twenty-four lives were lost in terrorist attacks bookended by the IRA bomb at Frizzell's fish shop on the Shankill Road and the UDA massacre at the Rising Sun bar in Greysteel.

I was a young reporter at the time, working for the *Daily Telegraph* and based in London. I was routinely sent to Belfast then for lengthy periods or at times of crisis.

It is not the chain of events I want to write about, however, but the mechanics and struggles of reporting them as a Northern Irish journalist working for an English newspaper.

I grew up in Dungannon where my teachers included Father Denis Faul, who somehow managed to juggle his human rights campaigning and efforts to end the hunger strikes with unorthodox religious education classes. I went on to university in London but returned home to become a journalist with the *Tyrone Democrat*, covering council meetings, sport and the routine day-to-day of the Troubles in East Tyrone. The Loughgall ambush was my first taste of a major story.

I reached Fleet Street in 1992, excited and passionate about landing a job on a major newspaper.

In the autumn of 1993, however, it felt awkward and sometimes uncomfortable to be an Irish reporter in the English pack. It was not that my colleagues were hostile – rather that many of those parachuted in from London were naive, incurious and happily ill-informed about the conflict.

I remember the sideways glances as an English reporter bellowed out my very Catholic name amid a funeral crowd on the Shankill.

London news desks don't like complications – the story has to be black and white, good and evil. That week in the North had to conform to the formula. It had to be 'maniacal sectarian killers destroy nascent peace process'. To me, however, it felt like this terrifying killing spree might be the death throes of the violence rather than its resurgence.

I know I did some good, honest reporting that week. It was impossible not to be moved by the funerals of the Shankill dead or the bloody aftermath at Greysteel.

However, the one thing that I took most satisfaction from was a single paragraph in the front-page report on the funeral of the Shankill bomber Thomas Begley.

I filed my copy from the ground, describing how Gerry Adams and Martin McGuinness had carried the killer's tricolour-draped coffin, and it was duly sent by the news desk to the political editor for his input. He topped the story with the orthodox Westminster lines of ministerial outrage and Downing Street distaste at the sight of the Sinn Féin leaders shouldering that casket.

On the third leg of the story, however, my paragraph of context survived. It attempted to explain what I called Adams's 'dilemma over his peace plans'. And it added, 'Sinn Féin leaders traditionally attend IRA funerals and carry the coffins of the dead. If Mr Adams had not done so yesterday he could have risked a split in Republican ranks'.

Of course, there was lots of intelligent incisive commentary on the political situation that week, but there was also the usual formulaic approach, which roughly translated as both tribes are mad and hate each other.

Not long after this, one executive floated the idea of my becoming permanent Irish correspondent, doing lots of whimsy and paddywhackery from the South as well as the grim news from the North. My then news editor had a different view: 'Forget all that, we're only really interested in bullets and blood.'

That attitude still persists in London. You only have to listen to the former foreign secretary, Boris Johnson, a hack on the *Telegraph* at the same time as me, blithely comparing the Irish border with the boundary between Camden and Westminster to know how deep that ignorance and carelessness runs. As Brexit looms and the border question rears its head again, I fear for the peace.

Sean O'Neill is chief reporter with *The Times*. He previously worked at the *Daily Telegraph* and *Tyrone Democrat*.

John and Pat Hume attend the funeral of five of the victims of the Greysteel massacre.

Torment in a country graveyard
Miriam O'Callaghan

There have many dark days in the troubled history of Northern Ireland, but those seven days in October 1993 were the darkest.

It began with the IRA bombing of the fish shop, Frizzell's, on the Shankill Road – nine people lost their lives that day and the bomber also died. I remember going there for BBC *Newsnight* to cover what had happened, and finding it very difficult to deal with the horror unfolding before my eyes.

Then exactly seven days later, in the tit-for-tat horrific rhythm of retaliation that became all too familiar to the people of the North, on both sides, loyalist gunmen burst into the Rising Sun bar in Greysteel, a village just a few miles from Derry, and shot dead seven people. Another devastating atrocity. It felt like Northern Ireland was descending into hell.

At that time I was also working south of the border in Dublin for RTÉ as a studio current affairs presenter, and in the run-up to that deadly seven days, I often found myself interviewing the SDLP leader John Hume, in particular about his ongoing talks with Sinn Féin's Gerry Adams.

Hume came under huge pressure to stop talking to Adams – criticism came hard and fast at him, from all quarters. Everyone had an opinion, and it was mostly that he was doing the wrong thing, that it was a very dangerous initiative, and that he should stop. Journalists constantly questioned his motives, attacked what he called his strategy for peace, constantly questioned his moral compass. I was one of those journalists, shooting from the comfort of my TV studio chair, arrogantly questioning the keenly-thought-out peace strategy he had been working on for decades.

Everything came to a head for him in the harrowing and bleak surroundings of the Greysteel graveyard as some of the victims of the pub massacre were being buried. I have since discovered from both John and his wife, Pat, that this was his lowest moment. This was the moment he almost gave up. Pat herself has told me that after Greysteel, she actually asked John to give up his pursuit for peace, to stop talking to Adams, and to forget about his dream of a Northern Ireland free from violence.

It was just all too much. The constant criticism, the attacks on their home, the pressure on their family, and then the continuing horrific violence, and John being blamed by many for it all. That day the Humes stood side by side in the Greysteel graveyard, there to show their respects to the victims and their families.

I was in that Greysteel graveyard, reporting on the funerals. All funerals are sad, but there was something particularly devastating about that day – some of the mourners were actually wailing. I remember looking over to my right at one point and seeing John and Pat Hume, and then I noticed that John was weeping, really weeping. It had all got to him. I felt incredibly guilty at that moment, as I felt I – along with many others – had put him under huge pressure, with our endless criticism and questioning.

Standing there at that moment, in that graveyard, after the seven wretched days of loss and grief between 23 and 30 October, I realised that John Hume was right – the alternative to what he was hoping to achieve was more of the hell that the North had found itself in. More funerals, more broken hearts. After that day, John Hume was hospitalised for stress.

Hope springs eternal though, and sometimes in life, people and places have to hit rock bottom for things to change. John Hume bounced back, more determined than ever that peace was possible. Northern Ireland too moved back from the brink of the abyss. Six weeks after those dark days that culminated in Greysteel, the Downing Street Declaration was signed, paving the way for a new beginning.

Miriam O'Callaghan is a current affairs presenter with RTÉ's *Primetime* and *Sunday with Miriam* on RTÉ Radio 1. She previously worked on the BBC's *Newsnight* programme.

Ten funerals in one working week
John Irvine

A journalist for thirty-five years, work has reduced me to tears three times.

Most recently in 2014, on board an Iraqi army helicopter that had taken supplies to a persecuted minority people called Yazidis. They were stranded on the top of Mount Sinjar, surrounded by bloodthirsty Islamic State fighters who wanted to wipe them off the face of the earth. Just before taking off empty from the mountaintop, the helicopter pilot unexpectedly gestured to a group of Yazidis, who rushed on board.

Eventually, a chopper with capacity for fifteen lumbered into the air with nearly sixty people crammed in. This was a life-saving flight and my tears flowed because of the raw emotion of those saved, and because I had just witnessed an act of compassion by the pilot that stirred the soul.

In 2005 I was part of an ITN team that spent more than a week in the mountains of Kashmir following an earthquake. It was rough living for everyone, particularly for the locals, who, unlike us, did not have a ticket out of there. The damage was so extensive that no one wanted to sleep indoors. Firstly, a high proportion of buildings had been brought down. And secondly, people were too frightened to stay inside the buildings still standing in case aftershocks collapsed them as well.

Flat ground on which to pitch a tent was at a premium. Frequently we found ourselves being moved on by people with a greater need than us. So often we were upping sticks to look for new campsites.

After four days and nights we found ourselves trying to drive pegs into the broken asphalt of an old car park.

We were tired, cold, hungry and wet. Uneven tarmac is not great to sleep on, and all of a sudden, as I tried to get over, I burst into tears instead. I was just miserable and feeling dreadfully sorry for myself.

The first time work reduced me to tears was in the early '90s. It was about 6.30 p.m. on a Friday. A pub at the bottom of Donegall Pass was a place of decompression for many of us working in the busy newsroom at UTV's Havelock House. I walked in and ordered a bottle of beer. It arrived and was duly paid for. Then, unexpectedly and suddenly, I found myself blubbering. A dam had broken.

During that working week I had covered ten funerals. As I wept I realised all the raw emotion and grief laid bare at those final farewells had exacted a toll on me too. Death was our stock-in-trade in those days. All aspects of it, from the way it was inflicted to its consequences for the victims' families, their friends and work colleagues. And finally came the funerals. It made sense for the reporter who covered a fatal attack to see that story right through to the end.

Everyone involved in the news business in Northern Ireland hoped that compassionate coverage would help bring it all to an end. We wanted to believe that people watching, listening or reading would eventually be persuaded that the violence and suffering were indefensible and could not go on indefinitely. The running joke was that eventually we might report ourselves out of a job.

The reporting of funerals was an emotive and delicate task. It's not a television reporter's job to get upset. The job is to stir the emotions of the viewer. To that end funerals could be extremely powerful.

That week, I covered all ten funerals with the same cameraman and sound recordist. At one burial a mourner stopped our dark-coloured Volvo estate car and asked if we were the undertakers. Mistaken identity for sure, but only just, or so it felt.

Those funerals were of people who'd been in the wrong job, were of the wrong religion, or who'd been in the wrong place at the wrong time. They weren't the victims of a mass attack, or spectacular. History dutifully remembers Warrenpoint, Enniskillen, Omagh, Teebane, Greysteel and Loughinisland. The chronicle has tended to ignore the lone murder victim, the single lives cut short with dreadful regularity, night after night.

Who, apart from his or her family and friends, remembers the poor soul, who but for the grace of God or good fortune, could have been us? Killed at home, or on the way home.

The paramilitaries and the security forces may have been the adversaries, but the death toll was highest among the civilian population amidst which that low-intensity war was fought. More than 52 per cent of the people killed during the Troubles were civilians. Looking back it seems like a lifetime ago. In truth it's more than 3,600 lifetimes ago – the number of lives wiped out during that bloody time.

I wept that Friday evening because I was overflowing with the sadness I had witnessed at two funerals a day for five days.

Like all of us doing that job at that time I did my best to make each report telling and respectful. In each broadcast, every priest and minister officiating was given time to express their revulsion and the hope that it would never happen again.

My tears came as a complete surprise. An involuntary spasm of utter sadness. How I hoped the viewers felt it too.

Covering Nelson Mandela's passing a few years ago, I learned that those South Africans who entered this world after the end of apartheid are known as 'Born Frees'. Perhaps people in Northern Ireland born after the paramilitary ceasefires should be known as 'Trouble Frees'?

I worry they don't know how lucky they are.

John Irvine is senior international correspondent for ITN. He previously worked for UTV and the *Tyrone Constitution*.

'The safest place to be was on the pitch'
Gerry Moriarty

The most apposite quote about the November 1993 World Cup qualifier in Belfast between Northern Ireland and the Republic of Ireland was uttered by Portsmouth player Alan McLoughlin: 'The safest place to be was on the pitch,' he said.

That night I felt a cold dread as soon as I entered the sectarian cauldron of Windsor Park with the £10 ticket I bought from a tout for twenty quid. Armed RUC officers patrolling the ground and stands; a cacophonous noise blasting from the tiered seating, creating an atmosphere of genuine fear and loathing; Northern Ireland goalie Tommy Wright and manager Billy Bingham rousing the crowd to act as the wired-up twelfth man.

The scene was set eight months earlier in Lansdowne Road in Dublin where the Republic defeated Northern Ireland 3–0, the home crowd adding deep insult to injury with the taunt, 'There's only one team in Ireland.'

Bingham executed his mind-game revenge on the eve of the Belfast match by describing Irish players with English and Scottish accents – such as Andy Townsend, John Aldridge and Ray Houghton – as 'mercenaries', not good enough to make the England and Scotland teams. Before the end of the night Jack Charlton was apologising to the Northern Ireland manager for an 'up yours too, Billy' riposte in the verbal jousting.

That was football, gamesmanship, to be expected in a crunch encounter. But there was a far deeper and more sinister tension poisoning the night.

Just weeks earlier there had been more Troubles horror in Northern Ireland, the IRA Shankill bombing killing ten people including the bomber, Thomas Begley – retaliation coming just a week later with the Ulster Defence Association Halloween 'trick or treat' killing of eight people in Greysteel, County Derry.

Out on the pitch, black players such as Paul McGrath and Terry Phelan got the monkey-chant treatment; Alan Kernaghan who played for Northern Ireland as a schoolboy and finally opted for the Republic, was condemned as a 'Lundy'; and others, such as Roy Keane and Niall Quinn, were merely being described as 'Taigs', with lots of adjectival expletives added for oomph and emphasis.

It was an awful time and an awful night, so bad, in fact, that for security reasons the Republic team had to fly by Aer Lingus to Belfast rather than drive the hundred miles up from Dublin. The UDA 'trick or treat' refrain was shouted out by some of the crowd. There is no way to gild it, that's how twisted it was.

But forgive my warped soul – as a journalist I found the occasion exhilarating and exciting, if also bloody terrifying.

This wasn't the first international I'd attended when the Troubles had intruded. Seventeen years earlier, in 1976, I travelled as a twenty-year-old from Galway to Dublin, caught a train to Dún Laoghaire, and then the overnight ferry to Holyhead in Wales, where I was questioned by the anti-terrorism police.

They looked at me suspiciously, searched my bag and flung some questions at me, trying to figure out if I posed a threat to the realm.

What was my name?

Where was I from?

Where was I going?

'I'm heading to Wembley to see the Republic of Ireland beat England,' I told them.

They convulsed in laughter, one of the cops actually holding his sides. 'Republic of Ireland beat England,' they spluttered. 'Oh my, oh my, that is the best ever.'

I held my tongue. They sent me about my lawful business, sure that while I was not a terrorist I was delusional.

It ended up, as some of the London papers reported – I still have the cuttings – England 1, Éire 1. England scored first through Manchester United's Stuart Pearson, his clubmate Gerry Daly equalising with a penalty. The astonished British sports journos acknowledged England were lucky to manage a draw. But it wasn't at all surprising to me considering some of the Irish line-up: David O'Leary, Johnny Giles, Liam Brady, Gerry Daly, Steve Heighway.

So, I had skin in the Windsor Park game. Primarily what I was interested in was the football rather than the tribal clash, not that you could escape the rage and hate. A defeat would put the Republic out of the World Cup and I desperately wanted them to qualify. But I had to be wise. I had to apply what John le Carré calls fieldcraft. I didn't want my neighbours in and around seat twenty-two of block Q of the lower deck of the north stand to sense my anxiety or hear my flat Offaly tones.

Some Republic supporters – and several hundred did turn up incognito – adopted English, American and what they thought passed for Northern accents to disguise themselves. I just tried to keep my mouth shut.

147

When Northern Ireland's Jimmy Quinn cracked a beautiful volley past Packie Bonner I decided that if the stadium was erupting I better erupt with it, rising from my seat with the electrified crowd, an expression of pseudo-celebration like a rictus on my face. That's hard to do, but I did it.

It looked like the Republic were doomed. Try smiling through that. Then five minutes later, in the seventy-first minute, wonderfully, gloriously, Alan McLoughlin chested down a poor Northern Ireland clearance and fired it to the corner of the net. I shot from my seat in exultation, starting to punch my arm in the air in delight and relief, adrenalin pulsing through me all the stronger because of the fervour I was unnaturally restraining.

But even in that rapid movement my survival instinct kicked in, causing me to stall in the mid-vertical. My diplomatic skills and cover were blown to pieces. In this S-shaped, almost crouching, position I was neither up nor down. Taking a cautious look to my right and left I saw those beside me eyeing me with disdain and disgust.

What to do? I never managed the full vertical. Slowly I sat down, perhaps emitting a whimper or two as I descended. My response and my exposed true allegiance spurred the northern supporters around me even more loudly and vehemently to exhort Northern Ireland to stick it into the Fenians. But otherwise I was treated as someone with a contagious antisocial disease and I was glad of that reprieve.

Back then I could never have imagined that twenty-three years later in a peaceful Northern Ireland I would be following and writing about the northern Green And White Army of supporters at the Euros in France in 2016, or attending family-friendly games in Windsor Park and wishing the best for Northern Ireland, notwithstanding that my primary loyalty always would be to the Republic.

It's a funny old beautiful game. Virtually everyone understands that football is one of the few areas where men feel free to liberate their emotions publicly. Your team scores a goal, you jump from your seat, whoop and holler, and maybe, in the moment, embrace the unknown spectator sitting beside you. But such normal camaraderie was impossible at Windsor Park.

Jack Charlton described the night pithily: 'It was unhealthy, it was nasty.' But, still, thanks to Spain defeating Denmark in Seville that same night the draw was enough to get the Republic though to the World Cup in the US.

I left the ground an emotional mess, inwardly elated but sensible enough to curb that feeling of sporting ecstasy, my true feelings suppressed until I got to surer ground. Approaching the Lisburn Road the first person I met who I knew meant me no harm was the *Guardian*'s Belfast correspondent, Owen Bowcott, a good colleague but with a typical English reserve.

I suspect he is still trying to make sense of the huge bear hug of finally-ventilated joy and relief that I smothered him in that bitter night in November 1993.

Gerry Moriarty is northern editor of the *Irish Times*.

The Chinook air tragedy
David Walmsley

Looking back, 1994 was as big a year as any for the Troubles. I had the privilege of being the subeditor for the *Belfast Telegraph* on 31 August that year. My duties included writing the front page headline before transmission to the press room. On that momentous day the headline was written for me by Ed Curran, the editor. I typed in the two most important words of the era: IT'S OVER. The IRA had announced a cessation and the loyalists followed suit.

Peace had all seemed so uncertain. Too much bloodshed in late 1993 and the early parts of 1994 overwhelmed the hope and growing political signs of a breakthrough.

I reported from the scene of many atrocities. More than I care to remember but I remember them all. What happened on 2 June 1994, however, was of a scale beyond my experience.

An RAF Chinook helicopter – carrying 25 passengers and 4 crew from RAF Aldergrove to Inverness, Scotland – crashed. All on board died at the scene, on the Mull of Kintyre. It was at the time the RAF's worst accident. The 25 passengers – 10 RUC Special Branch, 9 soldiers, 4 MI5 spies, a member of GCHQ and a Northern Ireland Office civil servant who briefed successive secretaries of state on the everyday chaos – all died. It was as big a story as Northern Ireland has created.

As the helicopter flew low over the north Atlantic it was spotted flying at a reasonable speed by a sailor. The top of the Beinn na Lice headland on the Mull of Kintyre lay ahead, patchy with fog but from the sea the land was clearly visible. Minutes later the Chinook slammed at high speed into the hillside. There were no eyewitnesses, no final radio call, no radar trace, no survivors. The aircraft had hit the first piece of land. Why?

I was the most junior reporter at the *Belfast Telegraph* back then but news editor Murray Morse sent me and my colleague Darwin Templeton to the scene.

It was the perfect resting place for conspiracies. Access to the crash site, near to the lighthouse on Beinn na Lice, was only possible by a single track road the authorities had closed. The weather was foul, the authorities at Westminster and Stormont and police HQ were truly stunned and coming to terms with the loss. US Navy Seals stationed at nearby RAF Machrihanish helped Strathclyde police with the recovery of the bodies and sensitive documents. What had happened in this desolate, lonely, unforgiving terrain?

Some things are beyond journalism. We had to let the air accident investigators do their work. I admitted defeat pretty early on in my quest to assess the loss. Even today, all these years later, nobody has been willing to explain what the twenty-four men and one woman actually did. There have been some accounts about individuals. Susan Phoenix wrote a book about her husband Ian's work in Special Branch. Covering the Loughgall inquest as a reporter I heard that another passenger, Maurice Neilly, had been involved in that police and army operation that killed the east Tyrone IRA unit. Some of the soldiers belonged to the frontline undercover 14th Intelligence Company.

But as the months passed, the thing that kept me curious was the story of the four men flying the helicopter. Who were these three Englishmen and one Scot and what happened? A year after the crash the government announced they had the cause.

Gross negligence by the two pilots. The two navigators in the back were absolved. It was a clean line supposed to end the coverage and I was the one who broke the story after obtaining a copy of the confidential crash report. Overexcitedly, I wrote that such was the outrageous behaviour of the Special Forces-trained pilots that even in death their actions could not be excused. Then David McKittrick, the veteran reporter, called me to say I had missed a contradiction in the report, which he had also got a copy of.

The report had actually concluded neither pilot should be blamed but upon review two senior officers said the burden of rank forced them to make a tougher decision. The pilots were to blame and had they survived would have faced manslaughter charges. I became focused on trying to understand why the Board of Inquiry was overruled.

I have always been blessed to have worked with strong journalists. The standard-bearers for our industry are always reporters who are fair and brave. The news editors are the guardians of that pact. Belfast punches above its weight on both scores. Among the lessons drilled into me as a young reporter was that if you break a story you stay on it come what may. As the *Belfast Telegraph*'s most junior employee I took that instruction very seriously. Little did I know my question of why the board was overruled would take me on a story lasting seventeen years.

For the first fifteen months after the crash the pilots' families did not speak. Finally, by chance, I was lazily reading the letters' page of *The Times* and I noticed a modest few paragraphs from a reader saying he could not understand the decision to blame the pilots.

I tracked the writer down and he vaulted me into journalistic hyperdrive by providing the home phone number for John Cook, the father of the co-pilot Flight Lieutenant Rick Cook. John was a retired Concorde pilot for British Airways and understood aviation. He told me that conclusions of pilot error were traditional conclusions when another explanation was absent. But he couldn't accept his boy was grossly negligent, not without the evidence. I learned a lot from that first call. Later I met Flight Lieutenant Jon Tapper's father, Mike. It was at the Paisley courthouse outside Glasgow where a fatal accident inquiry into the crash was held, lasting four weeks. Mike had been a defence analyst and knew the machinations of the Ministry of Defence well. It was dawning on me that if there was one silver lining from the tragedy it was that the pilots would have a chance, posthumously through their fathers, to have a right of reply.

I did a documentary for Channel 4's *Cutting Edge* on the crash. I wrote countless articles and, when the newsroom budgets weren't available for the story, I spent my own money in my own time turning over rocks, such was my desire to understand what happened that June evening. The sources I relied on risked their livelihoods to give me information and such is the sensitivity I still cannot reveal their identities. Some really would surprise you. Their motivation was singular – to show the cause of the crash was far from clear. My gut was attracted to the greyness and the ambiguity. Little involving Northern Ireland's violence is clean so it followed that the truth wouldn't be simple. Officialdom's whitewash created a deep allergic reaction within me.

It never crossed my mind that the finding of gross negligence would ultimately be upheld but I could not predict when it would evaporate. I shed many tears on the frustration of this story and the wider curse of the Troubles. Chinook changed me. It made me a better journalist and a stronger man. In my heart my motivation was consistent. All I could do, even years after leaving the UK, was to be loyal to the story.

I provided the reader with as much evidence as I could. At one point, now living in Canada, I called Sir Patrick Mayhew who had been the Northern Ireland secretary of state on the night of the crash. I will never forget his silence as I laid out the technical problems with the aircraft. He had never been told. John Major and Malcolm Rifkind both conceded they had been party to an injustice when in government and they too fought for the finding to be overturned. Even with the former prime minister and defence secretary involved, it still took years to budge the permanent, largely anonymous, extremely powerful government of Whitehall.

Principled men (all the politicians were men) in opposition abandoned common sense and adopted the same script of intransigence once they were in office. From Conservative to Labour and back again – it didn't matter. There were exceptions – James Arbuthnot, Crispin Blunt and Robert Key for the Conservatives, Martin O'Neill for Labour and Menzies Campbell for the Lib Dems seized the fight and worked across party lines. It was Establishment v. Establishment and it led to unnecessarily dizzying complexity. But as with so much of Northern Ireland, it was clear the answer lay in SW1, London.

When the end did come, it was by way of a formal apology to the families from the House of Commons dispatch box. The MoD conceded finally they had been wrong to blame the pilots. Honour restored. It came too late for too many. John Cook and Flight Lieutenant Tapper's mother, Hazel, had both died in the intervening years.

As I reflect back on 1994, a couple of things come to mind. The bravery of whistle-blowers, the difficult nature of fighting against a government apparatus that can make *Yes Minister* seem naive and, at its core, the fundamental confirmation that journalism matters.

Among the scores of discoveries unearthed by journalism was the fact the Chinook fleet had been grounded the day before the accident, that flight lieutenants Tapper and Cook appealed to their superiors to not fly the doomed machine, that the RAF'S own test pilots had refused to fly it, that the engine control system was subject to litigation because it wasn't fit for its intended purpose, and I suppose most damningly, that even Boeing who made the Chinook wasn't supportive of the government conclusions.

At the end of the day, the two reviewing officers had overruled the innocence finding with no evidence whatsoever.

An historic footnote to the remarkable campaign came with the appointment of Andy Pulford as chief of air staff for the RAF, the first helicopter pilot to reach the highest level of the air force. Andy had presided over the Board of Inquiry that had originally cleared the pilots. Once in high office he knew the burden of rank didn't allow him to overrule accident inquiries. Indeed, as a result of the injustice of Chinook, blame is no longer apportioned. Prevention and not finger pointing is the focus.

My mind is never far from the family members of the pilots. I came to care deeply about them and the unforgivable injustice meted out posthumously to their loved ones. The children of the pilots are adults now.

Like so many during the Troubles they lost their fathers at far too young an age. All their dads were doing was their best. It is recognised that at that time, the four-man crew was among the finest ever assembled. The SAS had created a brand new role devised specifically to recruit Rick Cook full time outside the RAF stream. He was due to take the posting in the September. As his commanding officer wrote after his death: 'Rick was not someone to go down lightly.'

The cause of the accident, like so much that happened during the dirty war, remains unknown.

David Walmsley is the editor-in-chief of the *Globe and Mail* newspaper in Toronto. He worked for the *Belfast Telegraph*, *Daily Mail* and *Daily Telegraph* before leaving for Canada in 1998.

David Trimble – the unlikely peacemaker
Ken Reid

It was the first time I'd ever met John Major and the first time I'd ever heard anyone ever predict that David Trimble might be a potential peacemaker on behalf of the unionist community.

It was October 1994 and I was in Bournemouth for a Tory party conference the day after loyalist paramilitaries had announced their ceasefire in Belfast, two months after a similar move by the IRA. Of course Bournemouth is probably one of the last places on the planet that you'd ever associate with a peace breakthrough. But as it turned out, what I heard in the popular seaside resort on England's south coast that evening portended an unlikely game-changer in the notorious stalemate of Northern Irish politics.

The Tories were buoyant that year, still riding on the crest of a wave from their unexpected election victory in 1992, and I was at their conference working for UTV, having just returned north of the border from the *Cork Examiner* newspaper. Another first in Bournemouth had been a chance encounter with David Trimble, and over coffee I invited him to an ITN party the next night. His image at the time was that of an uncompromising hard man whose views were firmly entrenched in far-right unionism.

But Prime Minister John Major made a beeline for him at the reception. Trimble introduced me to Major but was then called away, leaving me with the Tory leader, who surprised me with what he said next. 'I think David is going to have a considerable say in the future of your country, Ken.'

What stunned me about his remark was that no one back home had Trimble marked down as a future leader of the Ulster Unionist Party. But Major's prophecy clearly showed that the British government had identified Trimble as a leader-in-waiting. Suddenly things were adding up. A short time earlier in Dublin the Irish premier, Albert Reynolds, had confided to me that the fledgling peace process was doomed to fail without unionism on board and that Jim Molyneaux, the UUP leader of that era, was 'impossible to deal with'.

The sense was that something had to change. But still no one saw Trimble as the man to do it. In 1995 he wasn't given a hope of becoming the leader that would succeed the departing Molyneaux. The smart money was on Ken Maginnis or John Taylor being elected by the party's council. And few people will ever forget the shock as the name of David Trimble was read out from the stage of the historic Ulster Hall, sending a shudder through nationalism, which saw him as the least pragmatic of the leadership candidates.

Trimble did indeed play the part of the hard unionist for some time but when he went into the negotiations it became clear to me he was for real and knew that there had to be a deal.

However the chemistry between him and Gerry Adams and Martin McGuinness didn't add up. But the bottom line for Trimble was that, without compromising his unionist principles, he knew that Northern Ireland could not go on the way it was. Peace to him was the most important thing, coupled with his desire to keep Northern Ireland in the United Kingdom.

People talk about the transformation of Paisley and McGuinness but I think Trimble's journey was just as remarkable. And significantly, where he led in the realms of compromise, others followed.

His relationship with the SDLP's Seamus Mallon was always difficult, indeed it was embarrassing at times. I got on well with Trimble but he wasn't easy. He never made small talk. But he did occasionally talk to me about his love for the music of Van Morrison and Elvis Presley. I was one of only three journalists he spoke to, to any great extent. The others were Victor Gordon of the *Portadown Times* and Frank Millar of the *Irish Times*. I don't think he really liked journalists and he was always more comfortable at Westminster than in Northern Ireland.

One of his greatest weaknesses was that he didn't realise when his time was up. When he lost his seat in 2005 he telephoned me and said, 'I just didn't see it coming.' But overall I think history will be kind to David Trimble.

And I can reveal a little secret about what he tended to do during breaks from negotiations at Stormont. People would see him going off to a quiet corner to open up his computer. And there was all sorts of speculation about who or what he was consulting. He was playing patience.

Ken Reid is the political editor at UTV. He previously worked for the *News Letter*, *Sunday News* and *Cork Examiner*.

Clinton's men tried to arrest me under the Christmas lights

Eamonn Holmes

The American secret-service men took me down in the blink of an eye. They'd spotted me running away from President Bill Clinton and his wife, Hillary, who'd come to Belfast to support Northern Ireland's fledgling peace process.

What the US security guys who tackled me NFL-style outside the City Hall in November 1995 didn't know was that I'd just introduced the Clintons to upwards of one hundred thousand people who were there to see the couple switch on Belfast's Christmas tree lights, and to hear them talk peace.

I'd felt deeply honoured to be asked to welcome the Clintons but my bosses at GMTV in England wanted me back at work the next morning. And that's why I was sprinting towards the rear exit of the City Hall to jump into a car bound for the airport and the last flight to London. The Americans had other ideas. Until a senior local police officer recognised me and told them, 'It's okay, we know him.'

Good news, I thought. But no. The secret service thought the policeman was in fact saying that I was a known terrorist. Thankfully the officer put them right and I was allowed to go on my way and to reflect on what was history in the making. It was the first time in Northern Ireland that we'd dared to believe the Troubles might be over.

Usually people who gathered outside the City Hall in large numbers were there to protest. But that night was different. It was all about rejoicing and about happiness, and there was a palpable feeling of relief.

Sadly the next time Bill Clinton was in Northern Ireland was after the Omagh bombing in which twenty-nine people and unborn twins were killed shortly after the signing of the Good Friday Agreement in 1998.

I was in Belfast when the bomb went off and I was watching the latest football scores come in on a beautifully sunny Saturday afternoon. I knew GMTV would want me to be in Omagh that night. And so it proved.

The first thing I remember in the town was the smell of smoke and the noise of glass under my feet amid the quietness and sadness, the like of which I'd only felt in one other place before – Dunblane, Scotland, with the shooting of sixteen schoolchildren and a teacher in 1996.

With Omagh, as I prepared to broadcast to a national audience, I thought back to when I was a teenager and I wanted to become a journalist to explain what was going on in Northern Ireland.

That's precisely what I was being given a chance to do in Omagh. But you know what? Northern Ireland is very hard to explain, even to those of us who understand it. I can't ever say that Northern Ireland was just another story to me. It's always been more than that. Northern Ireland is me and it's everybody that I know, and therefore any reporting or any commentating I do is done from that perspective.

I'd grown up with the Troubles in Belfast and when I started presenting the teatime news bulletin for UTV I got to report on them. I quickly realised, however, that I was happier in the studio than on the road. The funeral of IRA man Charles English in Derry in 1985 confirmed my feeling that I didn't want to be a riots reporter.

Tensions were high even before the funeral because of speculation that Martin Galvin, the leader of NORAID who raised funds in America for the IRA, was going to turn up in defiance of an exclusion order that banned him from entering Northern Ireland. As my camera crew set off on foot they told me to follow them in the car with all the spare videotapes and so on, but I'd never driven an automatic before. This meant that when it came to changing gear, I put my foot firmly down on what I thought was the clutch, only to discover it was the brake! So instead of accelerating, the big Ford Granada came to a screeching standstill. Not surprisingly, soldiers stopped the car and pulled me out, forcing me to the ground, putting rifles to my head and demanding to know who I was. After a lot of expletives they eventually let me go – but just at that moment Galvin appeared and shots were fired over English's coffin, which was the cue for the police and the army to move in.

Within minutes a full-scale riot was erupting and I was in the middle of it, thinking UTV were not paying me enough for this. Bizarrely a kid suddenly appeared from a house and, recognising me from the TV, offered to let me out the back door, but said it would cost me a tenner. I only had a twenty-pound note on me but it was the best twenty quid I ever spent, escaping from the bricks and the batons.

Back in the studio, which I was determined to make my working base, things weren't always easy as I conducted live interviews with all the incredibly prominent people of the day. I was only in my early twenties and, looking back, I shouldn't have been doing that. It was a tremendous responsibility.

Some of the political figures were very, very charming. Others were very, very frightening. I defy anyone to say that Ian Paisley in his prime was not scary. And, believe me, when you are sitting down at twenty-two or twenty-three, starting out in your career, with a man as seasoned as he was, with a voice like his and an astute political brain like his, it was a terrifying situation.

It was all a baptism of fire for someone like me but that's what I was paid to do. I wasn't being paid for when it went right; I was paid for when it went wrong. As for adrenalin, I don't think those first few years at Ulster Television have ever been topped in my working career.

Eamonn Holmes began his career with UTV before moving to England, where he has worked on entertainment and news programmes for the BBC, Sky and ITV.

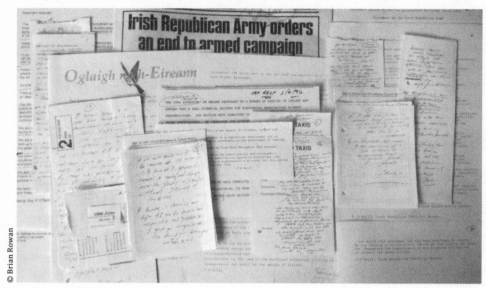

Take a note – a record of some of Rowan's contact with P O'Neills over the years.

The five 'P O'Neills' who briefed me about the IRA
Brian Rowan

I spent twenty-plus years of my working life meeting them at all hours and in all sorts of places. Meeting them and noting statements and briefings on whatever scraps of paper I had with me on those many occasions – often hurried notes scribbled on to taxi receipts, into my cheque book, on to the corners of newspaper pages and, a couple of times, on to a church bulletin. There were other occasions when a typed statement would be passed to me in an envelope. I would remove the statement and give the envelope back – this to ensure no trace of fingerprints. These were not ordinary or routine reporting times, nor was there much notice given before those many meetings with 'P O'Neill' – the *nom de guerre*, or assumed name, of the authorised spokesman for the IRA leadership and organisation. In a period spanning the mid to late 1980s to February 2010, I met with five P O'Neills; and, through those statements and briefings, you can track the journey from conflict to what we now call peace; follow the words from bombs and bullets into the stories of ceasefires, arms decommissioning, and the search for the remains of the Disappeared who were executed and secretly buried – some of them still not found. Then, there are the stories of political agreements and disagreements and, eventually, the formal ending of the IRA campaign. The name P O'Neill – sometimes with a dot after the P, other times not – appears on major IRA statements. A name that will be forever attached to our war and peace.

How secret was it all?

Those many meetings were certainly intended to be as discreet as possible; organised to be kept under the radar and away from the listening and watching apparatus of the Special Branch and Security Service MI5. Did it always work that way? The answer is no.

Remember back to 1996. The collapse of the IRA ceasefire in the screaming headlines of the Docklands bomb in London; the dead of that night and that explosion added to the body count of a decades-long conflict. The peace and dreams of the 1994 ceasefire had been shattered. I am told that on that February day in 1996, the P O'Neill of that period had travelled to Dublin after an IRA meeting that had stretched into the early hours; the purpose of his business in the Irish capital was to deliver a last-minute message through a contact to Taoiseach John Bruton that the ceasefire – declared in August 1994 – was over.

Months later, in June 1996, as the British and Irish governments attempted to construct another talks process, some in politics believed another IRA ceasefire was possible. On two occasions in the early days of that month, I met with P O'Neill. Twice he told me that the prospects of any new cessation were remote in the extreme. In this same period, I bumped into RUC deputy chief constable Ronnie Flanagan. Flanagan used an initial during our brief conversation, letting me know he knew the identity of the man who had briefed me. This is an example of the mind games that are played. I did not respond, but later learned that there had been an eavesdropping intercept of a conversation involving the P O'Neill of that time and Gerry Adams. There are very few secrets in war and, always, the possibility of being heard.

The new talks began on 10 June and, five days later, a blizzard of glass and rubble swept through part of Manchester; a bomb that was the IRA's way of underscoring the words it had spoken in those two P O'Neill briefings of 3 and 5 June. Two hundred people were injured. There would be no new ceasefire until July the following year and, by late 1997, there would also be a new P O'Neill – the third I was to meet.

My first meeting with Peter (not his real name) was on Sunday 9 November 1997; a briefing after an IRA convention that had been intended by some as a coup, an attempt to dislodge the Adams/McGuinness leadership and to bin their peace strategy. The plan failed but, in the fallout, we were to witness the emergence of a new dissident republican threat – this the beginning of events that would lead to the Omagh bomb of August 1998, that dark Saturday after the hope of the political agreement of Good Friday that year.

In November 1997, I noted my meeting with Peter on four bank lodgement slips and two cheques. The information confirmed that a convention had happened. Such meetings are rare and, in the decision-making processes of the IRA, there is no higher authority than a General Army Convention. I was told that 'the vast majority of those present endorsed the strategy and the Army Council position on the cessation [of July 1997]'. Adams and McGuinness had survived.

It was the P O'Neills who followed Peter – Conor and Tomas (again not their real names) – who would deliver the numerous briefings and statements, detailing firstly arms inspections, and then the beginning and ending of a four-year process of putting arms beyond use.

Have all guns been decommissioned? The answer is no – not by republicans or by loyalists, and nor has the security and intelligence apparatus of the conflict period been completely dismantled. There is no such thing as a perfect peace.

The IRA statement on Thursday 28 July 2005, formally ordering an end to the armed campaign, was given to me in an envelope by Tomas. A DVD was also enclosed, showing the statement being read by one of the IRA's former longest-serving prisoners, Séanna Walsh, whom I later asked to sign it. The statement has a green heading, Óglaigh na hÉireann, and, on the copy given to me, you now see a running blue from that green lettering; smudge marks caused by rain dropping on to the paper as I broadcast live into the BBC's coverage that lunchtime from a street off the Falls Road. So as there is no confusion, Séanna Walsh was not P O'Neill.

I also asked Gerry Adams to sign the relevant page in that week's edition of the republican newspaper *An Phoblacht* – because this was such an important moment in our history. All IRA units had been ordered to dump arms and the statement set out the path to the most significant acts of decommissioning that, weeks later, would be witnessed by Father Alec Reid and former Methodist president, Harold Good. These orders and acts of July and September 2005 represent a significant contribution to our unfinished and imperfect peace. Yes, there are blemishes, but we are in a better place.

The P O'Neills have now melted into the background, their work in that role now finished. There are, of course, untold stories – how the IRA initiated a sequence of events that produced the proof of their secret contacts with the British government that ended in such acrimony and argument in late 1993 being perhaps the most fascinating. The proof came in the form of a document – an aide-memoire or speaking note – that a British official mistakenly left with the late Brendan Duddy, a Derry businessman who was the critical link between government officials and the republican leadership. From there it came into the possession of the IRA. Eventually the document would end up with DUP MP William McCrea who shared it with journalist Eamonn Mallie. Neither McCrea nor the others used in that chain of events knew this situation was being manipulated by the IRA. Republicans wanted the story out to challenge the contradictions in the British government position of no place for Sinn Féin in peace talks unless there was a credible end to IRA violence.

Yet behind that public position, that same government – albeit at arm's length – was in secret contact with the IRA. In the method chosen to get the story out, republicans were covering their tracks and shielding the real source of the leak. The full details, only confirmed to me in 2017 and 2018, are for another page and another time.

Brian Rowan is a freelance writer and broadcaster. He was previously security correspondent for BBC Northern Ireland.

Orange Order parade, Drumcree, July 1997.

How Drumcree changed my home town
David Armstrong

The grainy old newspaper photograph shows Orange lodges parading through the once-busy Castle Street in Portadown.

The lodges were on their way back to Carleton Street Orange Hall after their annual parade to Drumcree Parish Church. The photograph was taken about lunchtime and there isn't a spectator in sight. The parade had been taking place since 1807 so it wasn't going to be front-page news. The townspeople had all gone home after the Sunday morning services in their respective churches.

It was the early 1960s and Portadown, celebrating its successes in the province's Best Kept Town Awards, was still priding itself as the 'Hub of the North'. It was just a few years before I started editing the *Portadown Times* and they were exciting times in the town. The Craigavon New Town Plan had just been launched. New houses were springing up and the town was seeing the last of what former *Times* editor and BBC reporter David Capper once headlined 'the little hells of Portadown': the slum houses bordering the centre of the town that are now the site of a major shopping centre.

Many of the families from those houses were moving into modern new homes being built on the site of the world-famous McGredy roses on the Garvaghy Road – the road that leads to Drumcree Parish Church and the road that was to have a major influence on my forty years editing the *Portadown Times*.

It was the road the Portadown Orange District paraded along on their way home from the Drumcree church and, because of the movement of population and growing political unrest, it turned into one of the most publicised roads in the world. Reporters from all over the globe flocked to Portadown to cover the ongoing impasse over the disputed Garvaghy Road parade.

Journalists from Australia, Canada, South Africa, Denmark, Austria, France, everywhere, arrived at the *Times* office on a daily basis, initially to find out where Drumcree was, and then to try and gain some understanding of what the dispute was all about.

Editing a newspaper is never easy but it was particularly difficult in Portadown as all the staff were from the town, all well known and all vulnerable to the daily pressures of dealing with a dispute that often threatened to boil over and throw Northern Ireland into the worst violence it had ever seen. And this was on top of reporting more than two hundred murders in an area that became notorious as the Murder Triangle.

The *Times* was the only one of the twenty-three papers in the Morton Group to write opinion articles and I suppose we were making a rod for our own backs with these editorials. But we had the full backing of our owner, Jim Morton, who was years ahead of his time in producing newspapers, and not a week passed without the *Times* commenting on the Drumcree issue, preaching moderation all the time and encouraging both sides to engage in talks to resolve the issue. We didn't always win, of course, but our stand on the issue was widely respected, and the circulation of the paper rose in both sides of the community, which said something of our impartiality.

I was fortunate to have a reporting staff that knew the town inside out, a courageous and immensely able staff that stood by me on all occasions and, as a team, tried to play some part in preventing situations going from bad to worse. We never sought kudos but it was encouraging when our efforts were recognised and, on my retirement ten years ago, one clergyman, Canon Tom McGonigle, remarked: 'Enjoy your retirement, David. You and your team kept the lid on this place.'

The staff should be mentioned at this stage – deputy editor Victor Gordon, senior reporters Brian Courtney, a young Ivan Little, Niall Crozier, Mairead Holland, Gail Bell and photographer Tony Hendron. All gifted staff who could have held down a job on any paper.

Our editorials weren't always respected on both sides and there were frequent threats against the staff. On one occasion on my way home from reporting on a football match at Shamrock Park I was told there was a bullet waiting for me. Later I was told it was a case of 'mistaken identity' – how many people lost their lives for that reason. Other staff members were threatened with violence.

I remember one day in particular. The Orange parade down Garvaghy Road had been banned but when the decision was reversed hundreds of the Garvaghy Road residents and their supporters turned out to protest. The road was lined with police and army Land Rovers and there were hundreds of security force personnel on duty. I thought I could gauge the situation if the army allowed me to walk down the road between the Land Rovers, which they did, having warned me that I did so at my own risk.

Bottles and bricks cascaded over the Land Rovers and I was forced to make a hasty retreat. I have never seen such venom, such vitriol. I knew many of the protestors – many I didn't know as there were outside influences on both sides. But I grew up with some of the local protestors. I played football with many of them. I didn't want to see this. This wasn't the Portadown I knew. And this isn't a criticism of the protestors. Nor is it a reflection on the Orange Order. Both sides had sincerely held beliefs.

The town's name was being blackened because of a disputed parade. But behind the stark headlines, behind the politics, I know that an immense amount of good, positive, community work goes on and this we tried to reflect in our columns.

Portadown has had its fair share of trouble – the murders, the bombings, and Drumcree. They all changed the dynamics of editing a local paper. And they were all a far cry from my early days in the papers when one of the yearly assignments was to cover the local agriculture show, sitting in the changing rooms at Shamrock Park with a typewriter and carbon paper writing about 'best apple tart in show', 'best cow in show', 'best knitted garment', 'best young calf'…

Drumcree – and the Troubles – changed all of that.

David Armstrong was editor of the *Portadown Times* for more than forty years. He previously worked for the *Belfast Telegraph*.

A birthday present for Billy Wright
Noreen Erskine

The funerals of victims of the Troubles were always uncomfortable to cover. Like many of my colleagues, I dreaded intruding on bereaved families at such times of intense distress and grief.

The funeral of Michael McGoldrick was especially poignant. A thirty-one-year-old Catholic, he was shot by a loyalist paramilitary group in July 1996 as tension rose between nationalists and loyalists during a five-day stand-off over an Orange Order parade at Drumcree outside Portadown.

Two days before his murder, he had graduated as a mature student from Queen's University in Belfast with a degree in English and politics. His lecturers described him as 'dedicated' and 'an ideal mature student'. At his funeral Mass, his seven-year-old daughter, Emma, carried his degree scroll to the altar.

During the years of conflict journalists seeking interviews with a victim's family after a shooting or bombing normally held back from making an approach at the funerals. Unusually, Michael McGoldrick's family indicated that his father, also called Michael, wanted to speak out after the funeral at St Peter's Church in Lurgan, County Armagh.

Standing in St Colman's Cemetery near Michael's grave, a group of journalists, including me, listened to his father's anguished appeals to both communities to halt the violence and bloodshed. His pain was stark, his words were clear.

'As I bury my son, both of you bury your pride. I don't want any mother or father going through what my wife and I have went through today. I've watched my daughter-in-law, I've watched my grandchild go through hell. Don't do it. Please stop this. Bury your pride with my boy. To those who've done this, I and my family forgive you.'

Born in Glasgow to Northern Irish parents, Michael (junior) moved from Scotland to Lurgan with his wife, Sadie, also from Northern Ireland, two years after the birth of their daughter. Sadie was pregnant with their second child when he was killed.

Michael had been working part-time as a taxi driver to fund his university studies. A pub quiz enthusiast, he had told a fellow taxi driver that if his application for a temporary teaching post was successful, he would stop driving taxis. Before clocking off that Sunday night, he collected two passengers from outside a cinema complex in a loyalist area. Colleagues at the taxi firm's depot in Lurgan raised the alarm when he didn't check in again. Early next morning a passer-by found his body slumped over the wheel of his car near the village of Aghagallon, about three miles from Lurgan. He had been shot at least twice in the head.

Lost Lives, the epic reference book chronicling the stories of those who died in the Troubles, relates how his parents, Michael and Bridie, first heard about their son's death as they watched television while on holiday at their caravan at Warrenpoint, County Down. His father later said, 'It was our only son, our only child. We were so shocked that we just started screaming and shouting. I ran out of the caravan. I remember going down on my knees and hitting the ground with my fists.'

In an interview in 2002, Michael McGoldrick (senior) spoke again about his son's murder. 'I was a Christian before, but not a fully-fledged one. After Michael's death, I had a conversion. Before they put the lid on my son's coffin, I put my two hands on top of his and said, "Goodbye, I'll see you in heaven."

'From that moment my whole life changed. I realised then how much evil there was in Northern Ireland. I wanted to turn my life into something good, something positive.'

Michael McGoldrick died four years later after becoming ill while delivering supplies to Moldova for the Christian charity that he helped found. He was sixty-four.

Security forces cited in *Lost Lives* said his son Michael was killed by renegade Ulster Volunteer Force members who later formed the breakaway Loyalist Volunteer Force headed by Billy Wright. Senior security personnel said they believed that Wright, who was later shot dead inside the Maze prison by a prisoner from the republican paramilitary group the Irish National Liberation Army, had been involved in planning Michael's death.

In 2003, Clifford McKeown, forty-four, from Craigavon, was jailed for twenty-four years for Michael's murder. During the trial, Belfast Crown Court heard that the killing was 'a birthday present' for Wright.

Passing sentence, the judge said Michael's murder was a 'chilling execution', which was arranged to 'secure a random death based on religious persuasion'. Michael, he said, had become a victim 'simply by the chance of his taxi firm's rota'.

I never met Michael, but I felt a thread of connection to him. Michael was an only child. So am I. He wanted to become a teacher. I am a teacher's daughter. It is only a tenuous connection, but perhaps explains why he lingers in my mind.

Noreen Erskine has worked for BBC Northern Ireland, and the *Daily Mail* and *Belfast Telegraph*.

George Mitchell – the man who lit up the peace process
Trevor Birney

The annual convention of the National Association of the Advancement of Colored People isn't an event where you'd expect Northern Ireland to be on the agenda. But there, in the blistering sun in July 1996, President Bill Clinton was willing to not only discuss the state of the health of the peace process, but to get into the detail of the worrying situation developing at an Orange Order parade in Drumcree outside Portadown.

Twice in his speech in Charlotte, North Carolina, he referred to Northern Ireland.

He asked, 'What is leading to all this terrorism around the world? What does it have in common, when the Hutus and the Tutsis just slaughter each other in Rwanda or Burundi? What does that have to do with people rioting in Northern Ireland?'

Outside, as he left, I took the opportunity to raise Northern Ireland with him. Was he hopeful of a new IRA ceasefire? Was he concerned about the stand-off at Drumcree that had paralysed Northern Ireland for several days?

He replied, 'I'm talking to all the leaders and I hope that a peaceful solution will be found at Drumcree. We're working to restore the IRA ceasefire. The peace process is very important, we're going to keep at it.'

Looking back, there was no small element of professional pride that I'd managed to get a response from Clinton, and that was probably a lot do with my own journalistic journey.

I'd only become a reporter due to the faith shown in me by the *Impartial Reporter* newspaper and its editor, Denzil McDaniel. Under his guidance I'd covered many terrorist attacks along Fermanagh's border.

Now, not only was I in America at the invitation of the US State Department but I was also getting answers from the leader of the free world as Northern Ireland was entering an exciting era of change, one where everything and anything was possible.

That encounter in Charlotte led me to take a deep interest in America's involvement and, in particular, Clinton's role in the developing peace process. I was lucky enough to come to know many US officials who came to Belfast, and some of those who worked in the White House. They included people, like Nancy Soderberg at the National Security Council, who were willing to take phone calls. It was incredible access, and she still retains a deep interest in our affairs.

The high point of that period and that feeling of hope was the visit to Belfast by Bill and Hillary Clinton in November 1995. Even the most cynical of journalists and politicians could not fail to be impressed with the level of planning by the White House. Not a single political box was left unticked in a masterful display of diplomacy.

Their final engagement, the lighting of the Christmas tree at Belfast City Hall, remains the only moment peace was truly celebrated on Northern Ireland's streets. Thousands turned out to see the president flick the switch. Carried live on television at home and abroad, it felt as if the world was joining in, cheering us on as we tried to leave behind our dark past. It was a euphoric moment.

The US diplomats who came into Belfast in the mid-'90s became friends to not only senior civil servants and politicians but to community leaders, and even journalists. They offered a vital external perspective on the issues that consumed the peace process, often acting as guides, offering reassurance and encouragement. I felt they were glad to be here.

The diplomatic master of them all was Senator George Mitchell, a man of the highest moral integrity who, with his soft, authoritative tone, never ceased to challenge us to do more and be better. History will record him as being the best friend the peace process and Northern Ireland ever had. He'd agreed to become Clinton's economic envoy. Later he drafted the Mitchell principles on non-violence and then led the negotiations that ended with the signing of the 1998 Good Friday Agreement.

Twenty years later, in April 2018, he returned to Belfast for the twentieth anniversary of the deal. Now in his mid-eighties, he reflected on his personal relationship with Northern Ireland. A hushed audience heard him tell how his father was born into an Irish family but knew nothing of his roots. Mitchell helped to bring political stability to Northern Ireland but in doing so, he had reclaimed his father's heritage. He retains an ability to connect and communicate with Northern Ireland that has come from a deep understanding of its people.

I've been fortunate to hear him speak many times, on both sides of the Atlantic, telling how he came to know the people from the North whatever their religion, political persuasion or paramilitary association.

His contribution helped transform lives and he made friends far beyond politics. While many others involved in the peace process moved on with their lives, George Mitchell was a constant, ready to lend a hand or to provide a word of encouragement in tough times.

His experience in Northern Ireland impacted on him deeply. He named his daughter Claire after a young woman, Claire Gallagher, who was blinded in the Omagh bombing.

Having been tipped to take a seat on the US Supreme Court, he instead came to Belfast and never judged anyone. He has come to embody the peace process and, in particular, the American contribution that has been so vital in Northern Ireland's search for a lasting peace.

Trevor Birney is a documentary producer. He previously worked at UTV, Downtown Radio and the *Impartial Reporter*.

We were uniquely privileged to do this work
Susan McKay

My daughters were small during the Drumcree summers of the 1990s. Sometimes they'd cling to my legs at the front door as I went out to work. I'd prise their little hands off, tell them I'd be back soon, kiss them goodbye. I'd feel torn.

Part of me wanted to stay at home, snuggle up on the sofa and read them a story. But the journalist part of me needed to tell other stories, Portadown stories. I would drive off, feeling guilty, reminding myself to bring them back cherry scones and tray bakes from the home bakeries of County Armagh.

I would never tell them about my work, the notebooks in my bag packed with a scrawled record of hatred and grief, but one day I heard one of them solemnly telling a visitor to our house that 'the orange men don't like my mummy'. She said it like she understood the men to be the colour orange.

It was true that the Orangemen did not like me, because I wrote about sectarian murders carried out by men and women motivated by the hatred unleashed by their Order's protests of those years, in favour of dominance and against the peace process.

The protests were ostensibly about the right to march through nationalist areas despite opposition from residents. All roads in Northern Ireland were the Queen's highway, according to the Order. One day at the church at Drumcree a leading figure asked his little grandson to sing me a song.

'I'm bringing him up to the gun,' he told me. 'Sing the girl a song, son. Sing her "The Billy Boys".'

The child stood to attention. Then he sang, 'We are, we are, we are the Billy Boys ...' When he sang the line, 'We're up to our necks in Fenian blood,' his grandfather grinned, patted him on the head, and punched the air.

You walk to the front door of the home of someone who has just been murdered and you have to steady your heart. This is one of the most daunting things a reporter has to do. You are crossing a line, a stranger from the ordinary world, asking for a glimpse into lives that have just been plunged into overwhelming pain.

You know it is a lot to ask. You know that whoever comes to the door would have every right to tell you to go to hell. I did it many times, too many times. I looked around me at the beautiful Mourne Mountains soaring over Annsborough village, braced myself, and knocked. Justin and Philomena Morgan invited me in to their house as if I was a friend. Their beloved child, sixteen-year-old James, had been brutally murdered. He'd gone out, a carefree teenager on a summer day, never to return.

He had been abducted, beaten with a hammer, set on fire, and his body had been dumped into a pit used to dump the carcasses of dead farm animals. An Orangeman from the nearby town of Newcastle had walked into a police station the next day and confessed.

By 1997, the peace process was well advanced. The Rev. Ian Paisley's DUP denounced it as a sell-out to republicanism. In mid Ulster, the party's Rev. Willie McCrea warned that nationalists would 'reap a bitter harvest' after he lost his seat at Westminster to former IRA man Martin McGuinness. (Paisley would echo his words at Drumcree in 1998, warning nationalists that there would be 'a price to be paid' for their defiance.) But the Morgans had taken their family to County Kerry for their holidays with the light-hearted feeling that the Troubles were all but over.

James had a ball, Philomena told me, running around, going to discos, meeting up with girls, swimming in the Atlantic. She was glad he had that time. They showed me his photo, a smiling, mischievous, dark-haired boy, long limbs stretched out in the sun, his life in front of him.

Then Justin said something devastating. 'I only hope the first hammer blow killed him,' he said. I will never forget the look on his face as he spoke.

They sent me to meet his friend Nathan, who talked while he cried and laughed at the same time about how James had brought him back a bottle of aftershave from Kerry: 'Well, half a bottle actually.' Nathan told me that he and James used to do daft things like trying to overturn resting cows in the fields. They'd lie on their backs on the slopes of the mountain behind us, looking at the stars, talking. After James's murder, Nathan and his brother had named a constellation after him.

I would go home to my daughters and hug them tightly and cry, as if I was returning from some far country after a long, long time. I think as Troubles journalists we were uniquely privileged to do this work. It was an extraordinary honour to be able to write about James, to be trusted by his family to capture something of the beloved boy they'd lost.

But I also believe it left us with a residue of sadness that is never entirely dispelled.

The Orangeman, who had been out of his brains on drink, drugs and sectarian hatred, was not expelled from the Order. After he was convicted, he resigned from it. (He was released from prison after eighteen months under the terms of the Good Friday Agreement.) The more powerful man, who was with him when they picked James up, was never charged. He has been linked to other murders and attacks, but appears to enjoy some sort of immunity.

I rarely pass through Annsborough but when I do I call in to see Justin and Philomena. Sometimes it has been to ask their reaction to some political development, sometimes just to say hello.

For a moment on the doorstep I fleetingly glimpse that old, raw agony. I am afraid that seeing me must pitch the Morgans back to the time I first came. But they always greet me warmly and ask about my girls. Once, talking to me about how they had managed to survive James' murder, Philomena said that the priest, Father Brian D'Arcy, had given them a lot of support.

'One of the things he said to us was "if you get a good day, take it",' she said.

And, as time went on, there were good days. On the mantelpiece, the photograph of James is beginning to look old-fashioned, surrounded now by pictures of little boys and girls who are his nephews and nieces, laughing, playing, the lovely children of a new generation in the family. 'They like looking at his picture,' Philomena told me. 'We say that's your Uncle James and we tell them what he was like.'

Susan McKay is an award-winning freelance journalist and author from Derry. She is a former Northern Ireland editor of the *Sunday Tribune*, and currently writes for the *Guardian/Observer*, *London Review of Books*, *New York Times* and *Irish Times*.

David Trimble and Seamus Mallon with Tommy Canavan (Bernie Canavan's brother) in Poyntzpass, March 1998.

An epitaph of sorts
John Mullin

It is one of those villages in Northern Ireland, unnoticed before and unremarkable since, that, through the horrors of the times, and the luck of some macabre draw, is linked forever to tragedy. Think Greysteel; think Loughinsland; think Poyntzpass.

Two died when the gunmen burst into Bernie Canavan's Railway Bar in the County Armagh village of Poyntzpass twelve miles away from the renegade Loyalist Volunteer Force's stronghold in Portadown.

By the warped standards of the Troubles, that would have barely flickered on the Richter scale of terrorism, except the time – March 1998 – and the circumstances meant otherwise.

Eight died at Greysteel in County Londonderry in a hail of bullets in the so-called trick-or-treat massacre of Halloween 1993. Six more perished in Hugh O'Toole's pub in Loughinisland, County Down – cut down as they celebrated Ireland's victory over the hosts Italy at the World Cup in June 1994.

Both were tough stories to cover, when, just before the dawning fingers of light, the darkness was inky black. Before the IRA and loyalist ceasefires later in 1994 finally brought some release, the place was gripped by the particularly malevolent death throes of madness.

Four years later, the old certainties were ebbing and peace was taking a stuttering hold. It lost its grip from time to time, and as the remarkable political talks continued – haltingly – through the winter of 1997–98, there were still shameful sectarian murders. They were sporadic now, sinister reminders of those waiting in the shadows ready to resume their part centre stage if the other actors fluffed their lines.

When the call came about the shooting at a pub in Poyntzpass, the instinctive question was 'where?' And it was a challenging drive in the dark, pre-satnav. It was the usual gruesome, frenzied journey: sad, scared, excited, and most journalists working in Northern Ireland had felt this way scores of times.

Filing copy had changed, even then. I didn't have to concentrate through the drunken aggression of a fellow Glaswegian smashing up the phone box as I'd had to once when I was filing from outside a theatre elsewhere after I had watched an amateur thespian succumb on stage to a heart attack. Nor did I have to secure access to a friendly resident's phone, as when a child had gone missing in the west of England ten years earlier, sparking a massive police operation. We had mobile phones by Poyntzpass, but you still had to file off the top of your head to make the next edition.

Aside from a successful door-knock – and in Northern Ireland, the success rate on those was gratifyingly high – there was no greater adrenalin shot as a reporter than filing good, tight running copy. Within maybe fifteen minutes of parking up by the Railway Bar, interviewing all in sight, loitering ready for reporters' interrogation, my front page story had been phoned over, without so much as a jot of it noted down, aside from quotes recorded in shorthand.

It told how best pals Philip Allen, thirty-four, and Damien Trainor, twenty-five, had been enjoying a drink – orange juice for them both – when the LVF gunmen entered, shouted, 'Lie down, you fucking bastards,' and opened fire. They got off twelve rounds, injuring two others.

The human factor? Philip had just told Damien he was getting married later that year, and had asked him to be his best man. The rub? Philip was a Protestant, and Damien a Catholic.

At this time, in this place, that represented a strange sort of serendipity: a terrible vicissitude, of course, for the men who died and the families left behind. But it was the greatest of all galvanising forces for the fraught political negotiations, stymied through the winter and liable to be blown out of the water at any time.

You could see it the next day in the village when David Trimble, the Ulster Unionist leader, and Seamus Mallon, the deputy leader of the SDLP, came to pay their respects to the bereaved. While Mallon always came across well, Trimble was an odd cove. He was awkward, and not just because he found himself in an incredibly difficult position as the leader of unionism when it was torn down the middle as to its approach to Sinn Féin.

But here were Trimble and Mallon – and no one could remember political leaders across the divide speaking together in quite the same way – answering as one, saying all the right things, with a mutual respect and a new-found purpose.

I remember being struck for the first time that day that the political process not only could not fail, but would not fail.

Amazing, it was only five weeks later that the Good Friday Agreement was sealed. Trimble was to be first minister, and Mallon his deputy. There would, of course, be terrible times ahead, at Omagh especially, and, twenty years on, the challenges are there, still.

But it truly felt that day, in a hitherto unremarkable village of four hundred souls, that something fundamental had shifted. It was a fulcrum, a point of no return, when politicians proved their mettle.

Of scant consolation to those grieving folk they left behind, but it is an epitaph of sorts. We remember you, Philip Allen and Damien Trainor. Rest in peace.

John Mullin was Ireland correspondent of the *Guardian* and is a former editor of the *Independent on Sunday*. He is deputy head of sport at the *Daily Telegraph*.

Good Friday – a day and night like no other
Sister Martina Purdy

I thought the rain would never end. It was relentless that day, like the Troubles, always there, oppressive and depressing, something to be endured while life, with all its bitter-sweetness, carried on. For hours water just fell, thousands of tears, I thought, for thousands of victims; rain, as one songwriter put it, like a bad memory, a tragedy, a new emotion.

The ground was soaked, and the green grass around Castle Buildings, an ugly brown building where the politicians were working behind a wire fence, had been tramped into mud. I was corralled in a little media village of Portakabins out front, along with journalists from home and around the world, watching, waiting, wondering: would there be a deal?

The answer it seemed was blowing in the wind.

Midnight, Thursday 9 April 1998, was the deadline for agreement, set by the American talks chairman Senator George Mitchell, the smiling, steely diplomat from Maine.

But like so many deadlines, it had slipped, the drama of a deal delayed until dawn, Good Friday.

What a dawn it was, one of the most vivid days of my life – after a very long night.

The negotiations had been a see-saw: unionists down and nationalists up, and vice versa. In the midnight hour, Sinn Féin's chief negotiator Martin McGuinness was furious. He wasn't the only one.

The DUP's Ian Paisley – with whom McGuinness would eventually share power – had come in the night, with supporters, to protest. We could hear police dogs howling and angry voices rising on the other side of the estate. It was eerie. Soon the DUP pack had bolted through the gate. They held an impromptu press conference, which was effectively hijacked by jeering loyalists who were involved in the talks process. Paisley bellowed, 'Sell-out,' but the loyalists were no longer listening.

'Dinosaur,' they shouted. 'Go home!'

This public showdown was one of the signs that a deal was indeed tantalisingly close.

Who could sleep that night?

Inside, the two prime ministers, Tony Blair and Bertie Ahern – a dynamic duo who had arrived by helicopter to rescue the talks from collapse – were pressing for a compromise, amid whispers that 'progress' was being made and claims paramilitary prisoners might be released in a year or two. Key figures from the IRA and loyalist paramilitaries were now inside Castle Buildings.

I remember being so tired I literally slid down the wall of the Portakabin. Every so often, we would go out for air or hear of some move: Sinn Féin's Gerry Adams and Martin McGuinness were chatting and circling the fenced car park beside us. What could it mean? Then the SDLP leader John Hume was taking a walk, mouth saying nothing, demeanour saying deal.

Information was harder to come by then. We had the prime minister's official spokesman, among others. But Twitter and Facebook had yet to be thought up. The internet – like the mobile phone – was in its infancy.

Talks had begun, at a snail's pace, two years earlier, with the DUP in and Sinn Féin out. Midway, the DUP was out and Sinn Féin was in. At times, standing outside Castle Buildings, it was mind-numbingly tedious. The *Irish News* correspondent Billy Graham once parodied Yeats' famous poem on Irish history, declaring, 'A terrible boredom is born.'

In the end, it was anything but boring.

What I remember most is the humanity: Bertie Ahern coming to help from his mother's funeral, Tony Blair's patience, the SDLP's Seamus Mallon choking back tears, David Trimble's sheer guts, George Mitchell's satisfied smile, Monica McWilliams' unshakeable faith, David Ervine's exuberance, and the little brothers, Alex, four, and Patrick Huston, two, who came with balloons marked 'Peace, please.'

What was remarkable too was the Christian symbolism of Easter.

As the sun rose that Good Friday, the mood was changing. Some emerged with some cautious news. When Sinn Féin's Mitchel McLaughlin came to the big Portakabin with a statement saying earlier problems had been resolved, it became clear the party – linked to the IRA – was on board for an agreement, though details were still being worked out.

There were frantic calls to news desks, amid loud tapping on laptops about a breakthrough, with details still being worked out. As a journalist I needed to stay detached but as a citizen – who dreaded waking up to hear about another shooting or bombing – I had a lump in my throat. I had hope.

There was to be a final all-party session around noon, but beyond Castle Buildings, there was mixed reaction to the news.

Members of the Orange Order turned up amid rumours the unionists had gotten cold feet. I recalled what one Irish official had said a few days earlier:

181

negotiating with unionists was like nailing jellyfish.

Instead of a lunchtime closing session in front of the camera, the press pack lined up for a picture with the Secretary of State Mo Mowlam.

An air of gloom was about the place as we waited, and waited. We found out later that the US President Bill Clinton was working the phones from Washington.

My colleague Barry White, an affable pessimist, confirmed his reputation as the guy who turned the light out at the end of the tunnel. He had covered the ill-fated Sunningdale Agreement in 1974. 'Even then I knew it was too good to be true,' he said mournfully.

I was feeling the same.

By mid-afternoon, I was starving and had ordered a pizza. As I waited at the security gate an RUC woman turned to her colleague. 'Isn't that strange?' she said. 'Look at that cross – it's Good Friday and it's nearly three o'clock.' I thought rather unkindly that she needed a day off more than I did. But, sure enough, two streaks of cloud had formed a very large white cross over Castle Buildings.

I was too tired and irritated to get a cameraman. I've always regretted missing that shot.

The Ulster Unionist leader's nerves were finally settled with a comfort letter from the prime minister, agreeing that decommissioning should happen straight away. However, MP Jeffrey Donaldson, Trimble's colleague and negotiator, walked out.

Trimble's final press conference was bizarre. Amid a hailstorm, he waved his finger, demanding to know from Gerry Adams whether 'the IRA's dirty little squalid terrorist war' was over. The tone was far from peaceful – he was no St Francis – but I admired his risk-taking.

I showed Blair's letter to a Sinn Féin negotiator – who read it and pushed it back at me dismissively. Decommissioning would become one of the biggest stumbling blocks.

The cameras for now were focused on all the politicians around the table, with Senator Mitchell, for a closing session, ready to go forward with the document now dubbed the Good Friday Agreement.

Years later, I interviewed the boy with the balloon. Alex Huston was now a politics student. What about the Agreement then? 'The worst deal we could really get,' he said. 'But it was better than the alternative.'

I think politicians did the best they could in the circumstances. The Agreement offered hope, and a way to work things out without violence. Little did I realise the Omagh bomb, the worst atrocity of the Troubles, was already being planned. We didn't quite have peace yet but we had a roadmap.

Peace, I would learn later, is a person. Peace is Christ.

I know this too: I will never have another Good Friday quite like it.

Martina Purdy was political correspondent for BBC Northern Ireland. After twenty years in journalism she joined the Congregation of Adoration Réparatrice in Belfast and is now Sister Martina of the Blessed Sacrament.

Omagh remembered
Jane Loughrey

'You can get bitter or you can get better' were the words spoken to Claire Gallagher by her mum, Marie, as Claire learned that she would spend the rest of her life in complete darkness.

The fifteen-year-old's optic nerve had been severed by a piece of metal – just the size of a matchbox – from the Real IRA car bomb that exploded in the centre of Omagh at 3.10 p.m. on Saturday 15 August 1998 ... with devastating consequences.

I was the duty reporter in UTV on what began as a very ordinary day. Even the weather was fairly unremarkable, cloudy and dry as I remember it, but as I arrived back in the newsroom from an Ancient Order of Hibernians march in Kilkeel, the duty news editor Barbara Graham told me a bomb had exploded in Omagh. UTV was about to broadcast an appeal for off-duty doctors and nurses to head to the Tyrone County Hospital in the town and for blood donors.

In the days before social media, news took time to come through. 'There may be as many as eight or ten dead' someone whispered as I headed to Omagh feeling sick inside about what lay ahead.

Memories of standing on the Shankill Road in 1993, watching people frantically digging in the rubble, searching for the dead and injured after a no-warning IRA bomb exploded in Frizzell's fish shop came back to me. Nothing, I thought to myself, could be worse than that. But over an hour later, as I stood behind the police tape in the centre of Omagh, the horror of what had happened in this bustling market town, crammed with Saturday shoppers, emerged.

What struck me first was the smell of burning that hung in the air and the deafening silence, broken only by the wailing of alarms. Shops, cafes and bars had been blown apart like they were made of matchsticks. A thick, white dust covered the walking wounded, police, fire service and rescue workers. Their faces all bore expressions of exhaustion, shock and pain.

My colleague Niall Donnelly, who had rushed to the scene to help, stood with me, both of us aghast at what was unfolding before our eyes. We knew then that people were dead and dying in the ruins.

I left him there and made my way to the hospital. Roads were closed and it was impossible to get a phone signal. Chaos, confusion and fear stalked the streets.

Nothing could have prepared me for the sounds, smells and scenes in the Tyrone County Hospital, where staff were struggling to cope with the vast number of casualties. Doctors and nurses fought valiantly to save lives and treat the wounded. Staff, splattered with blood from the dead and dying, stopped only to gasp for breath. Every ward, corridor and waiting room was filled with the sound of cries of agony and the smell of burning. It was as I stood there with other journalists that we heard for the first time that Spanish children staying in Buncrana had been caught up in the blast and might be among the dead

With an incorrect warning given by the Real IRA, hundreds of people had unwittingly fled from the courthouse down to where the car, loaded with its deadly cargo, had been parked. When the five-hundred-pound bomb exploded, men, women and children were killed and maimed.

I felt useless standing in the hospital as I watched anxious families gather, sobbing and desperate, to find out if their loved ones were there. Some even thought we might know, but we shook our heads. I felt even more useless.

Some of those families, their faces etched with fear and pain, were redirected to the leisure centre, which in just a few short hours had been transformed into a makeshift information hub.

In the midst of the madness my phone rang. My newsroom had been trying to get through to me to tell me I had to do a live broadcast for a UTV special in a matter of minutes. Night was beginning to fall. I ran to the Dunnes Stores car park where our satellite dish had been set up. Out of breath, I began to talk to our presenter Mike Nesbitt about the horror that was unfolding in this town. I tried to explain as best I could what I had heard and seen that day. As I began to talk about the children who had almost certainly been killed in this atrocity I found it increasingly difficult to speak.

The following day, assisted by the *Ulster Herald*'s John McCusker, I arrived outside the door of Michael Gallagher. We had heard his son Aiden was missing. Opening the door Michael said his twenty-one-year-old son was no longer missing. He had found the body of his beloved Aiden in the morgue three hours earlier.

Weeping, he invited me in. Sitting on the sofa beside his daughter, Michael recorded his first interview during which he paid many poignant tributes to his amazing son Aiden who had only gone into Omagh to buy a new pair of jeans ... never to return.

This was the first of many families I would interview in the coming days. Raw with grief, they were driven, I think, by a desire to let the world know –

a world hungry for news about this massacre – about their loved ones who had been so cruelly taken from them.

Perched on the edge of a bed, in a house crammed with mourners, I spoke to Stanley McCombe who had lost his wife, Ann, in the atrocity. In a voice strangled with emotion he asked how, after twenty-five years together, was he going to be able to go on without her.

Bill Harper, the principal of Omagh High School, wept as he heaped praise on pupils Samantha McFarland, Lorraine Wilson and Alan Radford. Close friends, Samantha and Lorraine had been working together in the Oxfam shop in the centre of the town when the bomb went off. Alan had been shopping with his mum who would, in the following days, invite me into her home as she waked her child. It was a tragic scene repeated throughout this town that had been plunged into unimaginable raw grief.

Over two hundred people were injured. Some left without limbs, some disfigured. Claire Gallagher, who was robbed of her sight, explained to me how music was helping her to heal.

In the dark days and months after the explosion, the decision the fifteen-year-old took to get better rather than bitter led her to play the piano for President Clinton and pop stars, graduate from Queen's University, get married and become a mother. Like all the survivors of this atrocity her courage is beyond belief.

I first met Donna-Marie Keyes as she was preparing to be discharged from the Royal Victoria Hospital in Belfast. With 65 per cent of her face and body covered in third degree burns, few thought she would survive. Donna-Marie had been shopping for shoes for her flower girl, Breda Devine, when the bomb exploded. Little Breda was one of the youngest victims of the atrocity. She was twenty-one months old. Twenty-nine people were murdered that day in August. Nine were children. Unborn twins too were denied their right to draw their first breath.

The following week the sound of sobbing filled the air as Omagh began to bury its dead. Roads and streets were thronged with mourners following coffins. The tiny white coffins didn't require pall-bearers. Broken parents or close relatives shouldered that unbearable task alone. For me and my colleagues – Niall, Mark McFadden and Jeanie Johnston – finding words to adequately report on each one of those very personal final farewells was incredibly difficult.

Father Kevin Mullan and the Rev. Ian Mairs, the Presbyterian minister, attended many of the funerals together. They were greeted with applause. Little glimmers of hope in the bleakest of weeks.

In her first media interview, just before she left hospital, Donna-Marie courageously told me she was determined to defy the bombers, and her wedding, which was meant to take place a week after the explosion, went ahead the following March.

As her wedding day dawned I found myself drying dishes in her home, as my cameraman Donovan Ross washed them. Laughter replaced tears that day as Donna-Marie and Garry McGillion exchanged their vows in the Sacred Heart Church. The people of this shattered town spontaneously applauded outside. This wedding was a symbol of hope. Out of the darkness a light that would not be dimmed was shining.

In the wake of the Good Friday Agreement that April, the summer of 1998 had begun with such hope. Peace appeared possible. It ended in horror.

But from the midst of the carnage and despair in that Tyrone town emerged stories of remarkable courage, determination and defiance. I feel privileged to have been trusted enough to tell many of them.

History records the Omagh bomb as the single biggest atrocity of the Troubles. I record it as the day a town's heart was torn asunder – a town that has gradually been pieced back together by an incredibly brave community that refused to be either broken or divided.

Jane Loughrey is a correspondent at UTV.

And then there was Omagh

John Coghlan

When I was a young photographer at the beginning of the Troubles I had a naive belief in the goodness of man, and I believed that by showing people the horror and cruelty of war I might play some small part in bringing about peace. I was sadly mistaken. As a result, for over thirty years, my TV footage of bombs, bullets, fires and funerals was the staple diet for an ever-more-wearying public; a public that became increasingly immune to the sights and sounds of communal violence.

Sadly, having filmed over three thousand killings, bombings and funerals in Northern Ireland it's almost impossible to differentiate one incident from another. Was the Shankill bombing worse than Bloody Sunday? Was the Loughinisland massacre worse than the Whitecross massacre? Were the tortured, bloated bodies of so-called IRA informers lying on a remote border road more gruesome than the tortured victims of the Shankill Butchers? I honestly can't remember. Maybe it's a mechanism the mind has developed to protect itself from the horror of it all.

Each atrocity brought ritualistic condemnation from politicians, sometimes sincere. However, very often the condemnation was qualified with words of seeming justification, along the lines of: 'If they hadn't started it ...'

There's a hidden linguistic code in Northern Ireland, almost genetically understood by the members of the two communities, which belies and negates rational language. Whenever politicians ritualistically condemn an atrocity then feel the need to qualify their condemnation with the words 'but I understand why they do it', then I believe that they are effectively saying, 'I support what you are doing' – and I believe that this is what the terrorists hear and are meant to hear.

Bizarrely what do come to mind are random thoughts. An unguarded Gerry Adams in despair at John Major's announcement in January 1996 that the IRA would have to fully disarm before Sinn Féin would be allowed to take part in peace talks. In a bleak Sinn Féin office in Twinbrook, Adams lamented, 'The Brits and unionists are erecting one obstacle after another to frustrate every attempt at peace and deliberately threatening the ceasefire. I can't deliver on disarmament.' Or the UVF's Gusty Spence singing peace songs with a cross-community group of school children in the grounds of Stormont Castle

Buildings on the day of the signing of the Good Friday Agreement.

However the event that is indelibly printed in my memory, and which had the biggest effect on my career, happened at 3.10 p.m. on Saturday 15 August 1998, when the Real IRA detonated a bomb that devastated the centre of Omagh, County Tyrone. Twenty-nine people were killed in the atrocity: Protestants, Catholics, teenagers and children, Spanish tourists, a pregnant woman – ordinary people going about life. There was nothing in particular that I remember about the victims other than, I suppose, that they had dreams and plans, that they had been loved and loved others in return. The bombing took place barely thirteen weeks after the Good Friday Agreement referendum, in which most of the electorate had voted 'yes'.

There was a palpable feeling of hope in the community; hope that at last the conflict was over and peace was at hand. It was a hope that I bought into and dearly wished to be true. But alas it was not to be.

I was cutting the grass at home in Belfast when I got the call from a TV news desk. I was asked to drive to Omagh as quickly as possible and hook up with a satellite van for an input into the 6 p.m. news bulletin. It wasn't an unusual assignment for me. I'd covered bombings and killings in and around Omagh for years. The Provisional IRA had killed four off-duty soldiers in a booby-trap bomb in May 1973; then six weeks later three Provisional IRA men were killed in a premature bomb explosion on Gortin Road near Omagh; and there were also the usual scores of random killings and bombings. What was unusual for me was my reaction – for the first time in my career I refused to go! I can still hear myself telling the news editor, 'I'm not going.'

Why didn't I go? Maybe I was tired of seeing so much grief and anguish? Or too many bodies? Or too much political rationalisation?

However, at that moment of saying 'I'm not going' I felt an overwhelming sense of despair. It was personal. For me the despair of living with communal strife and hatred had become a normal way of life, but I found that living with hope and having it dashed was heartbreaking.

The Omagh bombing effectively signalled the end of my career. I plodded along for another two years. I covered the wars in Kosovo in 1998 and Ethiopia in 1999 but my heart was no longer in the job. My career officially ended in Ardoyne in 2001 when I was injured in a blast-bomb incident during the Holy Cross stand-off, and to be truthful it was a merciful release.

It's ironic that my breaking point wasn't the horror of war but the hope of peace. Hope in Northern Ireland can be a two-edged sword and is meant for a stronger person than me.

John Coghlan worked as a cameraman for RTÉ and BBC in Northern Ireland.

A touch of magic as Hume and Trimble collect their Nobel Peace Prize

Deaglán de Bréadún

Nostalgia ain't what it used to be. Having been on this earth a substantial number of years (let's not go into too much detail, folks), when I look back nowadays on the past it is no longer a case of being transported in a mental time-machine to relive my experiences in a simple and straightforward manner. The intervening years and related occurrences since that time inevitably place their mark on the initial event.

When I covered the presentation of the Nobel Peace Prize to John Hume and David Trimble in December 1998, one of the highlights was a concert where an array of musical stars played and sang. It remains a matter of pride to me that the best performance on that wonderful night in Oslo was given by an Irish band. I can still see, in my mind's eye, Dolores O'Riordan and the other members of The Cranberries giving a great rendition of their hits, with the woman from Limerick clicking her fingers to the music in a way that was particularly cool.

When I was asked to write this piece, I knew the Oslo concert would feature prominently. Little did I realise, however, that, by the time I got to the point of actual writing, Dolores would have been found dead in a London hotel at the early age of forty-six years.

Other musical performers at the Nobel gig included Canadian pop diva Alanis Morissette, Phil Collins, Shania Twain, Enrique Iglesias, Norwegian rock band A-ha, Elton John (on videoscreen) and two Irish artists, Derry legend Phil Coulter and celebrated flautist James Galway. The young people of Oslo were well represented on the night, as well as being much in evidence on other days. Here again, my memories have an overlay of sadness as I wonder how many of them were among the seventy-seven mostly young persons killed by the Norwegian mass-murderer Anders Breivik on that infamous day of bombing and shooting in July 2011.

Back in December 1998, the contrast between Norway and Northern Ireland was quite stark. After all, it was only four months since the horrific Omagh bombing in which twenty-nine people, including a woman pregnant with twins, were killed and more than two hundred others injured. Indeed in one of my dispatches from Oslo I wrote that the Nobel ceremony provided an example of a country with an advanced level of prosperity and social justice which decided 'to give something back by helping others less fortunate'.

In February 1997 I had taken up a position as northern editor of the *Irish Times* and spent the next fourteen months covering the lead-in to the Good Friday Agreement, which was concluded in April 1998. Three weeks after that historic pact, it emerged that the leaders of the Social Democratic and Labour Party (SDLP) and Ulster Unionist Party (UUP) had been nominated for the Nobel Peace Prize. Hume's instant response was, 'The only prize I want is peace.'

Later, on 16 October, it was announced that Hume and Trimble were to be the recipients of the prize which carried with it the sum of 7.6 million kr (Swedish crowns), equivalent at the time to almost stg £600,000, to be divided between them.

The prize for journalists was to get the assignment and I made sure to put in my application at an early stage, knowing that other colleagues might very well be interested. Having put in the hard yards involved in covering the ups and downs of the peace process, I felt I deserved the assignment and, happily, my employers gave me the green light to go ahead.

The ceremony was scheduled for 10 December and in the previous day's *Irish Times* I reported that the group of family and friends accompanying John Hume was being led by his legendary Aunt Bella, a resident of the Bogside in Derry. The Trimble entourage included another legend, Sir John Gorman, decorated for his actions as a tank commander in the Second World War and the only Catholic member of the Ulster Unionist Party in the Northern Ireland Assembly. As a young boy I had read about his wartime exploits, which were immortalised on the front page of *The Victor* comic.

There were about a thousand invited guests at the presentation ceremony in Oslo City Hall and the procession of dignitaries was led by Norway's King Harald and Queen Sonja. Hume's acceptance speech reiterated his oft-expressed belief in the need to spill your sweat and not your blood in the name of peace. And he once again recalled standing on the bridge at Kehl, between France and Germany, and meditating on the fact that these two countries, regularly at war in the past, were now working together in peace and harmony as part of the European project. He quoted W.B. Yeats, Louis MacNeice and, of course, Martin Luther King.

Trimble's oration – which had a strong input from the southern Irish commentator and former television producer Eoghan Harris (who also provided directions on when to look at the camera, etc.) – quoted the eighteenth-century parliamentarian and political philosopher Edmund Burke, 'the son of a Protestant father and a Catholic mother', as well as Amos Oz, 'the distinguished Israeli writer who has reached out to the Arab tradition'.

The UUP leader's most memorable line was his statement that unionists had built a 'solid house' in Northern Ireland, 'but it was a cold house for Catholics'. At the same time, he said that nationalists 'seemed to us as if they meant to burn the house down'.

There was a touch of magic about the occasion, with cockaded soldiers in fairy-tale uniforms blowing silver trumpets. The snow on the streets reminded us that Christmas was drawing near. Children in bright clothes sang about peace and lit eternal flames. Among those in attendance were Jean Kennedy Smith, former US ambassador to Ireland and member of the distinguished Boston family, and Bishop Edward Daly from Derry, forever remembered for his brave actions on Bloody Sunday in 1972.

At a social gathering afterwards, Hume and UUP treasurer Jack Allen paid tribute to their native city when they sang 'The Town I Loved So Well' together, accompanied on the piano by Phil Coulter, who wrote the song.

Then it was on to Stockholm for a peace seminar organised by the Olof Palme International Centre, named after the Swedish prime minister who was shot dead by a lone assassin in 1986. There was a surprise at the end as the lights were dimmed and a group of seven children, whose leader wore a crown made of glimmering candles, came in and sang hymns. For the moment at least, the drums of war were silenced by heavenly voices.

Deaglán de Bréadún was northern editor, foreign affairs correspondent and political correspondent with the *Irish Times*.

Rosemary Nelson's last interview
Steven McCaffery

For the first time in our hour-long conversation, Rosemary Nelson suddenly seemed uncomfortable.

'The threats? Yes, there are threats. Particularly when I am involved in highlighting issues, when there is a lot of attention ...'

The interview had focused on concerns for her clients, but now it veered into the widely publicised fears for her own safety.

'What type of threats? Well, death threats. Of course it's frightening, when you have children and a husband. It has to have some impact on your life.'

The forty-year-old solicitor was sitting in a plain upstairs room in her office: two chairs, a simple desk on hard-wearing carpet. Papers and files spilled in an arc in front of her. She sat with her legs curled, a cup of coffee clasped in her hands. 'The thing is that it is so sinister ...'

The phone to her right rang and she answered it. Minutes later a mobile in her bag buzzed for attention. A third telephone gave a muffled ring before she hunted it out beneath files to her left. Rosemary Nelson was a busy woman.

By then her killers were busy too. Their bomb would detonate under her car as she drove from the home she shared with her husband and three children in Lurgan, County Armagh.

That day in her office she chatted about her family. She had a young daughter and two sons. The boys had left on a school ski trip and she talked about her worries for them. But such ordinariness made the wider picture seem all the more surreal.

She lived in an area dubbed the Murder Triangle due to the sectarian violence seen around the towns of Lurgan, Craigavon and Portadown. Three cases there brought her to prominence.

The 1990s saw outbreaks of mass violence over controversial parades, with the most serious at Drumcree in Portadown, where Orange Order processions through the Catholic enclave of Garvaghy Road were opposed by the Garvaghy Road Residents' Coalition. Rosemary Nelson became the coalition's lawyer.

Prominent Lurgan republican Colin Duffy was jailed for the shooting of a former soldier in 1993, but he denied involvement and the murder conviction was quashed on appeal in 1996. His legal representative in the high profile case was Rosemary Nelson.

In 1997 Catholic man Robert Hamill was walking home after a night out in Portadown when he was fatally injured in a sectarian attack, while witnesses claimed police were parked nearby. Rosemary Nelson championed calls for a public inquiry.

This all took place in era of rising tension, when the hopes for peace were fragile and still beset by ongoing republican and loyalist violence. The course of events and her involvement in such prominent cases put her on the radar of violent loyalists and eventually set her at odds with the RUC.

United Nations Special Rapporteur Param Cumaraswamy met Rosemary Nelson and compared her situation to that of solicitor Pat Finucane, who was killed in 1989 by loyalists colluding with UK state forces.

In September 1998 Mrs Nelson testified at a hearing in the United States Congress in Washington: 'I have begun to experience some difficulties with the RUC. These difficulties have involved RUC officers questioning my professional integrity, making allegations that I am a member of a paramilitary group and, at their most serious, making threats against my personal safety, including death threats.'

Earlier in her life she had dealt with very different pressures. Her relatives would later explain that she was born with a large strawberry birthmark on one side of her face and from the age of ten endured weeks at a time in a Scottish hospital for skin graft surgery that continued into her teens.

The surgery left extensive facial scars that loyalists later used for propaganda purposes. Leaflets were circulated that falsely attributed the scars to her being a former bomber. It was the beginning of a process that saw her life become public property, one which accelerated after her death.

Rosemary Nelson's murder immediately sparked allegations that security forces colluded with her loyalist killers. The claims were strenuously denied but they attracted international attention and came as a special policing commission set up under the Good Friday Agreement was considering the future of the RUC. Her case became part of the battle over the reputation of the predominantly Protestant police force and so her name was exalted by some and attacked by others. In the end, her case had the effect of amplifying the calls for radical reform of policing. Was that her legacy?

As mourners left St Peter's Church in Lurgan to lay her to rest, there was no talk of legacy. A funeral procession moves as one, speaking to itself in a low voice. Its many feet drag to a destination that it does not wish to reach. On that day there was also an air of disbelief at a death that was foretold and perhaps could have been prevented. As the hearse turned the corner near her home, passing the spot where she died, huge crowds waited on either side of the road, like two human arms waiting to embrace the funeral cortege before melting into it. At the heart of the throng, a car carried a huddle of three confused children, cowering from the world.

But all this was yet to come.

Rosemary Nelson finished her phone calls. She brought the conversation back to her clients living on the Garvaghy Road. They included people whose homes were invaded by loyalist gangs at night. Families barricaded into bedrooms. Threats shouted up the stairs in the dark.

'I am a human rights lawyer,' said Mrs Nelson, almost angrily. 'I believe in the rule of law ...'

It was Friday 12 March 1999. Three days later the bomb planted by loyalist paramilitaries would explode beneath her silver BMW. Rosemary Nelson was about to pay a terrible price for her work.

Steven McCaffery is former editor of The Detail website, former deputy editor of Press Association Ireland and former news editor of the *Irish News*. He now works for the Social Change Initiative.

The authors of *Lost Lives* (L–R): Brian Feeney, David McVea, David McKittrick, Chris Thornton and Seamus Kelters.

Chronicling the lost lives of the Troubles
David McKittrick

In the 1990s a group of us, five journalists and academics, came together with the idea of chronicling each one of the thousands of deaths of the Troubles we were living through. The five were Seamus Kelters, David McVea, Chris Thornton, Brian Feeney and me.

We had no comprehensive files, no template and no publisher. We all had work and family commitments – we were busy people with growing families. But we did have much experience: between us we had, over the years, contributed to the *Belfast Telegraph*, *Irish News*, *News Letter*, *Irish Times*, BBC, London *Independent*, *Economist*, *New York Times*, *The Sunday Times*, *Le Monde* and other outlets.

As seasoned observers of the violence, we imagined it might take us a couple of years. In the event it took us well over a decade to research and write what became the million-word book *Lost Lives*. Eventually realising that we required assistance, we enlisted the help of dozens of people, including a further fifteen journalists.

The idea was for a chronicle of the fatalities, setting out the tales of those who died as unemotionally and objectively as we could. We adhered to that objective, but as years passed we came to realise that the facts, even when presented as dispassionately as possible, had great intrinsic power. They certainly had an effect on us, for along the way we shed tears. The words we wrote may read like journalism, but we quickly become aware that between the lines lay much grief and tragedy. Within the book's covers are more than 3,700 lost lives, testimony to what happens to a community that attempts to resolve difference through violence. To our knowledge there had never before been a work that set out to relate the circumstances of every single death in a conflict.

Since the deaths are listed chronologically, their sequence provides in effect an alternative history of the troubles. While standard history books concentrate on the broader sweeps of policy and events, and the deeds of leading politicians and paramilitaries, a reading of these entries in *Lost Lives* gives a unique insight into the huge political and emotional impact that deaths can have.

There are many heart-rending tales within its pages. There is, for example, the story of Royal Ulster Constabulary constable James Seymour who was shot in 1973 and for twenty-two years lay in a hospital bed, a bullet in his head, apparently conscious but unable to move or speak. On every day of those twenty-two years he was visited by his wife. He died aged fifty-five in 1995, bringing the vigil of two decades to a close: the strain and anguish suffered by him and his family can only be imagined. Many families have found that such scars may never heal.

Although the Seymour family suffered particularly severely, their protracted, heartbreaking tragedy is only one of hundreds arising from a quarter-century of death and destruction, affecting many types of people.

Among the wounded are many in wheelchairs or confined to bed, or who have suffered brain damage. Some are in constant pain. One senior policeman continued to serve in the force despite losing an arm, a leg and an eye in an explosion.

So many people have been treated unkindly by fate. At least two women have lost two life-partners, in both instances killed years apart. One woman survived a shooting but lost her unborn child who was buried, in a tiny light-blue coffin, in unconsecrated ground next to a graveyard only yards from her home. Over and over again the 'wrong' people died. A nine-year-old Londonderry boy, playing cowboys with his brother, upset a tripwire in his garden and set off a bomb that killed him. A man burst into a house in Belfast, shot dead the occupant and then exclaimed, 'Christ, I'm in the wrong house.'

A man was issued with a personal protection weapon after receiving death threats: within a few hours it went off by accident and killed him. A dying man plaintively asked his wife, 'Why did they shoot me? I'm not in anything.'

A bullet fired by a soldier during an altercation in a pub passed through the arm of a loyalist activist and killed a man having a quiet drink in a corner. A bullet fired by a republican passed through the arm of a policeman on traffic duty and killed a woman motorist.

One woman lost both her son, who was shot dead, and her husband, who collapsed and died when he heard the news. When a father of four was shot dead in County Armagh, his widow and her sister had to be carried into church for the funeral, since both suffered from multiple sclerosis. A man who had been drinking followed his wife to a police station where he became involved in an altercation with a sentry and was shot dead.

The character of some of the killers made many of the murders seem even more senseless. A loyalist, jailed for four murders, had been drinking two bottles of gin a day, which resulted in brain damage. He gave himself up to police after twice trying to commit suicide.

There are hundreds more stories in the pages of terrible deaths and terrible injuries, of shattered lives and shattered families, of widows and orphans whose suffering continues even though the guns have largely fallen silent.

We tried to be non-judgemental. Those who died in the Troubles included civilians, members of loyalist and republican groups, political figures, soldiers, joyriders, alleged drug dealers, judges and magistrates, those killed during armed robberies, prison officers, police officers, convicted killers, businessmen, alleged informers, military personnel, those who died on hunger strike, men, women, children, pensioners and unborn babies. They are all in *Lost Lives*.

We differentiated between the various categories of the dead but we did not judge them. All died in the Troubles so all are listed. Readers will bring their own attitudes to bear, ranking different categories as deserving of differing degrees of sympathy. It is human nature that this should be so: we saw our task as simply providing the facts that would allow readers to make their own judgements.

For years it was uncertain whether the book would ever see the light of day, for it was rejected by scores of publishers. One of the strongest impulses to persevere came from our colleague Seamus Kelters who died in 2017. He provided communal cheer and encouragement in the face of many difficulties, showing infinite energy and appetite for the most daunting tasks. We were writing about conflict, but Seamus's lion-hearted commitment meant that we never once experienced conflict within our group.

The reaction to the appearance of the book was for us a moving and humbling experience, with thousands of people buying it within weeks of publication. In one shop a book lay stained with mascara where a woman had wept on its pages. Stories reached us of families communally reading it around the kitchen table and reflecting together, sometimes for the first time, on the exact circumstances of the death of a loved one.

We know of both Protestant and Catholic churches where the book was used as the basis for sermons. In some places the book was placed on a lectern in front of an altar for all to read.

The book was awarded the Ewart-Biggs prize for the promotion of peace and reconciliation in Ireland, the judges declaring, '*Lost Lives* is both an enduring memorial to all those who died and a dramatic enterprise of historical recovery. It is both a deeply significant historical record and a labour of love – dedicated journalistic objectivity put to the highest use.'

David McKittrick has been reporting on Northern Ireland for the *Irish Times* and the *Independent* since the 1970s.

The tears of Martin McGuinness's mother
Katie Hannon

I missed the war. By the time I began making regular excursions across the border in my trusty little Renault Clio, it was to cover the often tedious business of ceasefire politics. There were some dramatic episodes to break the tedium. Dodging plastic bullets and flying missiles in Portadown. Tense stand-offs on the Ormeau Road. A colour piece from a Rangers supporters' club in Sandy Row. Another from the Felons club on the Falls Road.

But mostly I recall a blur of seemingly endless 'doorstep' interviews in a variety of car parks and hallways and footpaths and courtyards as the talks meandered along a very bumpy road.

And then it happened. I remember it now in freeze-frame. The overheated prefabs in the Castle Buildings car park. The dusting of snow. The jokes ('If I said you had a cross-border body, would you hold it against me?'). The talks, we were warned, were close to collapse. The talks, we were assured, were edging towards success. Silhouetted figures spotted hugging in a window. The hand of history. The sheer, blessed relief that the years of ill-tempered, patience-sapping negotiations had yielded a deal.

That felt like a big moment. It led to another big moment: when the man most closely identified with the IRA's campaign of violence became minister for education.

I was intrigued by Martin McGuinness. He was so affable and naturally at ease in a way that Gerry Adams wasn't. It was chilling to imagine what lay behind the engaging exterior. I would catch myself staring at him during those doorsteps, wondering what stuff he was made of, what dark secrets he had to be keeping. This got me thinking about his mother. What it would feel like to have raised this blue-eyed, blond-haired boy who would be so instrumental to both the beginning and the end of so violent a conflict?

In the way of these things, I knew a man who knew his sister. After some cajoling, a loose arrangement was made to facilitate an introduction and I pointed my car in the direction of the N2. Just how loose the arrangement was became clear when I arrived in Derry.

I couldn't contact this sister despite numerous efforts. Increasingly desperate, I headed to Elmwood Street in the city's Bogside where I hung around at the end of the terrace of red-brick houses waiting for word to come through to call in. It didn't come. With darkness falling, there was nothing for it but to chance my arm. A young lad helpfully directed me to the house where Martin McGuinness grew up. Conscious that turning up uninvited to the family home of the man some insisted on calling the 'Butcher of the Bogside' might not be my best-ever idea, I nervously tapped on the door. A smallish woman with a warm smile opened it. I launched into my convoluted tale about prior arrangements and missed messages. She shooed me into the front room without further ado.

Tea was made. This was a couple of days after Martin had been made a minister and I got the sense that Peggy couldn't quite believe it had happened. She described watching the scenes in Stormont in silence as the DUP Assembly members joined in with the hissing from the public gallery. She said she couldn't help wondering how long the arrangement could possibly last. She told me, 'Then the tears came and says I, "I'll just savour the moment." And I did. And the tears are still coming ...'

Indeed she had to dab at her eyes again as she talked about the 'complete surprise' of the news that he was taking up the education portfolio. 'I'm pleased and I'm scared. I don't know if I should say that but I worry about him.'

I knew that Peggy was a devout Catholic. But if she harboured reservations about her son's path in life, they didn't show. The woman I met was fair bursting with maternal awe at the boy she had raised.

'He never gave me one minute's trouble,' she said of the man who would grow up to be the key IRA commander during the bloodiest years of the conflict. If she had suffered sleepless nights over what her second-born might be getting himself involved in, it appeared these were now erased from her official memory. 'All my children were good but Martin was exceptionally quiet.'

Sitting in pride of place atop the television in the corner was a photograph of Albert Reynolds with Martin. Peggy was a big fan of the former taoiseach and what he had done for the peace process.

The news was on and the screen suddenly filled with Martin's face and Peggy reached for the remote control to raise the volume. A former teacher was describing a quiet, shy boy who never sought the limelight. 'You're right,' Peggy told the television, delighted. 'That's what he was.'

She recalled then that Martin had also impressed another teacher, disappearing upstairs in search of proof and returning some time later with an old leather handbag overflowing with old letters and mortuary cards. Despite a meticulous search, the glowing reference from Brother O'Sullivan couldn't be located and she had to fall back on her memory of it.

'There was something in it about him being sure that if Martin was given responsibility he would be able to take charge.'

After I took my leave from the Bogside I headed over to the watering holes of the Waterside, where the welcome for the new minister was less than enthusiastic.

'I think he's a bigoted, sectarian bastard,' Julie told me, while claiming to be 'the only Catholic drinking in this pub'.

Her friend worked in the Department of Education. 'I said at work today that I will not shake that man's hand. A lot of people were saying that at work. But then the trouble with this place is that people often say one thing and do the opposite.

'I've heard that he doesn't offer people his hand when he is introduced because he's had it snubbed so often. That suits me fine. I just couldn't shake a hand that had been involved in killing.'

Thirteen years later, I thought about that woman when I saw a photo of Queen Elizabeth shaking the hand of Peggy McGuinness's son. She hadn't lived to see it. But she had seen plenty.

Katie Hannon is the political correspondent for the RTÉ current affairs department. She previously worked for the *Evening Herald, Irish Examiner* and *Ireland on Sunday*.

The murder of Martin O'Hagan

Jim McDowell

It was late on a Friday evening, 28 September 2001, when Brian Rowan phoned me at home. He had worked with us running the Ulster Press Agency, before leaving to become the security correspondent for BBC Northern Ireland. It wasn't unusual for us to exchange information after a terrorist shooting, bombing or other atrocity, especially when deadlines were looming.

I'd heard there'd been a shooting in Lurgan, Martin O'Hagan's home town. Nothing unusual about that. The County Armagh town was a hotbed of strife; a place where, when you walked up the street, you could almost bite the sectarianism.

Brian was phoning about the shooting, fatal as it proved. And then came the bombshell. He sounded like he didn't want to ask. But he did.

'Jim,' he said, 'what age is Martin O'Hagan?'

Alarm bells didn't start ringing in my head, as the cliché goes. Big Ben started bonging instead. I didn't really know Martin's age off the top of my head.

Then Brian said that, although the police at that early stage weren't giving the victim's name, they were saying that the man 'down on the street' was aged 51.

Brian then told me where the shooting had occurred. It was the road in which Martin lived with Marie and their three daughters. Both the age and the address synched. But I still didn't want to even countenance that.

'Jim, I think it's Martin,' said Brian quietly.

It was.

My wife, Lindy, and I got into the car. We went to Lurgan, to the quarantined spot on the road that the police had cordoned off with plastic tape.

The police knew who I was. I ducked under the tape.

Martin's body was still warm. The blood that had poured out of seven bullet holes in his back pooled on the ground.

I was white with shock and horror. And burning red with rage. And then, even worse, just at this point an LVF mob gathered on a corner close to the murder scene. They began an obscene, sectarian chant, the main crass chorus of which was '... another Fenian dead'.

I went to move towards them. The police at the scene were already stretched, coping with the immediate aftermath of the murder. A uniformed officer put his hand on my arm. 'Sir,' he said, 'do you want a riot erupting here, with bricks and bottles flying over this lad's dead body?'

No. Definitely not.

Not with the terrible task still to be faced.

Going to the nearby O'Hagan home, to put my arms around a weeping widow, who'd just witnessed her husband being shot dead in front of her. Martin had been gunned down just a hundred metres from his own front door. He died a hero, protecting his wife, Marie, from the assassin's bullets of the LVF.

He and Marie had been at his favourite pub that night, Fa' Joe's, in Lurgan town centre, enjoying a few Friday night drinks. It was only about half a mile from the bar to their home, a leisurely dander, or stroll. They decided to walk, as they often did.

But there was a spotter in the bar. A terror-gang scout. He used a public phone in the pub to call his LVF boss as soon as Marie and Martin left. Two brothers were waiting in a stolen car. One had taken over from Billy Wright as godfather of the mid-Ulster LVF after 'King Rat's' murder in jail. Indeed, known as 'The Piper', he had been the lone bagpiper at the terror czar's funeral.

The brothers – one of them, ironically, born a Catholic in a different marriage from his kin – had worked out a meticulous plan with their cohorts in a flat in Lurgan earlier that day, when the murder weapon had been produced and loaded. The elder brother, 'The Piper', was to be behind the wheel for the Chicago-style drive-by shooting. The designated gunman was his younger brother.

Martin probably heard the car speeding up. The shooting started. He threw himself across Marie, covering her with the front of his body. Seven bullets tore into his back, killing him almost instantly.

Billy Wright's orders from the grave had been fatally and cruelly fulfilled.

'King Rat' had veered erratically from being evangelically Christian (allegedly), especially when incarcerated in jail, to being a junkie. After he himself had been ambushed and assassinated on a prison bus by INLA godfather Christopher 'Crip' McWilliams and two other INLA henchmen, John Kennaway and John Glennon, on 27 December 1997, he was found to have smuggled-in drugs in his system. But whether it was a religious vision or a drug-induced premonition, Wright himself knew he was going, at some stage, to meet a violent end.

And I was later to learn, after Martin's murder, that Wright had used Old Testament language to order that killing ... as revenge for his own death.

He told his killer cohorts: 'If anything ever happens to me, it is to happen to Martin O'Hagan tenfold.'

Around 10.38 p.m. on that Black Friday, Wright's vengeance on Martin O'Hagan was exacted. That meant that Wright would never face justice for the murder of a journalist, unlike the killers of another investigative journalist, Veronica Guerin, in Dublin.

And, much to my chagrin and regret, the LVF killers who stalked and shot dead our colleague Martin have never been brought to justice either.

In spite of us naming them numerous times in the *Sunday World*, often on the front page.

In spite of one of their LVF Lurgan mob turning supergrass, or police informer, and threatening to nail the drive-by killers in court ... only for the case to be withdrawn.

And the reason why they are still free on the streets and have escaped jail, in spite of being convicted of other criminal charges down the years? For some reason, they are deemed 'Untouchables'. But still not by me, or the *Sunday World*.

We will continue to name and shame the death-dealing LVF killers until their, or my, dying day. After all, those who campaigned for justice for Veronica Guerin succeeded. And, even an incredulous and shameful seventeen years on, we are (still) asking for nothing more, nothing less.

Simply justice for Martin.

Jim McDowell is a *Sunday World* columnist, having previously been northern editor for the paper. He also previously worked for the *News Letter*, *Sunday News* and Ulster Press Agency.

© Paul Faith

The Chuckle Brothers.

I could see the picture unfold before it happened
Paul Faith

A couple of officials from the Northern Ireland Office were standing over my shoulder as I was transmitting the photograph downstairs in a basement room at Parliament Buildings, and I could hear one of them say, 'Brilliant. That's what we want to see. They'll love this in London ...'

I don't know where the title 'The Chuckle Brothers' originated, but of the thousands of photographs I've taken in thirty years in this business, this is the one that seems to have stood out. It might even define my career. An ordinary enough shot. Two guys in fits of laughter. Two guys, once avowed enemies who could barely stand the sight of each other, but now the best of pals, and content to share this astonishing new-found friendship with the rest of the world.

I always got on well with them.

The relationship with Paisley stretched back to my formative days with the *Ballymena Guardian* – a time when he was causing all sorts of anti-establishment mayhem, and when he was not particularly well disposed towards the media, especially certain individuals in the print and broadcasting industry.

But the Rev. Dr Ian Richard Kyle Paisley, loyalist politician and Protestant firebrand preacher, the future Baron Bannside, always seemed to have a soft spot for me. He didn't mind me referring to him as 'the Doc', and even though his hostile attitude towards the press was legendary, he kept an eye out for me.

One night we were waiting for him in the town of Portglenone, County Antrim, where a crowd had gathered for one of his rallies in the aftermath of the signing of the Anglo-Irish Agreement in 1985. The blood was up, and some of his supporters were itching to have a go at a group of journalists. But once his armour-plated, bulletproof Granada pulled up, he emerged from the back and implored them to behave. I don't think he knew my religious background, but he pointed towards me, a fellow Ballymena man, and declared in that unmistakable tone, 'Leave him alone. He's with me. He's a good man.'

Everywhere Paisley went, I went, at all hours of the day and night. I recall waiting for him at his home as Eileen, his wife, served him porridge for breakfast before he headed out with his police bodyguards. It might have been to a demonstration somewhere, or out electioneering in North Antrim, with me following behind and trying to keep up in an old Vauxhall Nova.

Not everybody was aware of his empathy towards me, especially when he was on the warpath. Paisley in full flow could be a fearsome sight, and his supporters worshipped him. He had this aura. He could whip them into a frenzy, and I never doubted for a moment there could be a dark and menacing side to him as well.

I know some reporters, and one or two photographers, felt uneasy at times in his company.

At an Ulster Resistance rally in Ballymena he pulled on a red beret before saluting the crowd to provide me with an exclusive photograph. You could have cut the atmosphere with a knife. I was working for Pacemaker Press at the time, and I had a very uncomfortable feeling about where this would all end up.

Back in those days Northern Ireland was a terrible place. Working closely with the Doc was always difficult – the situation could change in a heartbeat and his followers weren't big fans of the press. At times I felt vulnerable – something I often confided to my wife, Margaret. But I had a family to feed and this was a job that needed doing.

Martin McGuinness was different. I'd known him as long as I knew the Doc. Although he was somebody with a questionable past, I left it to others to query his reputation and political credentials – and, of all the prominent figures, I found him probably the most accommodating.

I remember mourners getting pretty restless with the media at the funerals of three IRA men shot dead by the SAS near Carrickmore, County Tyrone. He could see I was a little anxious. After he stepped in and appealed to the crowd, I told him I was okay. He whispered, 'The locals don't always listen to the ones from Belfast ...'

At another IRA funeral in Crossmaglen, South Armagh, which was coming down with police and soldiers, he could see I was there for one particular photograph. Sure enough when the security forces were busy taking up places in and around the graveyard, an IRA colour party suddenly appeared beside the coffin outside the church, McGuinness shoulder to shoulder with them. He never spoke, but he knew I had the photograph I wanted.

He and I loved fishing and one day in Belfast he spotted a fly rod in the back of my car. He told me he'd been out the night before trying to catch sea trout in Donegal. He could hear the fish moving and jumping in the dark, but never got so much as a bite. And then just before daybreak, he caught this beauty. He was so pleased with himself. But then he said, 'Paul, what do you think I did next? I unhooked it, cradled it in the water, reviving it in the fast-flowing oxygen-filled river, letting it swim free, and disappear.'

That was typical of the Martin McGuinness I got to know in the later years of his life. Generous, softly spoken, and courteous. I remember a few years later, after I photographed him shaking hands with the Queen, he came up to me during the Irish Open golf championship at Royal Portrush and said: 'You've made me famous again.' He then insisted we pose for a photograph as a keepsake in the media centre.

After all these years it was obvious he and Paisley were at peace with themselves, especially in each other's company. So on that day at Parliament Buildings in May 2007 when they were sworn in as first minister and deputy first minister, everything just fitted into place.

Tony Blair, Bertie Ahern and Peter Hain were also there. They had been laughing and joking earlier in Paisley's room as they prepared to announce the restoration of the power-sharing executive. The Doc turned to Blair and said: 'Here's me, a man of eighty-four, preparing to enter office, and there's you, just fifty-four, getting ready to leave …'

The mood was so relaxed and it was such an exciting time to be in there with them. I was working for the Press Association and no other photographer was present.

And when they walked down the steps at the Great Hall to make the announcement, Paisley and McGuinness taking their seats beside the British and Irish prime ministers, I could already envisage the photograph. Paisley was tap-tapping the railing, and when Blair recalled the Doc's throwaway remark about him standing down as prime minister, I could see the picture unfold before it happened.

I held my finger on the shutter and captured one of the great moments in Northern Ireland's troubled history. It was just perfect.

Paul Faith is a freelance photographer. He previously worked for the Press Association, Pacemaker Press and the *Ballymena Guardian*.

Bringing Gerard Evans home to his mother
Suzanne Breen

It's the perfect place for a secret burial. I'm wading through muddy bogland near Hackballscross, County Louth, in pitch darkness with the map the IRA man gave me. The rain drives down relentlessly from a moonless sky. The wind shakes reeds taller than I am. My torch provides only limited light. I bump into a tangle of bushes.

It's a remote, haunting landscape just across the border in the Irish Republic that sees few visitors. It's here Gerard Evans's body lies, the IRA man says.

Gerard Evans, whom for thirty years the IRA has denied abducting and murdering. Gerard Evans who was only twenty-four years old when he left a dance in Castleblayney, County Monaghan, and was 'disappeared'.

'We held him for three days,' the member of the IRA's South Armagh Brigade says. 'He confessed very quickly to being an informer. He wasn't tortured. He pleaded not to be killed, and then he said his prayers. He was shot once in the back of the head.'

The republican standing in front of me knows the full truth of what happened to Gerard Evans because he was part of the twelve-strong unit that executed him. It's January 2009 and it's the first time anyone involved in a disappearance has spoken to a journalist.

The IRA man's directions to where the secret grave is located are precise: 'Take the road to Knockbridge. Pass Kirk's crossroads, continue until you see a narrow lane on the left. Watch the road carefully or you'll miss it.

'Walk up that lane, past the green field on the right and the stone mounds, and you'll see the bogland. After 150 yards of bogland, stop. Walk 30 yards into the bog – that's where the body is buried.'

It was in the dark of night, a night like this, the IRA man recalls, when Gerard Evans was taken to this godforsaken place.

Six miles down the road and back across the border in Crossmaglen, South Armagh, Mary Evans sits at home, desperate for information about her first-born child. Aged seventy-six, she wants to give him a Christian burial before she dies. 'Everything stopped for our family thirty years ago. We haven't been able to move on,' she tells me.

Mary speaks of her son with pride: 'He was a quiet lad. He liked the darts and the snooker and going fishing with his father.'

He was a good singer too. Mary was never in the pubs herself but she'd hear that Gerard would often take the floor at a session.

Gerard Evans, an unemployed painter and decorator, was last seen alive at 11.30 p.m. on 25 March 1979, by the roadside outside Castleblayney, trying to hitch a lift home. He'd been at a dance in the Embassy Ballroom.

Mary has had many crosses to bear. Her husband, also called Gerard, never got over his son's disappearance. On his sixty-third birthday, he walked into Kiltybane Lake and drowned himself.

The IRA man, who has contacted me through a third party, is Mary's only hope of closure. I'm instructed to go to a prearranged spot on the roadside at Lough Ross, a mile west of Crossmaglen, at a certain time of night.

A van pulls up and I get in the back. It's quite surreal. A garden chair is set up for me to sit on. I can see only the back of the driver's head, which is covered in what initially seems to be a black woolly hat. After ten minutes, we drive into a lock-up garage. The driver gets out and opens the door to face me. The black 'hat' has now been pulled down – it was a rolled-up balaclava. A well-spoken man in a black jacket, dark jeans and black shoes stands before me.

Later, people ask me if I was scared. The IRA man was the nervous one, and with good reason. His life is on the line. If the leadership finds out his identity, he'll be executed for speaking to me 'regardless of the peace process', he warns.

He tells me Gerard was marched across the bogland, given a few minutes to prepare himself, then shot from behind. He knew the lad personally, knew the whole family. The RUC had blackmailed Gerard into becoming an informer after he was involved in a robbery. Thirty years later, the IRA man still justifies the killing: 'There was a war on. He could have had volunteers arrested or killed. Nobody tolerates traitors in a war.'

It was only after the 1994 ceasefire that he began to believe something should be done about Gerard's body. When the Provisionals published an official list of people they'd disappeared, Gerard wasn't on it.

'I was stunned,' the republican says. 'I don't see why the IRA in other areas can admit disappearing people but South Armagh can't. There's an attitude down here: "We won't admit anything until hell freezes over".'

He cites the Provisionals' denial of the murder of Paul Quinn in October 2007 as a reason he's come forward. Every bone in the twenty-one-year-old's body below his neck was broken in a brutal attack with iron bars. 'I knew the South Armagh leadership sanctioned that but they denied it,' the IRA man says. 'Their denial was an absolute lie. I'm sick of lies. A certain morality is okay during a war but things should be done differently in peace.'

He wants to 'do the decent thing' and give the Evans family closure. But he should have done that years ago, I tell him. Even before the ceasefire, he could have passed word to the Evanses about Gerard's death or burial, anonymously. 'I'd more on my mind then. I was concentrating on the war with the Brits,' he replies.

I ask him if he wasn't wracked with guilt when he met Mrs Evans or other family members. 'From time to time I thought about what had happened but no, it didn't keep me awake at night. I have a conscience but Gerry was a casualty of war. I've no regrets about his execution or secret burial. I'd still defend that 100 per cent,' he says.

When Gerard didn't return from the dance and hours turned into days, Mary was demented with worry. She went to the police but nobody could help her. She still has her son's christening robe and shawl. All his clothes have been lovingly folded and stored in a suitcase in the attic. She places prayer cards and holy medals in the pockets, hoping they will bring him back.

She lost her faith for a while 'after so many knocks'. But 'you get your strength back, I don't know where from, but you get it back,' she tells me.

I publish the information the IRA man gave me and the map details in the *Sunday Tribune* newspaper. I meet the Independent Commission for the Location of Victims' Remains, the organisation tasked with finding the bodies of the Disappeared.

Later that year, they start digging. After sixteen months, they find Gerard and bring him home to Mary. His coffin is carried through the snow to St Patrick's Church in Crossmaglen three weeks before Christmas in 2010. I think of the South Armagh Brigade responsible for this war crime, and give thanks that at least one man in its ranks found the courage to break the *omertà* and finally do the right thing.

Suzanne Breen is political editor at the *Belfast Telegraph*. She previously worked at the *Irish Times* and *Sunday Tribune*.

My meeting with the woman twice widowed by the UVF

Hugh Jordan

As I slipped the lock on Marie O'Hara's gate, I was apprehensive. Several times before I had asked her to talk about her remarkable life story, but she had always declined.

Why would it be any different this time, I asked myself. But more in hope than anything else, I gently tapped the pane on her glass door.

'Come in, Hugh!' a strong female voice said from within. Marie had seen me through the window. A cheery mother, grandmother and great-grandmother, she was sitting alone in the front room of her beautifully decorated terraced home.

'Sit down,' she commanded. 'I've just sat down myself after clearing out those cupboards next door.'

After exchanging a few pleasantries, Marie – always straight to the point – said, 'Well Hugh, what can I do for you?'

I explained the purpose of my visit and as I did so, I handed Marie a box of Scottish oatcakes.

'Is this a bribe?' she asked, laughing out loud as she sat up straight in her seat.

I found it uplifting that even after all she had endured, Marie was still inclined to laugh, even just before discussing the most serious of subjects, the murders of her two husbands.

And a few days later, after a Mother's Day discussion with her five daughters, Marie agreed to speak to me. That day, Marie and the girls had booked a table at Zen, a popular Asian fusion restaurant in the trendy Cathedral Quarter district of Belfast.

Marie's eldest daughter, Tracy, is now 50 and the ages of the other four descend like steps and stairs – Cathy is 48, Natalia is 38, Seana is 37 and Maria is the youngest at 31. Maria and her mum share a birthday on Christmas Day.

In the cosmopolitan Cathedral Quarter, it's an easy step to imagine you are in Barcelona and not Belfast. And certainly, with her daughters around her on Mother's Day, Marie looked just like any other happy and proud mum.

But Belfast isn't Barcelona and Marie O'Hara isn't at all like any other mother. Even by Northern Ireland standards – where broken hearts linger around every corner – Marie O'Hara's story stands out. It is totally unique.

Born Marie Lyttle in 1948, she lived with her parents, sisters and brother, at Foundry Street, Ballymacarrett. She attended St Matthew's Primary School, in nearby Short Strand, a tiny Catholic enclave in largely Protestant East Belfast.

When she was fifteen, Marie got a job as a bacon packer. And a year later, she went to work for a large brewery, bottling beer. Around this time, Marie met Hugh Duffy, a quiet young man who was four years older than her. Hugh was a Venetian blind maker, but he secured himself a job in the same brewery, delivering beer to pubs.

'Hugh was quiet. He worked hard and he enjoyed a wee drink. He liked football, particularly Celtic,' Marie recalled.

The couple married in 1967 when Marie was twenty and they set up home in Arran Street, Short Strand. Their first child, Tracy, was born the following year and a second, Cathy, two years later.

'Despite the Troubles, we were happy. We were normal,' she said. 'But of course, we didn't know what was to come.'

Everything changed on 20 June 1975, when Hugh was shot and wounded while walking home from work. He died in hospital two days later, without regaining consciousness. He was thirty.

'Two UVF gunmen were waiting for him,' said Marie. 'They called out his name and when he looked, they shot him. He was totally innocent and he was killed simply because he was a Catholic.'

Hugh Duffy's killers were teenage cousins and one of them lived a stone's throw from Marie's mother. At their trial, when they were both convicted, the judge described it as 'a cold-blooded sectarian murder'.

After the funeral, at the age of just twenty-six, Marie was left to pick up the pieces of her shattered life. 'I had no other choice, Hugh. I had two daughters and I just had to get on with it.'

Four years later, in 1979, Marie met John O'Hara, a local man who was as a skilled heating engineer. They married the following year and moved into a new home. In time, Marie and John had three daughters together.

John O'Hara was a steady and reliable man who took work wherever he found it.

In 1991, with the building industry in England struggling, John came home to work as a taxi driver. On the evening of 17 April, he began his first shift with a firm based in the Catholic Markets area. And at 10.30 p.m. he drove to collect a fare in South Belfast.

At the pick-up point, four armed and masked men stepped from the shadows and shot him as he sat at the wheel. They ran off laughing. A nurse and a doctor who lived nearby raced to John's aid, but alas, it was in vain. John died minutes later. He was forty-one.

'I'm glad those kind people were with John when he died,' Marie told me, as tears welled up in her eyes.

Although the killing was claimed by the loyalist UDA, it later emerged it was carried out by members of the UVF – the same organisation that had murdered Marie's first husband sixteen years earlier. For a second time, Marie was left totally devastated by the actions of loyalist terrorists.

'I was consumed by grief and despair. I couldn't believe that this had happened again. I didn't know which way to turn and to be honest at times I lost it. I thought my world had ended. My faith remained strong though and my daughters – the youngest was only three – helped me survive,' explained Marie, her lip trembling as she spoke.

But the loyalists weren't finished with Marie and her family.

A teenage gunman appeared outside her home brandishing a weapon while one of her girls sat in the front room, but apparently spooked by something, he ran off without firing.

Marie was also subjected to a campaign of harassment through repeated abusive and threatening phone calls to the family home. But as she spoke to me all these years later, she still declined to go into any detail.

'I just couldn't bring myself to repeat what was said to me. It was disgusting.'

Hugh Jordan is a freelance journalist. He is from Glasgow, and has worked in Northern Ireland for more than thirty years, mostly for the *Sunday World*.

Missing the obvious
Tommie Gorman

Marie McConomy sat opposite me in her home at Dove Gardens, an estate below Derry's walls in the Bogside. She was gaunt with grief. On 16 April 1982, her eleven-year-old son, Stephen, was playing with pals in a street close by. He was wearing his good jumper, bought for his Confirmation two weeks before.

The plastic bullet that struck him fractured his skull. For three days he remained unconscious, hooked up to tubes at Belfast's Royal Victoria Hospital, until he slipped away.

During the inquest that followed, British Army witnesses did not claim the boy had been rioting. The jury decided he had been hit at a range of seventeen feet and that the gun used was defective.

As I interviewed his mother about the decision that no soldier would be prosecuted, she said she was thinking of going on hunger strike. The earthquake of loss had been compounded by a second bout of injustice.

Awkwardly I asked what purpose might that serve, given how the campaign by republican prisoners in Long Kesh had ended the previous year. She focused on my face.

'Thomas,' she said – she called me Thomas – 'look in my fridge. There's not much difference being on hunger strike and not being on it.'

In December 1982 Bishop Edward Daly was visiting rural areas of the Derry diocese when the INLA planted a bomb at Ballykelly's Droppin Well pub. The disco was targeted because it was frequented by members of the British Army from the nearby Shackleton Barracks. Eleven soldiers and six civilians, three of them teenagers, were killed by the blast. Thirty people were injured.

As I sat interviewing the bishop, he suddenly went quiet and began to shake. The tape recorder was switched off and Edward Daly, the man who raised the handkerchief on Bloody Sunday, sobbed like a child.

Twenty-three-year-old Harry Keys was involved in a cross-border romance. He was from Ballycassidy in County Fermanagh; his girlfriend lived in neighbouring County Donegal. He had been a member of the RUC reserve but gave up the job two years before, months after he had survived an IRA bomb attack on Armagh RUC station.

On 15 January 1989, the couple drove up the lane to her home between Ballintra and Ballyshannon. The gunmen were waiting. She was ordered from the car and the gang then sprayed it with bullets. She heard their whooping and cheering as they made off after killing her boyfriend.

More than numbers or dates, the human details stay with you. The awful things people do to each other when anger is in flood. In October 1989, we boarded a ferry in Dublin and headed to a new job in Brussels. In a way relieved to be leaving, unsure the cycle of killing would ever stop in our homeland.

Almost thirty years later, having worked from a Belfast base for sixteen years, a different version of hopelessness came visiting. GUBU was the acronym once coined by Conor Cruise O'Brien to describe a combination of grotesque, unbelievable, bizarre and unprecedented events. 'Perfect storm' is the cliché that is part of modern parlance.

Emboldened by a general election victory he didn't expect, David Cameron decided to confront Tory Eurosceptics. The June 2016 Brexit referendum buried Cameron and undermined the European dimension that provides ballast in Northern Ireland's unique architecture. Martin McGuinness then contracted a rare form of aggressive cancer and it ended his life within three months of diagnosis. A row over the DUP's handing of a renewable heat incentive scheme destabilised power sharing and, with acrimony in season, the Stormont administration collapsed. Theresa May's decision to call a snap general election, designed to strengthen her authority, produced a result that left her depending on the support of ten DUP members to remain in government.

There are days when one wonders how could fate contrive to deal such a bleak combination of cards?

A Westminster parliament where the likes of Fitt, Hume, Mallon and Durkan were such respected figures, left without an SDLP voice. A well-meaning border politician, with personal knowledge of the impact of violence, struggling to build on the strides made by her predecessors, Ian Paisley and Peter Robinson. A former foreign secretary, wannabe prime minister, who shows no understanding of the unique status of Northern Ireland in an EU and UK/Ireland context. And two former Northern Ireland secretaries of state, prominent Brexiteers, who bolster his ignorance.

And yet, maybe the most obvious is being missed. True, a society is being left without its own structure of devolved government and its future, in a

Brexit context, could be the problem without a proper solution. But the killing has stopped. Men and women are no longer going to their beds at night, dreaming of ways to kill their neighbours.

Maybe that is the secret miracle, the magic of the Good Friday Agreement.

Tommie Gorman is northern editor at RTÉ.

Remembering the victims in the postscript of peace
Gail Walker

In the end his heroism won't be remembered, save perhaps as the stuff of family legend and a cutting in the *Belfast Telegraph* newspaper library. His story would be hard to track down, though, and I'm not sure what you would search under even if you did want to find it. He didn't want his name used. In a dangerous city, he feared exposing his family to risk. There aren't any catch-all files for heroes.

The people whose lives he saved – who were to get up the next morning, put the kettle on, peer out of their kitchen window at another one of those Belfast mornings where the sky makes it seem like you are living under a sheet of aluminium and the day feels bleached of all colour before it's even underway – will never know he existed. They will have gotten on with the routine business of living, immersed in the extraordinary joys and sadnesses of day-to-day life, unaware of their remarkable good fortune. And that's exactly the way this quietly spoken grandfather would have wanted it. For, in journalistic parlance, he was 'hard to get to talk'.

His problem that Monday morning back in 1996 was that the story was out there. Such had been his courage – and the wonderment at it – that even in a place where the unthinkable happened routinely, the news was spreading fast among the network of streets on the Shankill Road where he lived.

Consequently, one of the flotilla of cleaners who early each morning swept across Millfield and into our newsroom in Royal Avenue, dousing the desktops with eye-watering sprays of disinfectant and running roaring vacuum cleaners the full length of it, had delivered the tip-off to me before 8 a.m. 'They said they'd shoot him; he said "go ahead". Never blinked. Not once. You get up there and you'll get a scoop.' Spoken like an ace news editor.

There were early stories to be filed for the main evening edition and it was after midday when I finally pitched up at his modern terraced home. He answered the door holding a saucepan full of potatoes that he was just about to put on to cook. Given what had apparently taken place three nights earlier, it's remarkable he answered the door at all. I must have said something about his act of bravery and he demurred. It wasn't a convenient moment; he'd to get lunch ready for the grandchildren. I took another approach. I knew there had been an element of faith in his story and so – I'll be blunt here – I tried that as my way in, reckoning he would feel he might need to share what was a kind of testimony. He opened the door and said he could spare five minutes.

It was 12 February. Three days earlier, at 7.01 p.m., the IRA had detonated a huge bomb in Canary Wharf, killing two people, injuring more than a hundred and causing £150 million of damage. Northern Ireland journalists have a particular reference point to this night as it was the annual Press Awards bash and many had to put down their drinks, leave the event and return to work.

A few hours after the blast, my reluctant interviewee was alone at home when a knock came to the door. Upon answering it, he found himself confronted by two loyalist gunmen. They said they wanted to avenge the attack and demanded the keys to his car so that they could drive to the Falls Road.

Without a moment's hesitation, the grandfather refused. 'No, you're not getting them. I'm not going to help you to do something like that to some poor innocent people. Away you go now.'

There began an extraordinary verbal tussle. The terrorists pointed the gun at him and threatened to shoot him if he didn't hand over the keys. Again, he refused.

'Do it now or we'll kill you.'

'No. No way. I'm not going to help you do that to some unsuspecting craturs.'

'Hand them over now.'

'No, I won't. Go ahead then, shoot me. I'm not worried, son, I know where I'm going. Tonight I'll be in heaven.'

In the end, they left. Thwarted by bravery, stubbornness, goodness – and what I think we like to call in this place 'oul decency'.

The brief for this piece was to write about a victim. Though I'd agreed to contribute to this book, in the weeks that followed I couldn't settle to compose my copy. I knew why, of course. I didn't want to mentally work through the faces and names of the lost and try to choose one story over another. Each, in their own way, are unbearably sad. The lives that were stopped. The lives of loved ones suspended in grief. The hearts that cry out yet for some form of justice. The hope of closure.

And then there are those like the gentleman whose story I have just retold. Collateral damage. He didn't die but he was a victim too. For all his dignity and bravery, his mind must have spooled the events of that night over and over. The 'what if' of it all.

In some ways, I didn't – don't – want to remember any of it. Which is not to say that one ever forgets. I don't know any journalist who worked through the Troubles, with its relentless cycle of murders and doorstepping the homes of the dead and funerals and yet more murders, who isn't haunted from time to time by being an eyewitness to evil, to heartache and, yes, to courage too.

Twenty years into peace, I am mulling all this over again, looking out from our modern new offices at Clarendon Dock. The city's skyline has been transformed, its new office buildings and hotels reflected in the water as if it is blinking back at itself in amazement at how well it has done.

But shiny glass and chrome edifices can only shape the future, they cannot take away the past. The city landscape is pockmarked by atrocity. Just imagine if a tea light was lit at every spot where a soul lost their life due to sectarian violence on a dark winter's night. Imagine what a satellite image of that would look like. In some places a single flame; in others clusters of twinkling lights. Pull back some more and imagine if tea lights were placed across Northern Ireland. Our shared suffering strung out like gorse fires breaking out, spreading down the length of our motorways, across the rolling hills of County Down and around a pub in Loughinisland; along the north coast; up over the Mournes; their flames like a vigil at a church hall in South Armagh, lighting up the long filled-in craters of the landmine blasts that killed RUC officers and soldiers.

In the same way that so many of our place names are synonymous with terror. A generation of us brought up in the Troubles still feel a collective involuntary shiver when we drive past a sign for Teebane or Claudy or Greysteel. Sometimes it takes very little – turning into a street, hearing an old pop song – to pull you up short and send you hurtling back to another time and place, to the stories that you can never forget even if you wanted to.

The 'collects' that you brought back to the office – the photographs of the dead loaned by weeping relatives. Their faces would stare back at you as you hurried back to work, and then a few hours later they would stare out from the front page of your newspaper, and their eyes would be glassy and unknowing, mercifully oblivious to the horror that was to engulf them.

In recent years there has been a cartoon stereotype of the reporter held up for vitriol – a hard-hearted, feckless, amoral villain – but I can't recognise her or him from the many I have had the privilege to work with. I could, however, give you the names of those whose profession cost them dear, driven near-mad or to drink or both with grief, outrage and the despair that comes from a feeling of helplessness amid the carnage.

I think of the photographer who stood with me in the neat living room of the home of a Catholic hairdresser who had been shot dead hours earlier. As his wife went upstairs to fetch a favourite photograph, her young son – only eight or nine years old – sat in mute shock. My snapper crouched down beside him, put his arms round his little shoulders, hugged him and said, 'You be a brave boy for your mummy.' I had to leave the room.

And that was just one of so many. Looking on as the dead were dug out from the rubble of Frizzell's fish shop on the Shankill Road. Days later, watching a sheet being pulled hastily across two workmen gunned down minutes earlier in Kennedy Way. Ringing the doorbells of their loved ones less than two hours later. Walking through the hospital in Omagh, its floors streaked with blood and the air rent with screaming ...

Legacy, its out-workings, how to navigate the demands of the head and the heart, continue to perplex in Northern Ireland. Unquestionably people have a right to justice and for remembrance. The failure to deliver on those two counts is one of the great failings of the peace process.

As journalism sweeps onward into the digital age, our past lingers along with the determined stubbornness of the righteous.

How will the press adapt to this new world? We could do worse than to remind ourselves that journalism is at heart about telling stories.

It is by its very nature an intensely intimate exchange that requires two things: someone telling the story and someone listening and intervening, clarifying, teasing out, and all the other elements of a true conversation. It is a process more profound, more nuanced in the pursuit of 'truth' than unmediated testimony. So-called verbatim accounts are often flat, featureless and ultimately unsatisfying, both for those seeking a window on to an experience and, crucially, also for the 'witness' who finds themselves abandoned in the narrative they may not have the skills to explore. A practised listener in fact can greatly enhance what is being told in its accuracy as well as its emotional impact. The journalist – the proper journalist – is all of us by proxy, allowing a story to be told in social context.

We here live in a strange situation. Having endured thirty years of violence and enjoyed twenty years of 'peace' – though at times it feels like a prolonged ceasefire – we are faced with a frightening dilemma and responsibility: what to remember and what to forget. It is a question not just for journalists but for our politicians and social and cultural groups, creative communities, right down to individuals, each of us.

Some will say that we should forget the past. Ignore it. Let it go. That it would be – ironically – the price of peace: a self-inflicted, self-imposed cultural amnesia that renders us, in the end, speechless.

That's a recipe for mass neurosis, delusion and moral hypocrisy – that, to keep the 'peace', we must inflict another kind of violence on survivors, censoring their stories, blue-pencilling the raw heart and hurt mind.

And it would be a dereliction of duty, especially for journalists. We need to remember and both to allow and to make it easy for others to do so. The painful truth for politicians and commentators is that stories of grief do not conveniently establish the rightness of this or that political position. That is why we should be careful not just to recall this or that story. We need, as far as possible, to allow and hear as many stories as possible.

We spend a lot of time, rightly, mourning the dead of the Troubles. We may need to spend even more time doing that before we're finished with that traumatic period. But we should also take time right now to remember all those who didn't die over the last two decades.

How many lives were saved by the Belfast Agreement? A hundred? Five hundred? Three thousand?

Look around – they are beside you in coffee shops, shopping centres, your workplace, your church.

The people who didn't get caught up in the bomb blast, who weren't shot leaving work, who didn't wander into the wrong street, who didn't end up as legitimate targets or handy messages to the other side. The people who were saved by an anonymous hero.

They could be you and me.

That is not a small thing.

Gail Walker is editor of the *Belfast Telegraph*. She joined the paper in 1990.

Acknowledgements

Our joint thanks go to:

All the journalists and photographers who so willingly and enthusiastically contributed to the book.

Our great friend Mark Jamieson, whose humour, advice and insights were sources of encouragement to us, but who sadly passed away just as the book was about to be published.

Helen Wright and Patsy Horton, Blackstaff Press, whose expertise and patience were limitless.

From Ivan Little, thanks to:

Siofra O'Reilly Little, whose administrative skills and morale-boosters were invaluable bedrocks.

Emma and Kevin Lawless for their ideas and willing assistance on research.

John Gumbley for helping to open doors to his journalistic colleagues in England.

Darragh O'Neill and Enda Mullan for their help every step of the way.

To Sinead Hughes, for her guidance.

From Deric Henderson, thanks to:

My wife, Clare, and two sons, Deric and Edward – even when the pressure was on to meet the publishing deadline, their support was unstinting.

Sam Smyth of the Irish *Mail on Sunday* in Dublin, who was especially helpful.

Brendan Wright (RTÉ) and Barbara McCann (UTV), who provided first-class assistance with photographic research.

Two of the finest photographers in the business, Paul McErlean and Trevor McBride, who granted us permission to use some of their work.

Peter McKittrick at the US State Department Office, Belfast, who was on hand to help in the early stages of this project.

Index

A-ha, 190
Abercorn restaurant, Belfast, 11, 22
Adams, Gerry, xii, 32, 62, 93, 94, 100,
    112, 129, 136, 138, 141, 156, 162,
    163, 181, 182, 188, 200
Adie, Kate, 75–7, 78
Afghanistan, 75
Aghagallon, County Armagh, 169
Ahern, Bertie, ix, xiii, 130, 181, 209
Aiken, Jim, 124
Alderdice, John, 130
Aldergrove airport, County Antrim, 41,
    76. *See also* RAF Aldergrove, County
    Antrim
Aldridge, John, 146
Allen, Jack, 192
Allen, Philip, 178, 179
Alliance Party, 41
Altnagelvin Hospital, Derry, 2, 25
Amerique, Herve, *xvi*, xvii
Amman, Jordan, 14
An Phoblacht, 163
Anchor Hotel, Dublin, 38
Ancient Order of Hibernians, 184
Andersonstown, Belfast, 29, 38, 94, 114,
    117, 119, 127
Andrews, David, xiv, *xvi*, xvii
Andrews, Thomas, 93
Anglo-Irish Agreement (1985), 80, 99,
    207
Angola, 75
Annsborough, County Down, 174, 175
Antrim Road, Belfast, 10
Antrim, County, 207
Arbuthnot, James, 153
Ardoyne, Belfast, 32, 58, 189
Armagh, County Armagh, 9, 87
Armagh, County, 45, 57, 90, 168, 173,
    177, 193, 198, 203, 217
Armaghbreague Church, County Armagh,
    89
Armstrong, Bertha, 102

Armstrong, David, 165–7
Armstrong, Julian, 102
Armstrong, Ted, 102
Armstrong, Wesley, 102
Arran Street, Belfast, 214
Associated Press Television News, xvii
Association of Cinematograph, Television
    and Allied Technicians, 19
Atkins, Humphrey, 83
Austin, Wendy, 61–3
Australia, 166
Austria, 166

B Specials, 5–7
    Brackey Platoon, 7
Bain, Robert, 87
Ballintra, County Donegal, 216
Ballycassidy, County Fermanagh, 216
Ballyclare, County Antrim, 69
Ballykelly, County Londonderry, 79, 216
Ballymacarrett, Belfast, 214
Ballymena Guardian, 207
Ballymena, County Antrim, 207, 208,
    209
Ballymurphy, Belfast, 5
Ballyshannon, County Donegal, 216
Ballysillan, Belfast, 96
Banbridge, County Down, 53
Bannside, Baron. *See* Paisley, Ian
Barcelona, Spain, 85, 213
Barry, Peter, 99
BBC, xi, xii, xiii, xiv, xvii, 7, 8–9, 17, 18,
    21, 22, 23, 24, 43, 45, 55, 57, 59,
    60, 61, 63, 65, 66, 67, 76, 77, 78,
    79, 84, 86, 89, 108, 109, 120–123,
    141, 142, 159, 163, 169, 183, 189,
    197, 203
Radio 1, 86
Radio 2, 23
Radio 4, 22, 84, 86
Radio Foyle, 78
Radio Ulster, 24, 66, 108

World Service, 86
Beck, Chris, *xvi*, xvii
Begley, Thomas, 138, 146
Beijing, China, 46
Beinn na Lice, Argyll and Bute, 150
Beirut, Lebanon, 29, 30, 114
Belfast Agreement (1998). *See* Good
    Friday Agreement (1998)
Belfast City Commission, 53
Belfast Telegraph, xi, xii, xvii, 7, 11, 12, 34,
    36, 45, 49, 54, 58, 60, 63, 69, 72,
    73, 74, 104, 105, 109, 150, 151,
    154, 167, 169, 197, 212, 219, 223
Bell, Gail, 166
Bell, Martin, 8–9, 78
Belleek, County Fermanagh, 113
Bessbrook, County Armagh, 34, 56, 57
Bingham, Billy, 146
Birney, Trevor, 170–2
Black, Alan, 56
Blackwater, River, 90
Blair, Tony, ix, xiii, 130, 181, 182, 209
Blevins, David, *xvi*, xvii
Bloody Friday (1972), xii, 16, 34–6
Bloody Sunday (1972), xii, 15, 16, 17,
    19–21, 34, 99, 188, 192, 216
Blunt, Crispin, 153
Boa Island, County Fermanagh, 113
Bogside, Battle of the (1969), xii, 98
Bogside, Derry, 16, 17, 19–21, 98–9, 191,
    200, 201, 202, 216
Bolton, Roger, 121
Bonner, Packie, 148
Bosnia, 78
Boston, USA, 192
Bournemouth, Dorset, 155
Bowcott, Owen, 148
Boyle, Harris, 53
Brabourne, Dowager Lady, *64*, 66, 108
Brackey Loyal Orange Lodge, 7
Bradford, Claire, 71, 72, 73, 74
Bradford, Norah, *70*, 71, 72, 73
Bradford, Robert, *70*, 71–4
Brady, Kevin, 112, 117
Brady, Liam, 147
Brandywell, Derry, 96
Breen, Suzanne, 210–12
Breivik, Anders, 190
Bridge Street, Belfast, 106

Brighton, East Sussex, 80, 82, 99, 125
British Army, xii, 8, 10–12, 16, 19, 20, 21,
    23, 25, 26–7, 28, 29, 30, 31, 34, 37,
    38–9, 42, 48, 51, 53, 54, 55, 65–7,
    71, 72, 75, 77, 78, 79, 81, 82, 83,
    84, 85, 93, 97, 98, 99, 101, 105,
    106, 107, 109, 112, 117–19, 128,
    134, 135, 136, 150, 151, 158, 166,
    189, 192, 193, 198, 199, 208, 216,
    221
1st Battalion Royal Highland
    Fusiliers, 10–12, 28
2nd Battalion, Royal Green Jackets, 26
3rd Light Infantry, 8
14th Intelligence Company, 151
Gordon Highlanders, 38
Inniskilling Dragoon Guards, 101
Inniskilling Fusiliers, 101
Irish Guards, 12
Queen's Own Highlanders, 67
Parachute Regiment, 16, 19, 20, 21, 66, 81
SAS, 117, 118, 120, 121, 128, 135, 153,
    208
UDR, 25, 26, 30, 54, 113, 134
British Forces Broadcasting Service
    (BFBS), 23
Broadcasting House, Belfast, 55
Brodie, Malcolm, 69
Brooke, Peter, 83, 125
Brookeborough, Lord, 31
Brown, Elizabeth, 88
Brown, Harold, 87–9
Brown, Harper, 9
Brown, John, 28, 29
Brussels, Belgium, 45, 217
Bruton, John, 129–30, 162
Bryans, John, 56
Buncrana, County Donegal, 25, 100, 185
Burns, Gordon, 41–3
Burundi, 170

Cadwallader, Anne, *xvi*, xvii, 84–6
Cadwallader, Jane, 85
Café Royal, London, 13
Cairns, Michael, 87–9
Caledon, County Tyrone, 90
Cambrai Street, Belfast, 58
Camden, London, 138
Cameron, David, 43, 217

McDaniel, Denzil, 101–3, 171
McDonald, Cathy, 50
McDonald, Henry, 50–2
McDowell, Billy, 62
McDowell, James, 53, 54
McDowell, Jim, 203–5
McDowell, Lily, 62
McDowell, Lindy, 203
McEntee, Paddy, *xvi*, xvii
McErlane, Paul, *xvi*, xvii
McErlean, Thomas, 112
McFadden, Mark, 186
McFarland, Samantha, 186
McFarland, Walter, 68
McGillion, Garry, 187
McGirr, Jim, 126–7
McGladdery, Daniel, 31
McGlade, Frank, xii
McGlade's bar, xii, 10, 49
McGoldrick, Bridie, 169
McGoldrick, Emma, 168
McGoldrick, Michael (Jr), 168–9
McGoldrick, Michael (Sr), 168, 169
McGoldrick, Sadie, 168
McGonigle, Canon Tom, 166
McGrath, Paul, 146
McGuinness, Martin, xii, 20–1, 32, 98–100, 130, 138, 156, 162, 174, 180, 181, 200–2, *206*, 208–9, 217
McGuinness, Peggy, 200–2
McIlwaine, Eddie, 68–9
McKay, Susan, 59, 173–5
McKeever, Terence, 109
McKenna, Eamon, *xvi*, xvii
McKeown, Clifford, 169
McKittrick, David, 151, *196*, 197–9
McLaughlin, Mitchel, 181
McLoughlin, Alan, 146, 148
McManus, Billy, 132, 133, 134
McManus, Jim, 132, 133, 134
McManus, Willie, 132, 134
McMichael, Ivan, 53–4
McMullan, Bishop Gordon, 90
McSorley, Jane, *xvi*, xvii
McVea, David, *196*, 197
McWhirter, James, 56
McWilliams, Christopher 'Crip', 204
McWilliams, Monica, 130, 181
Megahey, Deric, 26

Megahey, Edward, 25, 27
Megahey, Ted, 25–7
Megaw, Johnny, 100
Melville Hotel, Derry, 9
Metropolitan police, 12
MI5, 150, 161
Miami Showband massacre (1975), 53–4
Middle East, 8, 14, 28, 29, 30, 52
Millar, Frank, 156
Millfield, Belfast, 219
Milltown Cemetery, Belfast, 16, *110*, 111–12, 114, 117
Ministry of Defence, 26, 152, 153
Mirchandani, Prakash, 66
Mitchell, Claire, 172
Mitchell, Senator George J., ix–x, xiii, *xvi*, xvii, 130, 170–2, 180, 181, 182
Moira, County Down, 108
Moldova, 169
Molyneaux, Jim, 155
Monaghan, County Monaghan, 135–6
Monaghan, County, 86
Monde, Le, 197
Mooney, Mrs, 50
Mooney's bar, Belfast, 11, 50–1
Moore, Chris, 106–9
Moran, Paul, 128, 130–1
Morgan, James, 174–5
Morgan, Justin, 174, 175
Morgan, Philomena, 174, 175
Moriarty, Gerry, 146–9
Morissette, Alanis, 190
Morrison, Rob, 57
Morrison, Van, 156
Morse, Murray, 150
Morton Group, 166
Morton, Jim, 166
Moscow, Russia, 46
Mountain Lodge. *See* Darkley Pentecostal Hall
Mountbatten, Earl, *64*, 65–7, 108
Mourne Mountains, 174, 221
Mowlam, Mo, xiii–xiv, *xvi*, xvii, 182
Mulhall, Dan, *xvi*, xvii
Mull of Kintyre, Argyll and Bute, 150
Mullaghmore, County Sligo, *64*, 65, 66, 108
Mullan, Billy, 102
Mullan, Father Kevin, 186

Oxford Street, Belfast, 35